T0245535

THE
FRUGAL
ECONOMY

About Thinkers50 ▏**THINKERS** ▏**50**

Thinkers50 is the world's most reliable resource for identifying, ranking, and sharing the leading management and business ideas of our age. Since 2001, we've been providing access to ideas with the power to make a positive difference in the world.

The Thinkers50 definitive ranking of management thinkers is published every two years. Its Distinguished Achievement Awards, which recognize the very best in management thinking and practice, have been described by the Financial Times as the "Oscars of management thinking."

THE FRUGAL ECONOMY

A GUIDE TO BUILDING A BETTER WORLD WITH LESS

NAVI RADJOU

BESTSELLING COAUTHOR OF *JUGAAD INNOVATION*

THINKERS
50

WILEY

For general information on our other products and services or for technical support, please contact our Customer Care Department within the United States at (800) 762-2974, outside the United States at (317) 572-3993 or fax (317) 572-4002.

Wiley also publishes its books in a variety of electronic formats. Some content that appears in print may not be available in electronic formats. For more information about Wiley products, visit our web site at www.wiley.com.

Library of Congress Cataloging-in-Publication Data

Names: Radjou, Navi, author. | John Wiley & Sons, publisher.
Title: The frugal economy : a guide to building a better world with less /
    Navi Radjou.
Description: Hoboken, New Jersey : Wiley, [2024] | Includes index.
Identifiers: LCCN 2024020708 (print) | LCCN 2024020709 (ebook) | ISBN
    9781394273058 (hardback) | ISBN 9781394273072 (adobe pdf) | ISBN
    9781394273065 (epub)
Subjects: LCSH: Sustainable development. | Sustainable living.
Classification: LCC HC79.E5 R334 2024 (print) | LCC HC79.E5 (ebook) | DDC
    338.973/07—dc23/eng/20240601
LC record available at https://lccn.loc.gov/2024020708
LC ebook record available at https://lccn.loc.gov/2024020709

Cover Design: Wiley
Cover Image: © amtitus/Getty Images

SKY10082324_082024

*"The way to wealth is as plain as the way to market.
It depends chiefly on two words, industry and frugality:
that is, waste neither time nor money, but make the best use of both.
Without industry and frugality nothing will do; with them, everything."*

—Benjamin Franklin

"Nothing is lost, nothing is created, everything is transformed."

—Antoine Lavoisier

oṃ
*pūrṇam adaḥ pūrṇam idam
pūrṇāt pūrṇam udacyate
pūrṇasya pūrṇam ādāya
pūrṇam evāvaśiṣyate*
oṃ śāntiḥ śāntiḥ śāntiḥ

om
*That is Infinite, this is infinite
this infinite arises from That Infinite
when this infinite is taken from or added to That Infinite
Infinite only remains
om peace peace peace*

—Isha Upanishad / shlokam

Contents

Introduction: Respect and Break All Limits

These days, the media is awash with alarmist headlines like "Humans have crossed six of the nine planetary boundaries that make Earth habitable" (see Figure I.1).[1] Altogether, these nine ecological boundaries "define a safe operating space for humanity" (the green zone that appears as a sphere in Figure I.1) that should not be exceeded if we wish to maintain stable conditions on Earth.[2]

Consequently, businesses are asked to "respect planetary boundaries" and injunctions are issued to "link planetary boundaries to business."

There is no doubt that rapid economic growth and intensified agriculture and industrialization have depleted our planet's natural resources, acidified our oceans, polluted our atmosphere, and degraded our biodiversity.[3]

As climate change worsens, businesses bear a *moral responsibility* to respect the planetary boundaries and reduce the "negative externalities" of their economic activities. This is why all businesses are now being asked to **do LESS** (harm).

But here is the big problem: we humans are not born to do LESS. We are wired to **do MORE**.

Nothing in Nature is designed to do *less*. All creatures on Earth are animated by an evolutionary need to do – and be(come) – more.

Three and a half billion years ago, Earth was filled with single-celled organisms that were able to survive on their own. Yet, these unicellular life forms were driven to do – and *be* – more. They were animated by what the French philosopher Henri Bergson called the *élan vital*, a mysterious vital impulse immanent within all life forms that compels them to keep evolving. So these individual cells

1

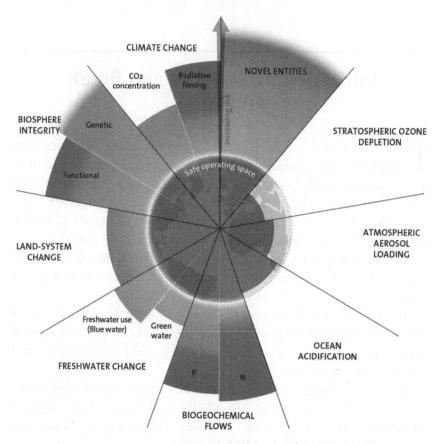

Figure I.1 The nine planetary boundaries defined in 2009 by a group of scientists led by Johan Rockström altogether delineate a safe operating space (the green zone that appears as a sphere above) for humans. In 2023, scientists found that six of these nine limits have already been transgressed as depicted in red.

Source: Adapted from Richardson et al., 2023.

aggregated together to form multicellular groups – starting with fungi, then animals, and finally us humans.

You are reading this sentence because your unicellular ancestors evolved and adapted to do more and better.

If you and I were to do LESS, we would be regressing back to the single-cell stage (which will be an insult to our ambitious mono-celled ancestors)!

What drives us to do more and be better? It is our desire to surpass ourselves and *break* the limits.

In 2014, I delivered a TED Talk titled "Creative Problem-Solving in the Face of Extreme Limits."[4]

I showed how millions of entrepreneurs in emerging markets in India, Africa, and South America overcome the scarcity of resources and use their *jugaad* (*ingenuity* in Hindi) to innovate faster, better, and cheaper. I explained how when you put a limitation on resources, you remove the limitation on creativity.[5]

Likewise, athletes, like those who participate in the Olympic games, are born to break the physical limits. "No limits for Usain (Bolt)" is how the Maths and Sport website described Usain Bolt, the "fastest man on the planet" who kept breaking his own 100-meter (sprint) world record.[6] Bolt didn't respect the planetary limit . . . for running fast! Scientists also don't believe "the sky is the limit" for their exploration. Otherwise, we would never have landed a man on the moon in 1969!

You get my point.

Certain limits – like planetary boundaries – are worth respecting and you need to "play within (those) limits" and DO LESS. But other limits – physical, mental, scientific – need to be crossed to push out the boundaries of what humans can achieve, so we can DO MORE. Especially, we need to break our self-limiting belief that "we are all small" and strive to BE MORE.

Spiritual traditions understood well human psychology. Christianity's 10 Commandments, which relate to ethics, are mostly about limits not to cross. That's why 8 of the 10 commandments begin with "Thou shall NOT'" to *restrict* what we can do.

Yet, akin to modern management thinkers (like me) who believe in "incentive systems," the Biblical leaders knew that morality and ethics in spirituality shouldn't just be *punitive* ("you will be chastened if you do X"); they also need to be *rewarding* ("you will be blessed if you do Y"). This is why Christianity identifies the seven deadly sins (vices) we must avoid ("do less") as well as the seven virtues we need to actively cultivate and practice ("do more"). See Figure I.2.[7]

From a Christian perspective – as well as a Hindu and Buddhist viewpoint – leading a **frugal life** consists in doing less harm (to people and Nature) *as well as* doing good (to others). A frugal life is about *living better with less*.

Vice	Latin	Virtue	Latin
Lust	*Luxuria*	Chastity	*Castitas*
Gluttony	*Gula*	Temperance	*Temperantia*
Greed	*Avaritia*	Charity	*Caritas*
Sloth	*Acedia*	Diligence	*Industria*
Wrath	*Ira*	Patience	*Patientia*
Envy	*Invidia*	Gratitude	*Gratia*
Pride	*Superbia*	Humility	*Humilitas*

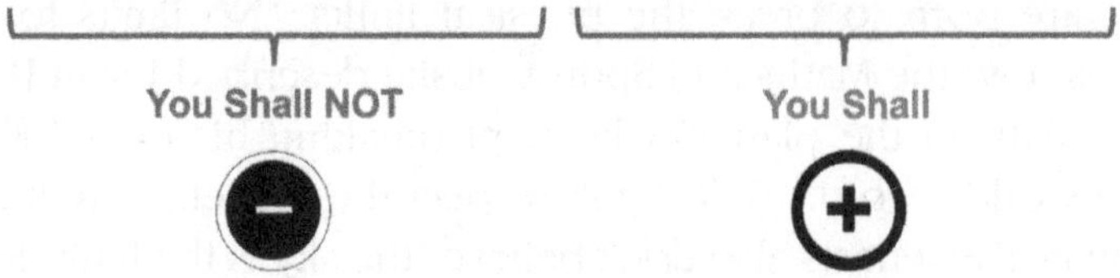

You Shall NOT   You Shall

Figure I.2 The seven virtues, which counterbalance the seven sins, form the basis of Christian ethics and offer humans a moral compass for leading an honorable life.

At this point, we need to revisit the evolutionary need of all creatures – including humans – to "do more." In fact, we aspire to not just do more, but "be" more. We want to break all physical and mental limits so we can experience . . . **infinity**.

All humans' *spiritual desire* – that's what it is all about – to reach infinity is beautifully captured in the very popular Hindu mantra (in Sanskrit):

> Om Asato Maa Sad-Gamaya
> Tamaso Maa Jyotir-Gamaya
> Mrtyor-Maa Amrtam Gamaya
> Om Shaantih Shaantih Shaantih

which translates into

> O Lord, Lead me from (the phenomenal
>   world of) Unreality to the Reality (of
>   Eternal Self)
> Lead me from the Darkness (of Ignorance)
>   toward the Light (of Spiritual Awareness)

> Lead me from this world of Mortality (world
> of Material Attachment) to the world of
> Immortality (of Self-Realization)
> Om, Peace, Peace, Peace.

This all sounds very nice.

Here is, however, the dilemma: we yearn to experience infinity while living on a . . . finite planet.

How do we resolve this quandary? By becoming aware of two things:

- ◆ "Infinite economic growth on a finite planet" is not sustainable.
- ◆ "Infinite development of *human potential* on a finite planet" *is* possible and worth pursuing as a noble goal.

Alas, gaining this awareness alone isn't enough. We need to fundamentally change our economic system, so it delivers a *qualitatively* different kind of growth that benefits all humans and enhances social and ecological harmony.

We must build a **frugal economy** that **does better with less**.

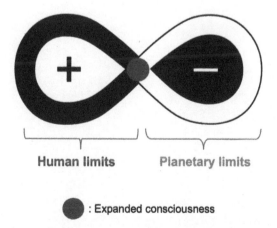

Human limits   **Planetary limits**

● : Expanded consciousness

Figure I.3 A frugal economy enables you to consciously surpass yourself within ecological limits.

A frugal economy will raise and expand our consciousness so we can all stretch our mental and psychic limits and become *better* human beings while harming *less* our environment and respecting the planetary limits. See Figure I.3.

The Stockholm Resilience Centre defines the planetary boundaries as "a set of nine planetary boundaries within which humanity can continue to develop and thrive for generations to come."[8]

A frugal economy will enable humanity to wisely "continue to develop and thrive for generations to come" while "playing" within the boundaries of our collective home: Earth.

CHAPTER 1

Doing Better with Less

In its March 2023 report, the World Bank warned that the economic forces that powered progress and prosperity over the last three decades are vanishing: "Between 2022 and 2030 average global potential GDP growth is expected to decline by roughly a third from the rate that prevailed in the first decade of this century – to 2.2% a year. For developing economies, the decline will be equally steep: from 6% a year between 2000 and 2010 to 4% a year over the remainder of this decade. These declines would be much steeper in the event of a global financial crisis or a recession."[1]

"A lost decade could be in the making for the global economy," presages Indermit Gill, chief economist of the World Bank.

The bank also offers suggestions for reversing this decline. "The global economy's speed limit can be raised – through policies that incentivize work, increase productivity, and accelerate investment."[2]

Unfortunately, these suggestions focus on increasing *quantitively* the economic growth of nations – as measured by GDP – without improving the *quality* of growth.

Today, we are all aware that the current growth model is not effective because it overexploits and depletes natural resources – aggravating climate change – and excludes people – worsening social inequalities. See Figure 1.1.

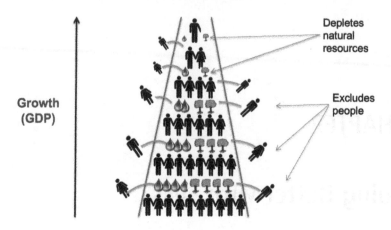

Growth
(GDP)

Figure 1.1 Today's growth model is not working because it excludes people and depletes resources.

Here is some shocking evidence to the fact that today's growth model is not working:

- In 2023, Earth Overshoot Day (EOD) – the date when humanity's demand for ecological resources and services in a given year exceeds what Earth can regenerate in that year – was on August 2.[3] In 2003, the EOD was September 12. We are borrowing (stealing, actually) more and more from our (ecological) future to fuel our economic growth, which is not sustainable.
- In the US, the richest economy in the world, 56% of adults are unable to cover a $1,000 emergency expense, according to Bankrate's 2024 annual emergency savings report.[4] In Europe, nearly 100 million citizens are at risk of poverty and social exclusion, which is about 22% of the total population.[5]
- In France, a disabled person today is three times less likely than others to find a job. Female entrepreneurs are 63% less likely than men to obtain venture capital (VC) financing.[6] In the US, black women receive less than 0.35% of all VC funding.[7]

Given this bleak scenario, experts are coming up with alternative growth models that claim to be more virtuous. A popular alternative much touted today is *decoupling*, whereby "continued growth in the economy is accompanied by a further contraction in CO_2 emissions."[8]

This so-called green growth model based on decoupling calls for companies to "**do more with less**," that is, keep producing more goods and services while "decarbonizing" their supply chains (see Figure 1.2).

In his book aptly titled *More from Less,* Andrew McAfee, a research scientist at MIT Sloan School of Management, argues that this decoupling has already occurred in the US. McAfee's book shows how the US has been able to increase productivity and drive more economic growth using fewer physical inputs since the first Earth Day in 1970. According to McAfee, "evidence from America shows that even though population and prosperity continued to increase steadily in the years after Earth Day (1970), resource consumption did not. Instead, it started to decline. The country now generally uses less metal, fertilizer, water, paper and timber, and energy year after year," even as output increases.[9] McAfee points to America's decoupling, that is the country's capacity to do "more from less," as evidence of the *dematerialization* of the US economy. In the same vein, proponents of the so-called circular economy today argue that we can do "more from less" by efficiently reusing and recycling existing resources and materials, instead of extracting more virgin materials from our depleted Earth.

Although *decoupling* could reduce the negative ecological impact of businesses, by curbing their emissions and resource consumption,

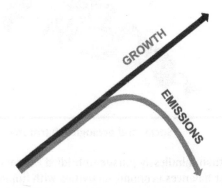

Figure 1.2 Decoupling aims to generate more economic growth while limiting and even reducing negative environmental impact like emissions.

it doesn't incentivize companies to radically change their existing business models or *positively* contribute to society.

I argue that what the world needs today is not decoupling but **recoupling**. It's time to "recouple" (reintegrate) economic activities with people, communities, and the planet. Rather than mindlessly dematerialize our economy using technology, we must intentionally *rematerialize* our economy, making its gains feel *real* for everyday citizens. Instead of decoupling to boost our productivity, we must do recoupling to boost our humanity.

Such tight recoupling will enable a *regenerative development* model that will boost human development and increase social and ecological harmony and will lead us toward a *conscious society* (see Figure 1.3).[10]

By engaging in – and actively shaping – this virtuous growth cycle, businesses could serve a noble purpose that is larger than just profit-making.

Here is the hiccup: our existing economic system, which is built on capitalism, lacks the right values and mechanisms to enable the recoupling of business and society/planet.

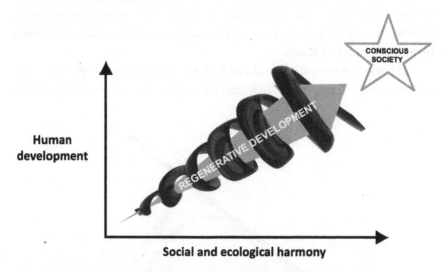

Figure 1.3 Rather than mindlessly pursue unbridled economic growth, regenerative development balances economic activities with human development and social and ecological harmony, hence leading us to a conscious society.

Here are four reasons why capitalism – the operating system that runs our modern societies – is unfit to drive the kind of inclusive and sustainable growth I just described[11]:

- ◆ First, capitalism exalts the virtues of private ownership, individualism, and competition, which motivate businesses to amass and hoard assets and compete ferociously with one another in a zero-sum game.
- ◆ Second, it pursues relentlessly economies of scale (efficiencies) through mass production and global supply chains, which are gravely polluting and resource-hungry, and lack the flexibility and resilience to cope with catastrophic disruptions like COVID-19 or water scarcity.[12]
- ◆ Third, it incentivizes businesses to maximize short-term profits exclusively for shareholders instead of creating long-term value for all stakeholders, including local communities.[13]
- ◆ Fourth, capitalism fails to hold businesses accountable for the harmful consequences of their operations – known as *negative externalities* – such as social inequality and ecological degradation.[14]

Given its fundamental and systemic flaws, we can't rely on a dysfunctional capitalist economy to power inclusive and sustainable growth. We need to totally upgrade and reinvent the economic system that undergirds our societies to make it more efficient and agile, socially inclusive, and ecologically beneficial.

To build and sustain radically new business models and industry value chains that are truly beneficial to people, society, and the planet, we need a new operating system that I call a **frugal economy**.

A frugal economy strives to expand human awareness and create greater economic, social, and ecological value simultaneously while wisely optimizing the use of all available resources.

In contrast with the "do more with more" capitalistic system, which gobbles up ever more resources to pump out ever more useless products, the frugal economy strives to **do better with less** by making the most of all existing resources to maximize the value for *all* stakeholders.

A frugal economy responds to the needs of thrifty and socially conscious consumers who seek a simpler, healthier, and more eco-friendly lifestyle and want to deepen their community ties through active local engagement.

This frugal economy is not a utopian vision.

Using more than **100 inspiring real-life examples** from all over the world, this book vividly shows how this **multitrillion-dollar** frugal economy is already emerging, fueled by **three megatrends** that will fundamentally reshape our societies in coming decades: business-to-business (B2B) sharing, distributed (decentralized) manufacturing and hyper-local value networks, and triple regeneration. See Figure 1.4. I will unpack these disruptive megatrends one by one in the first three parts of the book. In the fourth part, I will describe how these three megatrends are deeply reinventing the largest economy in the world: America.

In Part I, I will show how competing companies can learn to cooperate and share their physical and intangible resources to collectively maximize their value and have a positive impact on society and the planet.

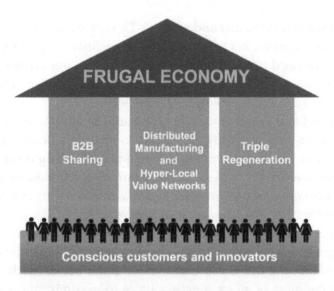

Figure 1.4 Conscious customers and innovators fuel the rise of a frugal economy that enables the sharing of resources, localizes production, and regenerates people, places, and the planet.

In Part II, I will explain how businesses, especially in developed nations, can gain in resilience and agility by *scaling out* manufacturing and producing goods and services much closer to customers, which will benefit both the local economy and the environment.

In Part III, I will reveal how businesses and communities can go beyond sustainability and regenerate people, places, and the planet altogether synergistically, hence boosting the health and vitality of citizens, communities, and natural ecosystems.

Finally, in Part IV, I will inspire you by showing how across America – the most *unfrugal* society in the world – enlightened entrepreneurs, businesses, states, and counties are building from the ground up inclusive frugal economies that truly benefit people, society, and the planet.

I believe that building a frugal economy will have a *civilizing* effect on companies, enabling them to break bad habits and adopt new virtuous behaviors. For instance, today businesses compete with each other brutally and hoard resources selfishly. Instead, what if they collaborated and shared their resources so they can cocreate greater economic, social, and ecological benefits for all? Excitingly, this is already happening, and it's called B2B sharing. Come discover it in Part I.

PART I

The B2B Sharing Revolution

CHAPTER 2

The Big Benefits of B2B Sharing

Every crisis begets an opportunity. The Great Recession of 2008–2009 gave birth to the sharing economy, enabling individuals to use digital platforms like Uber, Airbnb, and BlaBlaCar to share their unused or underused cars and homes with others, thus generating additional income while maximizing the value of their assets.

This peer-to-peer or consumer-to-consumer (C2C) sharing economy took off so quickly that, in 2015, the audit and consulting firm PwC estimated that 18% of US adults had already partaken in the sharing economy as a consumer, and 7% had participated as a provider. PwC projected this C2C sharing economy to grow from $15 billion in 2013 to a whopping $335 billion by 2025.[1]

In 2024, as the world grapples with a "polycrisis" (multiple intersecting crises at once), what if businesses started sharing their physical and intangible resources with each other? Such a business-to-business (B2B) sharing economy, potentially worth trillions of dollars, is already emerging, fueled by greater environmental and social awareness and new technologies like artificial intelligence (AI) and the Internet of Things.[2]

B2B Sharing Boosts Business Efficiency, Agility, and Innovation

By sharing resources, businesses can do the following:

- **Avoid big capital investments.** Rather than waste their precious capital to build new factories and warehouses, manufacturers can rapidly and cost-effectively expand their supply chain capabilities by leveraging on-demand industrial marketplaces like Xometry, Fictiv, and Protolabs Network and flexible storage networks like Flowspace, Flexe, and SpaceFill.[3]

Xometry, FacFox, Fictiv, and Protolabs Network are on-demand manufacturing marketplaces that connect thousands of highly specialized machine shops with global businesses, thus empowering the small industrial firms to keep their factories fully used, especially during a downturn.

Flowspace, Flexe, and SpaceFill are cloud-based, on-demand warehousing networks that link up businesses seeking warehouse space with firms that have underused storage space, enabling large companies as well as e-commerce startups to cost-effectively scale their distribution network and bring their products faster to customers. Flexe estimates that companies using its on-demand logistics services to fulfill online orders save 10% in warehousing costs, reduce last-mile transportation costs by 10%, and increase e-commerce revenues by 20% – all this without making a big fixed-cost investment.[4]

♦ **Reduce operating costs.** By pooling buying power and signing collective long-term contracts with shared suppliers, firms can curb their operating expenses while stabilizing the supply of critical materials. For instance, Civica Rx is a nonprofit group in the US that aggregates 1,550 hospitals' demands to reduce cost of generic drugs and vaccines by up to 90% for all its members and their patients. Likewise, rather than sign a long-term costly commercial lease, companies can rent additional office space on demand from workplace sharing platforms like Breather and LiquidSpace. Floow2 and Rheaply have built digital platforms that enable hospitals to share their underused medical equipment and services, thus maximizing their asset use, reducing operating costs, and boosting patient care quality. In the Netherlands, pharmacists use PharmaSwap to share with each other soon-to-expire drugs, hence reducing their waste and avoiding costly inventory write-offs.

♦ **Generate new revenue streams.** Thirty percent of all warehouse space in the US – and 50% in Asia – is unused at any time. Nearly 20% of office property across America today is empty, the highest vacancy rate since 1979.[5] Thirty-five percent of trucks on US roads run empty.[6] The owners of these underused facilities and vehicles can make money by renting them to other companies desperately seeking additional storage, workspace, or shipping capacity. Sennder, Vahak, TruggHub, and Trella are the Uber for trucking: their AI-based freight networks automatically connect shippers with carriers to move millions of truckloads effectively, helping shippers reduce freight cost and enabling truck drivers to earn more.

- ◆ **Maximize the value of intangible assets.** In today's knowledge economy, businesses can extract greater value from their intangible assets like intellectual property (patents, copyrights, and know-how) by sharing them with others. Each year, US firms lose $1 trillion in IP value because they lack a sound commercial strategy to monetize their inventions. IP-rich firms can leverage brokering services like yet2.com and NineSigma to generate profit from their unused intellectual assets like patents by licensing them to innovation-hungry businesses.

- ◆ **Boost agility and resilience.** During recessions and pandemics like COVID-19, as customer demand nose-dives, small manufacturers are stuck with idle factory capacity and underemployed workforce. On-demand industrial marketplaces like Xometry and Protolabs Network make these small firms resilient by linking them up rapidly with new clients so they keep their machine shops and employees fully used. Likewise, Hyver, Hydres, and Teambix are talent-sharing platforms that enable businesses to temporary "lend" their underused employees to other companies in need of additional human resources. They also facilitate the professional mobility of workers who wish to leave their current employers to expand their career elsewhere.

- ◆ **Innovate faster, better, cheaper.** Ninety-five percent of new consumer products fail at launch because they don't meet actual customer needs, leaving brands with costly unsold stock.[7] Instead of guessing consumer preferences and mass-producing the *wrong* products faster, brands could use platforms such as The Storefront and Appear Here to set up pop-up stores in multiple strategic locations to test a wide variety of new product concepts with customers. Brands can then selectively scale up the production of only those concepts that customers really like.

♦ **Satisfy customers seeking end-to-end solutions.** Instead of point solutions, customers are seeking end-to-end tailored solutions from multiple brands that extensively address their broader needs in mobility, finance, and wellness. For instance, there is a growing need for point-to-point mobility solutions that seamlessly integrate car sharing, train and bus rides, and rental bikes. By sharing and integrating data on their assets and customers with each other, companies from different sectors can synergistically deliver a seamless experience to their shared clients.

As these examples show, by sharing their physical and intangible resources with each other, companies can *do better with less*, that is, increase their revenue and agility while drastically reducing their operating costs and waste

Given all these benefits from sharing resources, it's not surprising that, according to a business.com survey, nearly 70% of companies today engage in the B2B sharing economy in one form or another at least once a month, with 26% using these services daily.[8] Forty percent said sharing resources with other companies reduced their expenses and 18% reported it saves them time.

B2B transactions – whether offline or online – are significantly larger in volume and value than B2C transactions. According to Statista, the global B2B e-commerce market is valued at $17.9 trillion in 2021, which is more than five times larger than the B2C market. In the past, B2B evolved slower than B2C. But the growing need for speed, agility, and sustainability is driving many companies to double down on B2B collaboration to serve their customers faster, better, and cheaper. As such, in the coming decade, I estimate that B2B sharing could unleash well over $3 trillion in economic value, dwarfing the C2C sharing economy, which will reach just $335 billion by 2025 (see Figure 2.1).

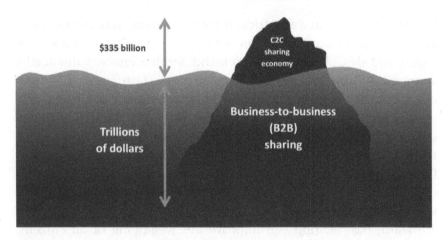

Figure 2.1 B2B sharing could dwarf the C2C sharing economy in volume and value.

The Social and Ecological Benefits of B2B Sharing

Beyond the purely economic gains for companies, B2B sharing can also have a major positive social impact, especially in historically excluded or underdeveloped communities, for several reasons.

First, B2B sharing networks and platforms catalyze the creation of new jobs, especially for marginalized groups, and help preserve local jobs and skills within regional economies. Take industrial symbiosis (IS), a sustainable practice whereby several colocated companies from different sectors share their materials, waste, and energy in a synergistic manner. IS initiatives like FE21 in northeast France and WISP in South Africa employ hundreds of underprivileged people to recycle their waste, hence regenerating local communities. Similarly, employee sharing platforms like Talent Sharing Platform in the east of England and Genesis in France avoid laying off underused workers and keep them fully employed by integrating them into other companies in the same city or region. In doing so, they also preserve valuable skills and know-how locally, hence avoiding a "brain drain."

Second, B2B sharing enables artisans, small farmers, and small and medium enterprises (SMEs) – the most valuable and the most vulnerable segments of our economy – to increase their resilience, agility, and performance by gaining access to assets and skills from other companies at lower cost. Take, for instance, the farming sector. Hello Tractor is an online platform that operates as an "Uber for small farmers" across Africa; it provides them access to tractors and other farm equipment on a flexible pay-per-use basis. This frugal and flexible tractor-on-demand service enables financially strapped African farmers to plant 40 times faster and 2.5 times cheaper than conventional manual methods, hence achieving 63% in savings and a three-time increase in yield.[9] Similarly, Digital Green is a knowledge-sharing platform that enables millions of small farmers in India, Africa, and South America to share impactful agricultural best practices and innovations directly with each other, which has resulted in an increase of 24% to 74% yield across various commodities.[10]

Third, B2B sharing can improve the well-being of all citizens. Take the example of digital platforms like Floow2 and Cohealo, which allow hospitals to share their medical equipment and services (hospitals use most medical devices only 42% of the time). Thanks to these platforms, anxious patients can get quality care faster by going directly to a hospital with the right equipment and readily available staff to treat them without delay. For instance, Intrakoop, the leading Dutch health care procurement cooperative, runs a sharing marketplace built on Floow2 technology that enables 550 hospitals and long-term care providers across the Netherlands to share their underused goods and services with other members. Likewise, Figure 1 is an online social networking service that enables 3 million health care professionals in 190 countries to share (anonymized) medical images and collaboratively and rapidly solve complex patient cases. Forty percent of clinicians who can't resolve a patient case on their own find a resolution through peer-to-peer collaboration on Figure 1.

Similarly, with most senior citizens' interest in "aging in place" – living in their own home independently and comfortably as long as possible – companies and local authorities can share their expertise and pool their resources through multisector initiatives like the MIT AgeLab C3 Connected Home Logistics Consortium to cocreate end-to-end wellness solutions to improve the quality of life of seniors at home. During COVID-19, pioneering B2B sharing initiatives around the world saved thousands of lives and enhanced the well-being of many citizens (see "B2B Sharing Battles COVID-19 and Saves Lives").

B2B Sharing Battles COVID-19 and Saves Lives

Here are three major B2B sharing initiatives launched in 2020, against the backdrop of the COVID-19 pandemic, that demonstrate powerfully the positive social impact that B2B sharing can achieve on a large scale in a region or an entire country:

China. In January 2020, as the COVID-19 pandemic engulfed China, hundreds of hotels, cinemas, and restaurants shut down and thousands of their employees were either put on furlough or laid off. Meanwhile, Hema, a digitally savvy supermarket chain founded by Chinese billionaire Jack Ma's Alibaba group, was facing a labor shortage as it struggled to keep up with a surge in online orders for groceries delivery. To solve its labor crunch, Hema entered into an employee-sharing agreement with caterers, hotels, cinemas, and restaurants to hire their idle workers on a short-term basis to prepare and deliver groceries. By late April 2020, 2,700 workers from 40 other companies were employed at Hema under the job-sharing plan. Inspired by Hema, other online retailers and supermarket chains in China like Ele, Carrefour, Walmart, Meituan, JD's 7Fresh also borrowed employees from restaurants and other businesses.[11]

US. On April 1, 2020, Ohio State Governor Mike DeWine announced the launch of the Ohio Manufacturing Alliance to Fight COVID-19 (OMAFC) to respond to the major shortage in the state of personal protective equipment (PPE) like face shields, isolation gowns, and masks. The OMAFC was co-led by the Ohio Manufacturers' Association (OMA), the Ohio Manufacturing Extension Partnership (and its partner organization MAGNET), the Ohio Hospital Association, and JobsOhio.[12]

(continued)

(continued)

The OMAFC acted as a large-scale B2B sharing platform by pooling demand data from hospitals and nursing homes from across Ohio to determine their specific PPE requirements and aggregating supply-side insights from 2,000 regional manufacturers to identify their existing capabilities and resources. MAGNET shared its engineering expertise with manufacturers to help retool their existing factories and repurpose their current products and materials to make PPE (for instance, ROE Dental Laboratory in Cleveland adapted its 3D printing facility to produce 1 million testing swabs and another group of manufacturers repurposed the plastics used in garbage bags to produce disposable gowns). JobsOhio offered regional support and financial assistance to scale up production and speed up delivery of PPE and other critical items to health care and frontline workers.

By rapidly connecting health care providers with thousands of regional manufacturers and widely sharing information, materials, and engineering expertise, the OMAFC enabled Ohio to fight COVID-19 with speed and efficacy by producing PPE at a cost-competitive price in the state without depending on other countries like China. For example, in mid-August 2020, the OMAFC announced it had successfully collaborated with Buckeye Mask and Stitches USA, two Ohio-based manufacturers, to repurpose their existing facilities and supply chains so they could co-effectively mass-produce 100,000 high-quality cotton face masks a day.

France. In March 2020, Kolmi-Hopen, the largest face mask manufacturer in France, was under pressure to

> mass-produce masks at its factory near Angers, but it lacked the operational skills to do so. Kolmi-Hopen was able to quickly identify and temporarily borrow experts in industrial processes from Scania, a heavy vehicle manufacturer located nearby. This sharing of employees enabled Kolmi-Hopen to reconfigure its factory and double its mask manufacturing in record time, thus saving the lives of thousands of French citizens.

B2B sharing will also have a considerable positive impact on the *environment*. By merely getting all its companies to share their waste – through a process known as the *circular economy*, which represents merely the Level 1 in the framework introduced in Chapter 3 – each country can reduce its carbon emissions by 39%.[13] If companies go one step further and start sharing physical assets – inventory, spaces, vehicles, equipment – the environmental benefits could be significant.

Take the case of transportation, the second largest contributor of greenhouse gases in the world after energy and electricity production. Road freight transportation, which carries 95% of the products we consume every day, accounts for 6% of the European Union's total CO_2 emissions.

In the US, heavy-duty trucks account for 20% of transportation sector emissions. However, 35% of trucks circulating in the US and 20% of trucks on European roads today drive empty because the drivers can't find enough shipments to completely fill their truck.[14]

These "empty kilometers" (or "empty miles") represent tens of millions of tons of CO_2 every year. Digital freight networks such as Convoy (owned by Flexport), Sennder, TruggHub, Trella, Uber Freight, and Vahak seek to make trucking more efficient and sustainable by connecting companies that want to ship goods directly with carriers (mostly small businesses), without going through intermediaries. By 100% automating freight procurement, these AI-powered digital platforms optimize truck fill rates by grouping several shipments into a single task for a driver, thus massively reducing emissions related to empty miles (and generating more revenue for truck operators). For instance, Convoy's Automated Reloads program could potentially reduce empty-mile emissions by 45% in the US.[15] In France, Chargeurs Pointe De Bretagne is a B2B logistics platform that pools shipments from agri-food companies located in the Brittany region to other regions. Since its launch in 2012, this platform has doubled the filling rate of trucks (which is good for carriers who earn more), reduced CO_2 emissions of shippers by up to 70% (which is great for the planet), and boosted the competitiveness of the agri-food sector in Brittany (which is awesome for the regional economy).

According to a study conducted in eight European countries by BlaBlaCar, Europe's leading consumer-to-consumer carpooling platform, its ride-sharing service saved more than 1.6 million tons of CO_2 per year in 2019 alone – the equivalent of the emissions generated by transportation in Paris in one year.[16] In 2023, BlaBlaCar helped reduce the ecological footprint of travel by 2.2 million tons of CO_2.

Similarly, by adopting B2B carpooling and ride-sharing services offered by players such as BlaBlaCar Daily, OpenFleet, Sixt, Share Now, and SoCar, businesses can significantly reduce the size of their vehicle fleet, offer flexible and affordable mobility solutions to their employees, and massively reduce their carbon footprint.

Solar Stewards is an inspiring project in the US that shows how B2B sharing can *simultaneously* generate economic, social, and ecological benefits for both communities and corporations. Solar Stewards is an online marketplace that enables companies to buy solar energy from underinvested communities located close to where they do business. This digital platform aggregates small solar projects installed at local schools, places of worship, and townhalls into portfolios of scale that are attractive to corporate buyers of renewable energy.

Solar Stewards is what I call a *systemic B2B sharing project* – a win-win solution that creates sustainable *value* for all stakeholders and promotes noble *values*. As Dana Clare Redden, founder of Solar Stewards, explains, "Frontline communities are eager to be a part of the renewable energy transition, which represents a generational opportunity for environmental rights and economic empowerment. Partnering with the private sector to enable both objectives is of great benefit to both stakeholders. These holistic value propositions achieve tangible and visible impact and deliver on both climate justice and corporate social responsibility initiatives."[17]

B2B sharing offers very compelling economic, social, and ecological benefits. To fully reap these benefits, however, businesses in capitalistic societies must unlearn their old habits of hoarding resources and competing brutally with each other and learn to cooperate and share resources.

This radical change in attitude – and especially in *mindset* – will not happen overnight. Companies therefore need a strategic road map to gradually transform their culture and to integrate their organization ever more deeply into the fledgling B2B sharing economy.

CHAPTER 3

Mastering B2B Sharing

I propose a holistic framework (see Figure 3.1) with six levels that can serve two purposes. First, it can be used both as a taxonomy to classify the various activities, associated with different kinds of resources, that take place in the B2B sharing economy. Second, it can serve as a "maturity model" to help businesses identify what strategies and capabilities they need to develop next to connect more deeply into the B2B sharing economy and achieve greater benefits.

As companies progress through each level, *they will gain more self-confidence and learn to trust their peers* in the B2B sharing economy. This, in turn, will encourage them to take more risk and share resources of even greater value and establish deeper strategic partnerships.

Level 1: Sharing Waste and Discarded Resources

A low-risk way for companies to get started with B2B sharing is by sharing waste, in a way that one company's waste streams become the raw materials for another firm. In Denmark's Kalundborg Eco-Industrial Park, for example, several colocated companies exchange material waste, energy, and water as an integrated closed-loop eco-system. At the center of this ecosystem is an electric power plant. This power station has supplied its waste heat (via a pipeline) to a nearby pharmaceutical firm and an oil refinery. It also captures its fly ash and sends it to a cement producer located in proximity. In turn, the oil refinery sends its warm cooling water effluent to the power

B2B Sharing: A Taxonomy-cum-Maturity Model

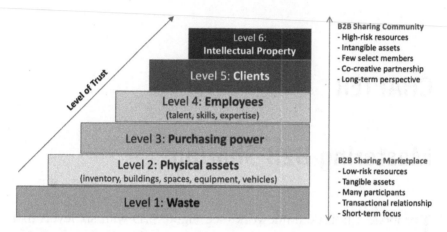

Figure 3.1 Firms can co-build trust and cocreate greater value by sharing a wide range of resources.

station for use as a boiler feedwater. The refinery has also supplied its excess flare gas to an adjacent drywall manufacturing plant to dry the gypsum boards made there. This cooperative and synergistic process of sharing industrial waste and by-products among a diverse set of firms is known as *industrial symbiosis* (which is a subset of a broader resource reusing and recycling paradigm called the *circular economy*). By recycling 62,000 tons of residual material, the Kalundborg symbiotic ecosystem has already reduced annual carbon emissions by 586,000 tons and water use by 4 million cubic meters. Since 2015, it has cut carbon emissions by 80%, and the local energy is now carbon neutral.[1]

Kalundborg's success has also inspired other Western governments to encourage industrial symbiosis. In 2003, the UK government launched the National Industrial Symbiosis Programme (NISP) to capture industrial opportunities from sharing energy, water, and waste materials. Working synergistically, the 15,000 corporate members of NISP collectively reduced carbon emissions by 42 million tons and redirected 48 million tons of waste from landfills for reuse, shrinking costs and creating more than £3 billion in revenue.[2] The NISP found that each ton of CO_2 saved costs members only about $1, which is far less expensive than, say, carbon trading, with its high transaction cost. The Organisation for Economic Co-operation and Development, an international organization that advises policymakers on driving inclusive and sustainable growth, declared the NISP to be a game-changer in waste management.

The NISP model is being replicated in 20 countries worldwide, including Turkey and Israel, which both have passed laws to encourage industrial symbiosis at the national level. ENEA, the Italian national agency for innovation, has created a digital platform (industrialsymbiosis.it) to enable Italian businesses to share their industrial resources with each other in different territories across Italy. So far, nearly 300 Italian firms, mostly small and medium businesses, have forged 1946 symbiotic partnerships to share 2,672 resources across multiple Italian regions. In 2020, 150 industrial symbiosis projects known as *écologie industrielle et territoriale* (industrial and territorial ecology) were active in all 13 regions across France.

In 2017, the European Union (EU) launched an ambitious project called SCALER (Scaling European Resources with Industrial Symbiosis). SCALER is an online platform that provided guides, best practices, and tools that enabled manufacturers to work together to speed up adoption of industrial symbiosis across 30 European regions. SCALER identified 38 industrial symbiosis opportunities in Europe that could generate €22 billion in added economic value and a total of 345,000 direct and indirect jobs.[3] In 2018, the European Commission has amended the European Waste Directive requiring member states to "promote industrial symbiosis" and "prioritize replicable practices of industrial symbiosis." In October 2020, the EU launched CORALIS, a project that will apply industrial symbiosis approaches to decarbonize resource and energy-intensive industrial sectors such as aluminum, food, steel, and chemical.

In North America, many states such as Washington, Tennessee, Ohio, Ontario, Michigan, and cities such as Austin, Texas, have built a regional- or city-level materials marketplace. This digital marketplace – powered by Rheaply's Resource Exchange platform – enables local businesses to share waste and by-products with organizations that can reuse and recycle them. By "valorizing" (enhancing the value of) waste – rather than sending it to landfills – this resource exchange enables major cost savings and energy savings and creates new jobs and business opportunities that benefit local communities. More than 840 organizations are currently engaged in Rheaply's public reuse marketplace. In recent years, Rheaply's platform has diverted more than 2 million pounds (1,000 tons) of waste materials to *higher and better use* in North America.

Let us focus on these last few words – *higher and better use* – which capture well the true purpose of a frugal economy, which is to do *better* with *less*. Just like alchemists can transform a low-value material (lead) into a high-value one (gold), by sharing their waste, companies can "transmute" (transform) their low-value by-product materials into new and better products of higher value. This alchemical process of turning waste into gold is known as *upcycling*. Here are some inspiring examples:

- ◆ **Floored.** Tarkett, a global leader in flooring solutions, recycles not only its own carpets but also those of other manufacturers and uses the recycled materials to make new well-designed carpet tiles.

- ◆ **Clothed.** Bilum, a socially responsible French company founded by Hélène de La Moureyre, recovers used materials (Heineken cartons, Club Med boat sails, gendarmerie jackets, Air France life jackets) and upcycles them into beautiful, more valuable products such as cool bags, accessories, or furniture.

- ◆ **Nourished.** Globally, industrial processes account for 31% of total greenhouse gas emissions. Startups like CarbonWorks and Twelve capture the CO_2 emitted by factories – before it is released in the atmosphere – and upcycles it into new valuable products. CarbonWorks has built a photo-bioreactor that contains microalgae that feed on the CO_2 captured directly at the source, such as factory fumes. By assimilating carbon, these microalgae multiply quickly and form a biomass, from which one can extract molecules with high added value that can be used for human and animal nutrition. Twelve has developed a suitcase-sized electrochemical reactor that transforms industrial CO_2 captured directly from their point of emission into critical chemicals that can be used to make sustainable aviation fuel as well as consumer products such as sunglasses, car parts, and laundry detergents.

♦ **Fueled.** Biotech startups Afyren and EcoCeres upcycle low-value agricultural waste into high-value materials and products. Afyren's industrial-scale biorefinery converts agricultural by-products sourced locally from sugarcane and sugar beet industries into bio-based organic acids. These natural high-quality acids are used as substitutes for fossil-based ingredients for various applications ranging from animal and human nutrition to cosmetics and lubricants. Similarly, EcoCeres's biorefinery transforms agricultural waste like corn cob and straw into a full range of high-value biofuels including sustainable aviation fuel (SAF) (by 2050 more than 70% of all aviation fuel powering flights leaving from European Union airports will be SAF). EcoCeres teamed up with Shenzhen Expressway Environmental (SEZ), whose parent firm processes more than 2.5 million metric tons of food waste across China. Under this partnership, SEZ will collect used cooking oil and waste oil from its kitchen waste treatment facilities and supply it to EcoCeres, which will convert the bio-grease into low-carbon and high-value biofuels.

Level 2: Sharing Physical Assets

Businesses with unused or underexploited physical assets – such as inventory, spaces, production capacity, equipment, vehicles – can share them with other firms seeking these things. This way, companies can keep their physical assets fully used and generate additional income.

SPACE

CBRE projects that Europe will need 300 million square feet of additional warehouse space by 2025 due to a surge in e-commerce.[4] Paris-based SpaceFill and Seattle-based Flexe are two startups that have developed digital logistics platforms that enable owners of underused warehouses to generate new revenue by quickly renting them out to large corporations or e-commerce startups in dire need of storage space.

According to Cushman & Wakefield, in the second quarter of 2023, Manhattan had a 22% office vacancy rate, the highest recorded since 1984. That's like 40 skyscrapers the size of the Chrysler Building staying empty.[5] Across the US, hybrid work will push office vacancies to a record 1.1 billion square feet by 2030. Headspace enables companies that own beautiful but underused spaces to rent them to other businesses seeking inspiring venues to host their meetings and conferences.

PRODUCTION CAPACITY
Manufacturers with idle factories can offer their unused production capacity to other firms by using platforms like MakerVerse, Xometry, Fictiv, Replique, and Protolabs Network.

SHIPPING
Digital freight networks like Convoy (owned by Flexport), Uber Freight, and Trukker help fleet operators keep their trucks fully used and earn more income by seamlessly combining loads from multiple shippers.

EQUIPMENT AND MATERIALS
In Canada, US, and the Netherlands, hospitals use digital platforms developed by Cohealo and Floow2 to share medical equipment with each other, thus maximizing asset use, reducing capital expenses, increasing availability, and improving patient care. Construction companies in North America use Dozr to share their unused construction materials and machines with their peers.

TRANSPORTATION
Seventy-four percent of French professionals go to work by car.[6] Private cars contribute to almost 16% of greenhouse gas emissions in France. Public transportation is not practical for all workers, as 40% of French people live in an area poorly served by buses and trains. Inspired by the great success of carpooling between individuals, the startups Klaxit and Karos have built B2B carpooling networks dedicated to companies, offering their employees a sustainable, comfortable, user-friendly, and frugal mobility solution. In 2022 alone, Klaxit (owned by BlaBlaCar) facilitated 2.6 million home-to-work carpools.

Karos estimates its carpooling service saves its business users two full tanks of gas per month and 26 minutes per trip.

Some businesses may be wary of sharing their physical assets in a marketplace that enables anonymous many-to-many relationships. These firms can get their feet wet in the B2B sharing economy by establishing a strategic partnership with just one trusted company – or a few select peers within their own industry – and share their assets exclusively with that firm first before engaging with other partners.

RIVALS UNITE

For many years, in Africa and India, rival telecom operators have shared mobile phone towers, which are managed by Tower Companies, also called Towercos, such as Indus Towers in India and Helios Towers in Africa. Now, Western telecoms firms are doing the same. For instance, Ericsson teamed up with Philips to combine city street lighting with mobile phone infrastructure. Integrating cell phone antennae into energy-efficient LED streetlights installed across a big city like Los Angeles helps carriers increase their network coverage in that city. Western firms are also learning from health care firms in Africa that piggyback on Coca-Cola's "cold chain" (a temperature-controlled supply chain) as a cost-effective way to preserve life-saving medicine and have it delivered rapidly to remote villages. In Belgium, Nestlé and its rival PepsiCo integrated their logistics capabilities to fill delivery trucks with both their companies' fresh and chilled products. By combining their supply chain resources, both Nestlé and PepsiCo reduced transportation costs by 44%, lowered carbon emissions by 55%, and improved customer satisfaction.[7]

Large enterprises, like industrial conglomerates, can also jump-start their B2B sharing journey by first sharing physical assets among internal units and trusted partners within their own ecosystem. For instance, since 2018, the energy giant Engie has piloted BeeWe, a collaborative economy platform that enables supply chain professionals among various Engie entities to pool and share industrial spare parts with each other. This cuts the need to produce costly new industrial parts (which would also have a negative ecological impact) and boosts the speed and agility of maintenance services. BeeWe already offers 360,000 items worth over €100 million in total and is used by 5,000 employees in 24 countries across Engie's global organization.

At Level 1 and Level 2, B2B sharing operates mainly as a **transactional marketplace**, connecting many cost-conscious "buyers" with multiple "providers" who want to monetize their underused physical assets and material resources on a short-term, tactical basis.

It should be noted here that *bartering* is also part of this logic of transactional exchanges at Levels 1 and 2. Bartering is the exchange of goods or services between companies without the use of cash. Bartering is thousands of years old and originated in Mesopotamia, the region currently known as Iraq. Today, bartering is a common business practice in Anglo-Saxon countries, Italy, Belgium, Switzerland, Greece, and developing countries. Now, companies in countries like France and Canada have also embraced bartering. In France, Korp is a well-established digital platform that facilitates inter-company bartering based on a virtual currency. In Canada, the BarterPay community boasts over 4,000 businesses that have conducted over Can$600 million in transactions, saving more than Can$200 million in cash. In the US, the total value of all barter transactions is $12 billion to $14 billion, according to the International Reciprocal Trade Association. Bartering is legally, accountably, and fiscally authorized in many countries, including the US, France, Australia, and Canada. Since 2020, when COVID-19 began, B2B bartering has taken off in countries like the UK, enabling millions of cash-strapped small businesses to buy and sell goods without using cash.

From Level 3 on, however, companies transcend the purely commercial logic and short-term financial interest. They move beyond tactical transactional exchanges of tangible goods and services that take place in an anonymous marketplace. Instead, firms begin to establish strategic partnerships with a select group of deeply trusted peers, forming strategic B2B sharing **communities**. Members of these close-knit communities pool and share highly valuable and intangible resources to cocreate long-term and large-scale economic value and positive social and ecological impact.

Level 3: Sharing Purchasing Power

Pooling buying power isn't new. For instance, government agencies as well as retailers form "purchasing cooperatives" that aggregate demand to get lower prices from select suppliers. But enlightened organizations can pool buying power to not only reduce the costs of procurement but also to increase their agility and resilience. In doing so, they can ensure the steady supply of critical goods that suffer from high price volatility and risk being disrupted by cataclysmic events like COVID-19 and climate change. In addition, these firms can boost their innovation capacity and contribute to the common good.

Consider the health care sector. US hospitals are experiencing chronic drug shortages. In 2023, 309 drugs were in short supply, the highest number ever.[8] These shortages are typically caused by product recalls, unexpected supply chain disruptions such as COVID-19 (80% of active pharmaceutical components in US drugs are sourced from China and India), or a big spike in demand during flu season or epidemics.[9] In 2019 alone, US hospitals had to invest 8.6 million in additional work hours, at a cost of $360 million, to deal with drug shortages.

In addition to shortages, hospitals in the US also face drastic drug price increases. In the first half of 2019 alone, the average price of more than 3,400 drugs rose by 10.5%, or five times the rate of inflation. In August 2023, AARP reported that list prices for the 25 brand-name drugs with the highest Medicare Part D spending have tripled since they first entered the market, thus far exceeding the rate of inflation.[10] This price hike explains why one in three US adults can no longer afford to take their medication as prescribed. Hospitals must also contend with wild price swings – when a pharmaceutical company breaks the price of a drug to wipe out its competitors, then drastically hikes the price, leaving hospitals and patients at its mercy.

Fed up with drug shortages and price gouging dictated by the pharmaceutical industry, more than 55 health systems representing more than 1,550 hospitals and one-third of all hospital beds across the US have joined forces to form Civica Rx, a nonprofit organization that ensures a steady supply of quality drugs at a lower price for all its members. Civica has pooled the buying power of its more than 55 members to negotiate a long-term agreement with generic drug manufacturers such as Xellia, and Hikma to produce more than 80 essential generic drugs at a fair and stable price and to supply them without interruption for several years.

All these drugs are being produced in the US, reducing dependence on global supply chains exposed to disruptions caused by pandemics like COVID-19, natural disasters related to climate change, or geopolitical tensions with China. Civica is also a boon for insurers, because it could save payers potentially $1 billion a year in drug costs. To date, 60 million patients across the US have been treated with Civica's medications. During the first two years of the COVID-19 pandemic, Civica and its supply partners were able to meet surge hospital demand of up to 400% for some COVID-19 medications. In 2024, Civica aims to produce insulin in large volume and reduce its cost from $300 to $30 per vial.[11] Civica is building its own state-of-the-art manufacturing facility in Petersburg, Virginia, that will produce dozens of low-cost drugs.

Dan Liljenquist, chairman of Civica's board of directors, explained to me that by pooling the purchasing power of 1,550 hospitals, Civica Rx wants to serve a noble purpose: to make drugs affordable and accessible to all Americans, which Liljenquist considers as their birthright.[12] Civica Rx therefore embodies **wise sharing**, a model of enlightened B2B sharing in the service of the common good (we will expound this notion of wise sharing in Chapter 4).

With climate change a clear and present danger, companies can also pool their purchasing power to buy clean energy at large scale to quickly decarbonize entire economies. Founded in 2013, the Clean Energy Buyers Association (CEBA) includes more than 400 big corporate energy buyers – such as Amazon, Coca-Cola, Google, McDonald's, and UPS – who collectively boost demand for solar and wind power, with a mission to create a 90% carbon-free US electricity system by 2030. Since 2014, CEBA's corporate members have procured 71 gigawatts of clean energy in the US, accounting for 42% of all wind and solar capacity added to the US grid during that period.[13] In 2022, these procurement deals represented 70% of the carbon-free energy capacity added to the US grid.

In the same vein, the First Movers Coalition (FMC) – created by the World Economic Forum and former US Special Presidential Envoy for Climate John Kerry – has more than 95 corporate members who aggregate purchasing demand for climate technologies to rapidly decarbonize emissions-intensive sectors like steel, chemicals, aviation, shipping, concrete, and cement. FMC members have collectively made more than 120 procurement commitments to buy $16 billion worth of emerging climate technologies and reduce annual carbon emissions by 31 million metric tons – all by 2030.[14]

Some Fortune 500 firms are leveraging aggregated power purchasing agreements (PPAs) to rapidly decarbonize their entire value chains by incentivizing the bulk of their suppliers to cost-effectively transition to renewable energy. An aggregated PPA enables multiple businesses – especially small and midsize enterprises – to pool their energy demand and collectively enter into a long-term agreement with a clean energy provider. In 2017, Walmart initiated Project Gigaton with the goal of reducing 1 billion tons of greenhouse gas emissions from its entire supply chain by 2030. As part of this initiative, in 2020, Walmart teamed up with Schneider Electric to launch Gigaton PPA, a program that aims to boost access to the renewable energy market by hundreds of Walmart suppliers by harnessing their collective buying power. In late 2022, five Walmart suppliers – Amy's Kitchen, Great Lakes Cheese, Levi Strauss & Co., The J.M. Smucker Co., and Valvoline Inc. – signed an aggregated PPA with the clean energy provider Ørsted to purchase annually during 12 years about 250,000 megawatt-hours of renewable power generated by Ørsted's Sunflower Wind Farm in Marion County, Kansas (this is tantamount to avoiding the emissions from more than 458,000 gasoline-powered cars during one year).[15]

My research shows that B2B sharing has grown considerably in countries all over the world since the public health and economic crisis of 2020–2021. Yet, most companies currently practice B2B sharing at Levels 1, 2, and 3. We can refer to these three levels collectively as **basic B2B sharing**. I strongly believe, however, that all nations can achieve significant economic, societal, and ecological gains by encouraging their businesses to progress to Levels 4, 5, and 6 of B2B sharing, what I call **advanced B2B sharing**.

Level 4: Sharing Employees

Companies can also share their human resources with one another, enabling them to gain access to a broader and more diverse pool of talent, skills, and expertise.

The 2015 Eurofound report identifies two kinds of employee sharing:[16]

♦ **Strategic employee sharing.** A group of businesses form a network that recruits one or more workers on a full-time basis and sends them on individual job assignments to the member firms.

  For instance, Vénétis is an association of 360 small French businesses that hires experts – in fields as diverse as industrial quality control and web marketing – as full-time employees and shares them on a project basis among its member firms, thus replacing precarious and poorly paid part-time jobs with stable and well-paid "shared-time" jobs.

♦ **Ad hoc (tactical) employee sharing.** A business that is unable to offer work for its employees temporarily loans them to another company, with full consent of the workers. This temporary mobility of workers is a win-win-win model. By loaning out underemployed employees, the lending company can maintain their employability, preserve valuable skills, and reduce personnel costs. The "host" business wins by gaining access to motivated and directly operational staff at lower cost. The employee is also a winner because they maintain their employment contract with their employer and 100% of their remuneration while diversifying and enriching their professional career in new work environments.

In France, digital platforms like Mobiliwork, laponi, and Pilgreem facilitate ad hoc (temporary) employee sharing among companies within the same or across different sectors. Hyver runs a B2B staff sharing marketplace in the UK. In South Africa, Teambix enables companies to loan out their skilled workers on a short-term basis to other businesses allowing, for instance, an accountant working in the banking industry to carry out an accounting project in the construction sector.

The twin health and economic crises in 2020 validated the value and merit of the talent sharing model on a grand scale and accelerated its wider adoption among businesses. For example, in April 2020, when COVID-19 was in full swing in the US, Accenture,

Lincoln Financial Group, ServiceNow, and Verizon jointly launched People + Work Connect, an artificial intelligence (AI)-based employer-to-employer platform that helped people laid off at one company quickly find employment at another organization, breaking the long and traumatic cycle of unemployment for these workers.

In France, the pandemic boosted the market for Hydres, a collaborative recruitment platform. Located in Trèves in the Cévennes National Park in southern France, Hydres accompanies the voluntary or involuntary professional mobility of employees within a network of companies that form the local economic ecosystem. The idea is to limit the impact of an employee layoff or resignation for all stakeholders while preserving talent and know-how in a territory.

Platforms like Teambix and Hydres also support the rise of the "boomerang" employee, that is, an employee who works three to five years in a company and leaves it to come back later, enriched with new skills and already familiar with the company's culture. This is a win-win model for both the employee and the employer.[17] In the US, 94% of senior executives are willing to rehire a former employee and 52% of workers won't mind rejoining a former employer. In France, 22% of companies rehired former employees during 2020. A global UKG survey in 2022 showed that 20% of people who quit during the pandemic had already returned to their old jobs.

Companies that feel too nervous to share their employees with other businesses can first experiment safely within their own organization. For instance, secondment programs – also known as *job rotations* – enable an employee with a specialized and valued skill to temporarily work in another team within a company, or an external organization, which is a smart way to cross-fertilize knowledge and find new inspiration. Australian collaboration software company Atlassian, ranked number 3 in Fortune Best Workplaces in Technology 2023, runs secondment programs for its personnel, which boost employee engagement. Eighty-six percent of employees at Atlassian consider it a great place to work compared to 57% of employees at a typical US-based firm.

A large consultancy with hundreds of thousands of employees in more than 100 countries teamed up with a world-leading freelancing and crowdsourcing marketplace to set up an internal talent-sharing platform for its global employees. This platform automatically matches employees with relevant skills with specific work projects. When managers urgently need a special skill for a project, they post their requirements on this platform and interested employees can bid to work on that project. This platform boosts employee motivation and engagement for two reasons. First, it enables multitalented employees to unleash their *multi-potentality* by applying their various skills in several projects across different practice areas. For instance, a risk management specialist in the insurance practice can lend their deep operations research skills to optimize a supply chain project in the automotive practice. Second, this platform gives global exposure to the consultancy's employees, so a London-based consultant can work remotely on projects led by teams in Bangalore or Shanghai.

Another way companies can jump-start employee-sharing is by leveraging industry-specific consortia or trade associations. In France, NextMove – an ecosystem of industrial firms and research agencies codeveloping next-generation mobility solutions in Paris and Normandy regions – set up Genesis, a digital platform that enables the sharing of goods and skills among member organizations colocated in the same region. Likewise, top French retailers Auchan, Boulanger, Decathlon, Jules, Kiabi, Leroy Merlin, and RougeGorge jointly leverage tipik, a platform that enables these retailers to share their employees with each other for one-off projects.

State and local governments are also investing in digital platforms to promote talent sharing among businesses within the same city or region to boost their attractiveness and competitiveness. The northwestern French region of Pays de la Loire has set up Solutions Partage, a platform for pooling and sharing all kinds of resources – facilities, vehicles, and even employees – between businesses in the region. About 15 cities in the region have adapted this platform to facilitate B2B sharing among companies colocated in the same *territoire* (county), hence forging *hyper-local value networks*, or HYLOVANs (we will explore HYLOVANs in Part II).

Similarly, the city of Tours, located in the heart of France, has launched the online platform Hub Eco, which enables local companies to share their competences and preserve local skills. In the UK, the New Anglia Advanced Manufacturing and Engineering group and the Cambridge Norwich Tech Corridor launched the talent-sharing platform (TSP) in early 2021. TSP enables engineering and manufacturing businesses within the East Anglia region to share their technical staff temporarily or "to co-employ niche expertise that may not be required on a permanent basis by an individual company."[18] TSP was set up to help businesses in East Anglia mitigate the negative impact of both COVID-19 and Brexit.

National government agencies are also jumping onto the employee-swapping and talent-sharing bandwagon. For instance, the US Department of Defense and private sector firms set up the public-private talent exchange (PPTE) to share high-performing mid-career professionals across organizations for short and well-defined assignments. PPTE has two major benefits: (1) it enables participating employees to gain exposure and experience in new settings and (2) it helps cross-pollinate innovative best practices across public and private sectors. Other government agencies – from the intelligence community to NASA – have launched their own PPTE programs to facilitate the sharing of talent in strategic areas like AI and aerospace technologies. Likewise, in 2023, the UK government launched the Digital Secondment Programme to temporarily hire AI and data experts from the private sector to boost the technological skills and productivity in government agencies.

The various employee-sharing mechanisms described in this chapter could deliver "flexicurity" – a synergistic balance of flexibility and security that will be highly valued by both employers and workers in the 21st century.[19] Talent sharing perfectly embodies the spirit of "doing better with less," the core operating principle of a frugal economy. By sharing employees and skills, companies collectively maximize their economic performance while minimizing waste of the most valuable resource: human talent.

Level 5: Sharing Clients

Competitively minded businesses have traditionally sought new ways to lock customers into their brands by building *vertical* ecosystems. But building a brand-specific ecosystem has become meaningless and even counterproductive today, as digitally empowered millennials and Gen Z customers can create their own personalized products without depending on established brands.

Given this new trend, visionary brands are forming *horizontal* ecosystems that integrate their capabilities and assets with those of other brands – including their rivals – to offer their "shared clients" end-to-end solutions and highly personalized experiences.

For instance, the French railway company SNCF joined forces with carmaker Renault to offer seamless end-to-end mobility solutions to shared clients – by, say, joining a long-distance train ride with last-mile travel in a rented electric car. SNCF also teamed up with Orange, Total, Air Liquide, and Michelin to set up Ecomobility Ventures, Europe's first multicorporate investment fund, which invests in promising startups that can jointly provide end-to-end solutions in sustainable mobility.

Noncompeting brands can also collaborate, not only to address the current needs of their shared customers but also to anticipate their future demand and proactively respond to it. For example, Orange, Kingfisher, Carrefour, Legrand, La Poste, SEB, and Pernod Ricard – seven leading companies from seven diverse industries – set up InHome, a cross-industry innovation incubator run by InProcess, an innovation consultancy. Through InProcess's ethnographic studies, InHome member firms first gain deeper insights into the future needs and values of typical families who will be living in tomorrow's homes. They then consider effective ways to integrate their respective offerings and core competences to synergistically serve their common customer of their future.

By participating in multisector innovation projects like InHome that are focused on the shared customers of tomorrow, explains Christophe Rebours, founder and CEO of InProcess, businesses competing directly in a capitalist market can unlearn their "competitive instincts" and cultivate the spirit of cooperation. "Companies can take off their 'industry blinkers' and see things from the point of view of their shared client; it is no longer increasing their own piece of the pie that motivates them but increasing the size of the whole pie for the benefit of all," elaborates Rebours.[20]

In coming years, McKinsey & Company predicts the rapid erosion of traditional industry boundaries and the rise of cross-sectoral digital ecosystems that deliver fully integrated, end-to-end customer experience. By 2025, the revenues flowing through these cross-industry ecosystems could exceed a whopping $60 trillion – or 30% of the combined revenue of global businesses.[21] Unless brick-and-mortar companies in established industries learn to join forces and code-velop cross-sectoral digital solutions for their shared clients, they will miss out on this $60 trillion market opportunity, to the benefit of digital giants like Google, Amazon, Meta, Apple, and Microsoft.

Level 6: Sharing Intellectual Property and Knowledge

Patents, ideas, best practices, and domain knowledge are the crown jewels of an organization. As a result, a company may be reluctant to share its intellectual property (IP) with other companies. However, it may make sense to do so for two reasons.

First, companies can monetize their unused or underused intellectual assets by sharing them. In the US, intangible assets account for 90% of the market value of the S&P 500 (the 500 US firms with the largest market capitalization). Each year, the US generates $7.8 trillion in IP – patents, copyrights, and know-how – which represents 41% of US GDP.[22] Yet, $1 trillion of it is wasted annually because US businesses lack a clear plan to obtain maximum value from their IP, such as new technology inventions.[23] Likewise, according to the European Commission's PatVal-EU study, 36% of European patents have not been commercially exploited. Companies can better leverage these underused patents, and generate new revenues, by exchanging them on IP-sharing platforms such as yet2.com and NineSigma with other innovation-seeking firms.

Second, progressive companies driven by a higher purpose can achieve "moral leadership" in their industry by sharing their IP with other organizations – including rival firms – to increase the collective social and ecological impact of their industry.

For example, R&D teams at consumer goods giant Unilever and apparel maker Levi Strauss had invented proprietary technologies to make their products more sustainable. Unilever's "compressed deodorants" use 25% less aluminum and half the amount of propellant, reducing the carbon footprint of each aerosol by 25%. Levi Strauss has developed 21 techniques to reduce water consumption by up to 96% in garment finishing. After deploying these green technologies successfully in their own supply chains first, these two firms have "open-sourced" their inventions with the aim of raising the environmental performance of their entire industry.[24]

Likewise, in 2019, the food giant Danone made its collection of 1,800 yogurt strains – including 193 lactic and bifidobacteria ferment strains – freely available to researchers around the world. In doing so, Danone wants to promote "open science" and help the world achieve the UN's Sustainable Development Goals faster, especially those related to ending hunger and improving nutrition and health.

When the COVID-19 pandemic began, enlightened health care providers shared their IP with other companies to co-innovate life-saving solutions. For instance, in March 2020, the medical device firm Ventec Life Systems shared the technology of its multifunction critical care ventilators with US carmaker GM. Both firms worked closely to rapidly scale up production of this life-saving device in a repurposed GM factory in Indiana. Similarly, the industrial giant Siemens teamed up with Medtronic, a world leader in medical technology, to code-velop a "digital twin" of a ventilator and made it available as open source on the internet so that anyone in the world could use it to make their own ventilators to help local COVID-19 patients.

IP is not restricted to patents. It can also be valuable knowledge – proven techniques and best practices as well as failures – accumulated by an organization or an industry over time. By *recombining* and *repurposing* the existing knowledge from diverse domains, companies can innovate faster, better, cheaper, and find novel ways to create sustainable value.[25] This ingenious process of creating something new and valuable by cleverly integrating different existing knowledge resources is called *combinatorial innovation* or *recombinant innovation*.[26] The creation of the iPhone is a perfect example of recombinant innovation. Steve Jobs's genius was to combine multiple technologies and ideas that already existed and integrate them seamlessly in a new well-designed mobile phone.

In the May 1998 issue of *The Quarterly Journal of Economics*, Martin Weitzman, who was a professor of economics at Harvard University, published a fascinating paper titled "Recombinant Growth."[27] Using complex mathematical formula, Weitzman demonstrated that innovation is a *combinatorial process*, that is any new "technology" or "idea" is in fact just a novel configuration of preexisting technologies and ideas. As such, if a nation wants to boost its economic growth, it needs to invest not so much in its ability to generate new ideas as in its capacity to combine existing knowledge to generate innovative ideas and bring them to fruition (interestingly, the word *frugal* stems from the Latin root *frux* meaning "fruit" or "value"; a frugal innovation is one that bears fruit, that is, creates genuine value and impact). A 2007 World Bank report titled "Unleashing India's Innovation" validated Weitzman's theory of recombinant growth in the context of the Indian economy. The report projected that India's economic growth can be as much as "4.8 times higher if (Indian) enterprises were to absorb and use the knowledge that *already* exists in the economy."[28]

As businesses share first their waste and physical assets, then their financial and human resources, and finally their clients and IP and knowledge with others, they will gradually build up their self-confidence and train their "trust muscle" as they learn to crawl, walk, and finally run in the B2B sharing world. B2B sharing could be the lynchpin of "stakeholder capitalism" and help us build inclusive, resilient, and regenerative societies in the 21st century.[29]

Mastering the Full Spectrum

At this juncture, it's critical to clarify two key elements about the taxonomy-cum-maturity model of B2B sharing depicted in Figure 3.1 and expounded in this chapter:

◆ Although this framework has six distinct levels, it does *not* imply a hierarchy. Sharing IP isn't "better" or "superior" in any way than sharing waste. Likewise, the fact that a company shares its IP – the top rung in the maturity ladder – doesn't mean it mastered the art of B2B sharing. The masters of B2B sharing are not the firms that can leap to – and remain at – the top of the pyramid in Figure 3.1. Rather, the winning companies that will lead their industries are those that have mastered – and keep practicing in a dynamic and synergistic manner – *the full spectrum* of B2B sharing activities.

◆ The various resources classified in Figure 3.1 are categorized by the level of general *risk* they carry if they were to be shared with other firms, rather than their intrinsic *economic value*. As such, sharing a low-risk resource like waste could also be highly valuable, that is, financially very lucrative, if a company

performs it strategically. Take the Tata Group, a global con-
glomerate with more than $150 billion in revenue headquar-
tered in India that is composed of 30 companies including
Tata Steel and Tata Motors, which owns Jaguar Land
Rover (JLR).

Tata Group companies are masters at turning waste into gold. Tata
Steel, for instance, generated more than $35 million in 2018 alone by
selling the 1.8 million tons of slag generated annually in its steel factory in India to other companies, who use it as a raw material to build
roads and produce cement and bricks.[30] Likewise, as part of its journey to zero emissions, JLR has launched Reality, a bold enterprise-
wide initiative to recover aluminum from used consumer products like
drinks cans and aerosols as well as end-of-life vehicles and upcycle it
to manufacture new vehicles, including an all-electric car.

Considering these two clarifications, Figure 3.2 offers a non-
hierarchical and dynamic representation of B2B sharing. It shows
what industry leadership in the 21st century entails: winning firms
will be those that can deftly navigate through and master the whole

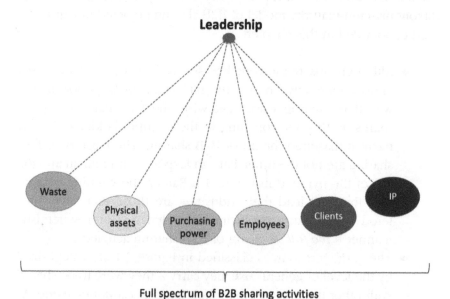

Figure 3.2 Leading firms will master the whole spectrum of B2B sharing to
capture its full value.

spectrum of B2B sharing activities. In doing so, leading firms will be able to unleash and capture the full value of B2B sharing. In Chapter 4 we will look at how organizations in a vital sector – health care – can harness the full B2B sharing spectrum to maximize the well-being of all citizens at lower cost.

CHAPTER 4

From Smart Sharing to Wise Sharing

As mentioned in Chapter 1, in 2023, the World Bank warned of a "lost decade" in global economic growth without bold policy shifts in labor supply, productivity, and investment.[1] Rather than rebuild the dysfunctional capitalist economic system, which has caused severe inequalities and environmental destruction, national and regional leaders could wisely use the next decade to construct a virtuous frugal economy that is socially inclusive and regenerates people, places, and the planet. Business-to-business (B2B) sharing would be a key pillar of this frugal economy – at national, regional, and local levels. However, to unlock B2B sharing's full potential and maximize its economic, social, and ecological impacts, businesses would need one critical element: *a noble purpose.*

In Chapters 2 and 3, I addressed the what and how of B2B sharing, that is, the different mechanisms through which businesses can share their various types of resources. But companies must also address the vital why question, that is, "why does our company want to engage in B2B sharing?" In other words, companies need to get their motivation right and make sense of – and give *meaning* to – their commitment to this path.

If, to the why question, most companies answer, "we want to share resources to save money or make more money," we will see the rise of what I call ***smart B2B sharing***, whose narrow purpose is to solely make the current capitalistic economic system, with all its deleterious dysfunctions, even more efficient. We don't want that. But if most businesses answer, "we want to make a positive social and ecological impact," then they can enable **wise B2B sharing**, whose noble purpose is to radically reinvent entire industries and accelerate the transition to a benign frugal economy in the coming decade (see Figure 4.1).

Here are two noble objectives that can motivate businesses to practice B2B sharing wisely and positively impact people, communities, and the planet.

Value Versus Values

B2B sharing can deliver a big shot in the arm for the financially stretched health care systems worldwide struggling to deliver better care to more patients at lower cost. This is especially the case in the US, where skyrocketing health care spending will account for nearly 20% of GDP in 2031, which is unsustainable, even as more Americans get sicker and don't live as long.[2] In 2022, American's life expectancy at birth was 77.5 years, down from 78.8 before the COVID-19 pandemic. As the Peterson-KFF Health System Tracker notes, "The

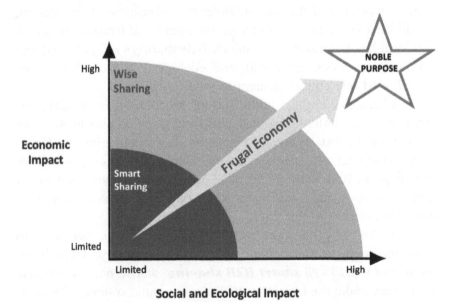

Figure 4.1 Wise sharing, connected to a noble purpose, can deliver greater impact than smart sharing.

U.S. has the lowest life expectancy among large, wealthy countries while it far outspends its peers on healthcare."[3]

Naively hoping to do better with less, a growing number of hospitals and clinics across the US are transitioning to value-based health care (VBHC), which is "an integrated care strategy focused on the value delivered to the patient."[4] In the VBHC model, currently being implemented in the US and Switzerland, multiple providers combine their resources and capabilities to optimize the care pathways and health outcomes for their shared patients. With pricing based on the quality, not the quantity, of care provided to the patient, VBHC aims to improve care delivery while reducing health care costs.

The efficiency-seeking VBHC model, however, is too narrowly focused on improving "health outcomes per dollar spent" and lacks a noble purpose that can deepen and broaden its impact. In a 2019 report titled "Defining Value in Value-Based Healthcare," the European Commission's expert panel on effective ways of investing in health (EXPH) noted, "Currently, 'value' in the context of healthcare is often discussed as 'health outcomes relative to monetized inputs,' aiming at increasing cost-effectiveness. This interpretation of 'value' is perceived by the EXPH as too narrow and the notion of 'values-based healthcare' seems more suitable in conveying the guiding principles underlying solidarity-based healthcare systems."[5]

By embracing the full spectrum of B2B sharing depicted in Figure 3.2, health care organizations can not only master value-based care but also evolve beyond it and pioneer *values*-based health care, a virtuous new care paradigm that is both rooted in – and powered by – cooperation and equity. As mentioned, hospitals can use digital platforms like Floow2 to share their underused medical equipment and services. Care providers can also pool their purchasing power – like the 1,550 hospitals who formed Civica Rx – to buy and even produce high-quality drugs at lower cost. Although sharing physical, financial, and human resources can certainly enhance health systems, it is by sharing their intellectual assets – patented technologies, best practices, and knowledge – that health care organizations can cocreate the biggest social impact both locally and globally.

As of March 13, 2023, three years after COVID-19 cases exploded globally, only 72.3% of people worldwide had been vaccinated against the virus.[6] This proportion drops to below 30% in many developing economies. By April 2022, only 12% of the African population was fully vaccinated against COVID-19.[7] To democratize access to mRNA COVID-19 vaccines in low-income countries, in June 2021, the World Health Organization (WHO) and the Medicines Patent Pool (MPP) teamed up with a South African consortium comprising the biotech firm Afrigen Biologics and the vaccine manufacturer Biovac to establish an mRNA vaccine technology development and transfer hub (the *hub*, for short) in Cape Town.[8]

This hub will develop mRNA vaccine technology and, through royalty-free licensing agreements, will share its technical know-how along with appropriate training with a global network of 15 low-/medium-income countries (LMICs). This transfer aims to empower LMICs to gradually build and sustain within their own countries the critical R&D and biomanufacturing capabilities and the skilled human capital needed to produce mRNA vaccines locally. It's worth noting that mRNA vaccines do *better* with *less*: they can be easily, speedily, and cheaply produced anywhere and yet are very efficient and can be swiftly updated (just like software) to tackle new virus variants.[9]

This hub, based at Afrigen in Cape Town, was inaugurated in April 2023 when Afrigen announced "the completion of the mRNA technology platform (which is) is housed within (Afrigen's) end-to-end mRNA vaccine development and production facility."[10] The first mRNA vaccine developed and produced at lab scale successfully by using this platform is AfriVac 2121, an mRNA COVID vaccine. AfriVac 2121, which will be tested on humans starting in late 2025, is the very first mRNA vaccine candidate developed end-to-end in the African continent. Biovac is working with Afrigen to scale up production of AfriVac 2121 to commercial batches as part of the completion of the Afrigen mRNA platform, which will be transferred by Afrigen to the 15 partner countries in the WHO-initiated mRNA technology transfer program.

Petro Terblanche, chief executive officer of Afrigen, explained to me the unique features of the mRNA technology transfer program that her firm is coleading:

> Many product-based tech transfer programs offer just a fish to LMICs. We, however, will transfer a platform capability that includes know-how and training of our partners in LMICs

how to fish – so they become fully autonomous and locally produce their own mRNA vaccines sustainably. To use a tech industry analogy, we don't give just an app to LMICs, we provide them an end-to-end platform they can use to build their own apps. And we show them how to build an amazing mRNA vaccine platform very frugally. The WHO and MPP investment made possible by the funders enables Afrigen's end-to-end R&D and our Good Manufacturing Practices (GMP) production facility is a fraction of the costs of similar or comparable facilities.

Also, our transfer program is bidirectional: our hub and spokes act as equal knowledge partners who all learn from each other. For example, some of our partners such as Incepta Vaccine (Bangladesh), Biological E Limited (India), Bio Farma (Indonesia), BioGeneric Pharma (Egypt) are experienced manufacturers with established GMP and quality management systems – so we learn from them. And with Bio-Manguinhos/Fiocruz in Brazil who has developed its own mRNA platform, we exchange information and will partner on joint development projects.[11]

Over time, this global sharing and cross-fertilization of knowledge and expertise will lead to new technologies that would drastically reduce the cost of developing and producing mRNA vaccines and enhance vaccine characteristics – such as durability, potency, and temperature stability – so they are better suited to LMICs. Beyond COVID-19, the WHO-sponsored mRNA technology transfer program has identified 30 diseases – including Dengue virus, hepatitis A and B, HIV, malaria, tuberculosis, and Zika virus – as potential priority targets for mRNA vaccines. The program is also creating partnerships to develop and test novel mRNA vaccine delivery technologies such as a microneedle array patch that lowers pain at application and eliminates the fear of needles for patients.

Achieving SDGs Faster, Better, Cheaper

The United Nations (UN) has defined 17 Sustainable Development Goals (SDGs), all of which aim to co-construct inclusive, healthy, and regenerative communities around the world by 2030 (see Figure 4.2). If implemented effectively, the SDGs could generate $12 trillion in economic value per year and create up to 380 million jobs by 2030 worldwide.[12]

To realize the SDGs' full potential, however, annual investments between $5.4 and $6.4 trillion will be required in sustainable development programs globally between now and 2030.[13] Sadly, developing countries face a $4 trillion annual funding gap.[14] In early 2023, the UN Chief António Guterres called for the world's most developed nations to increase to the tune of $500 billion their annual investment in sustainable development to achieve the 17 SDGs by 2030.[15] So much investment will be hard to marshal given the World Bank's prediction in January 2024 that over the next half-decade the global economic growth will be the weakest in 30 years.[16]

In the meantime, the social and ecological conditions globally are worsening. In early 2024, Oxfam reported that the five richest

Figure 4.2 The Sustainable Development Goals (SDGs) are a collection of 17 global goals that aim to improve the planet and communities and enhance the quality of human life around the world by the year 2030.

Source: United Nations / https://www.un.org/sustainabledevelopment//. The content of this publication has not been approved by the United Nations and does not reflect the views of the United Nations or its officials or Member States.

men in the world had their wealth doubled since 2020 while five billion people were made poorer in a "decade of division."[17] Oxfam predicted it would take more than 200 years to end poverty globally. Also, climate change has now become a clear and present danger in the richest countries. The Fifth National Climate Assessment, released in late 2023, warned that climate change is making it harder to "maintain safe homes and healthy families" in every part of the US even as extreme events such as heat waves, wildfires, and heavy rainfall are set to multiply as temperatures soar.[18]

With rising inequalities and climate disasters, the struggling world cannot afford to wait until 2030 to achieve the SDGs. It's time we reframe Sustainable Development Goals as **Shared Development Goals**. By *shared* I mean two things. First, businesses need to remove their "industry blinkers" and identify and leverage assets readily available in other sectors. By sharing resources across industry boundaries, businesses in different sectors can *collectively* achieve the SDGs faster, better, and cheaper.

For instance, in Africa, more than 50% of the population lack access to essential medicines.[19] As part of Project Last Mile, Coca-Cola shares its supply chain expertise and assets with nonprofit and government organizations that, for instance, piggyback on Coca-Cola's cold chain to deliver life-saving medicine like vaccines safely and promptly to remote African villages.[20] This example shows how cross-industry sharing of resources can (1) achieve SDG 3 related to "good health and well-being" faster, better, cheaper and (2) bolster SDG 17, which aims to "revitalize the global partnership for sustainable development."

Second, rather than tackle the 17 SDGs separately and individually – which is costly and time-consuming – companies must adopt a single shared strategy that can achieve multiple goals systemically and synergistically. In principle, the 17 SDGs should collectively "enable sustainable development in its three dimensions – economic, social, and environmental – in a balanced and integrated manner." But here is the reality: most companies find the sheer number of SDGs – 17 – overwhelming. So, they cherry-pick among the 17 SDGs a few goals that they believe they can realistically achieve by 2030. And even then, their few selected goals tend to favor the economic or environmental dimensions of sustainability at the expense of the social impact or vice versa. By adopting an integrated SDG strategy, however, businesses can cocreate win-win-win solutions that generate more economic *and* social *and* ecological value simultaneously by cleverly leveraging all existing resources.

Take the Solar Stewards marketplace mentioned in Chapter 2, which enables businesses to purchase renewable energy generated by small-scale solar units located in historically excluded communities in the US. By buying clean power through this marketplace, a multinational company can achieve the SDG 13: Climate Action for its own global organization as well as empower underprivileged communities to achieve many SDGs at a local level: SDG 7: Affordable and Clean Energy; SDG 8: Decent Work and Economic Growth; SDG 9: Industry, Innovation, and Infrastructure; SDG 10: Reduced Inequalities; SDG 11: Sustainable Cities and Communities; SDG 12: Responsible Consumption and Production; and SDG 17: Partnerships for the Goals.

■ ■ ■

In capitalist societies, businesses operate with a scarcity mindset and engage competitively with each other in a zero-sum game ruled by the formula 1 + 1 = 0. In India, however, people believe *ek aur ek gyarah*, that is **1 + 1 = 11**. Given their vast cultural diversity but also the debilitating scarcity of resources they face daily, Indians are attuned to cooperation. As Mahatma Gandhi said, "Interdependence is and ought to be as much the ideal of man as self-sufficiency. Man is a social being. Without interrelation with society, he cannot realize his oneness with the universe or suppress his egotism. His social interdependence enables him to test his faith and to prove himself on the touchstone of reality."[21]

As they face greater complexity and scarcity, businesses must eschew competition and embrace cooperation. 1 + 1 = 11 is a win-win formula that, when applied in the business realm, can enable *cocreation*, whereby two firms, even competitors, surpass their differences and combine their resources to cocreate something of greater value than they can individually. As Athena Aktipis, an associate professor at Arizona State University who studies cooperation across systems from human sharing to cancer biology, notes,

"Cocreators pool risk and share resources to produce a much larger pie for everyone to share, as opposed to fight for a teeny piece of a modest pie."[22]

The B2B sharing embodies this spirit of cocreation. By sharing wisely their physical and intangible resources – as explained in this chapter – pioneering firms across sectors and regions are cocreating trillions of dollars in economic value, boosting social inclusion, and accelerating their ecological transition.

B2B sharing is the first pillar of a frugal economy that is rooted in, and promotes, the spirit of cooperation among companies. By cooperating – instead of competing – companies can do "better with less": they can collectively boost their efficiency and agility, innovate faster and better, and drastically reduce their emissions and waste. The unfolding B2B sharing revolution promises not only to upend industries and reinvent our economies but also to help us build inclusive and sustainable societies in the 21st century.

In this first part of the book, I showed how businesses can unlearn their competitive mindset and cultivate a collaborative attitude. The next part looks at how companies can overcome their obsession with "scaling up" their operations globally and learn to "scale out" their activities by producing goods and services and cocreating value locally.

PART II

Distributed Manufacturing and Hyper-Local Value Networks

CHAPTER 5

Scaling Out Manufacturing

England and Europe through the 19th century, both America and Japan during the 20th century, and China in recent decades have all achieved exponential economic growth by vertically scaling up their manufacturing. In this context, scaling up means two things: (1) concentrating industrial activities in a few geographical locations where labor and other resources are cheap and abundant and (2) centralizing production in increasingly larger and ever-more efficient factories.

It is by scaling up cotton manufacturing that the city of Manchester in England went from being an insignificant town of 9,000 citizens in 1700 to becoming the world's first industrial city in the early 19th century.[1] Nicknamed *Cottonopolis*, Manchester gave birth to the British industrial revolution (1760–1840).[2] Already by 1774, 30,000 people were working in multiple cotton factories in Manchester. These mills were all modest in size. Then things changed. Murray's Mills, a vast industrial complex built between 1798 and 1806, housed the world's earliest and largest steam-powered cotton spinning factories that employed 1,200 workers at their peak.[3] "Here are buildings seven to eight stories, as high and as big as the Royal Palace in Berlin," enthused the Prussian architect Karl Friedrich Schinkel in 1825.[4] Do note that in 1860, more than 80% of the raw cotton used in Manchester mills was grown by African people laboring as slaves on plantations in the southern US.[5]

During the first half of the 20th century, the US scaled up its manufacturing to build a global industrial empire, especially in the automotive sector. In the late 19th century, the US car industry was more of a cottage industry. In 1899, 30 US auto manufacturers produced a total of just 2,500 motor vehicles, all made in small shops.[6] Most of these early US carmakers couldn't survive as they couldn't find a mass market for their pricey vehicles. In the early 20th century, 125 auto companies emerged in Detroit, which was only America's 13th largest city in 1903 when Henry Ford founded the Ford Motor Company.[7] A "frugal innovator," Henry Ford wanted to market a "frugal" vehicle that was affordable to US consumers as well as cheap to produce. In 1908, Ford introduced the Model T, dubbed as *everyman's car*, priced at $850 (rival models cost $2,000 to $3,000).[8] Within days, 15,000 orders were placed for the Model T. By 1918, half of all the cars running on US roads were Model Ts.[9] In 1925, the 15 millionth Model T came out of Ford's giant factory in Highland Park, Michigan, which mass-produced this vehicle.

Having mastered *standardization* with the Model T, Ford shifted his focus to *vertical integration*: he wanted his company to own and control the entire production value chain, from extracting raw materials from mines to making all individual parts to assembling the final vehicle. To achieve his vision of "a continuous, nonstop process from raw material to finished product, with no pause even for warehousing or storage," Henry Ford developed, between 1917 and 1928, a giant industrial complex in Dearborn, Michigan, along the River Rouge. The Ford River Rouge complex, as it came to be known, became the world's largest integrated factory. Measuring 1.5 miles (2.4 km) wide by 1 mile (1.6 km) long, the River Rouge complex comprised 93 buildings with 16 million square feet (1.5 km2) of factory floor space.[10] "There were ore docks, steel furnaces, coke ovens, rolling mills, glass furnaces and plate-glass rollers. Buildings included a tire-making plant, stamping plant, engine casting plant, frame and assembly plant, transmission plant, radiator plant, tool and die plant, and, at one time, even a paper mill. A massive power plant produced enough electricity to light a city the size of nearby Detroit, and a soybean conversion plant turned soybeans into plastic auto parts. Each day, workers smelted more than 1,500 tons of iron and made 500 tons of glass."[11] At its peak in the 1930s, more than 100,000 worked at the vertically integrated River Rouge factory, which rolled out a new car every 49 seconds, or 4,000 vehicles a day.

Following the lead of England, Europe, and America, China also massively scaled up its manufacturing to become "the world's factory." In 1990, China accounted for barely 3% of global manufacturing output by value.[12] In 2021, China's share of global manufacturing was 30%.[13] *The Economist* reported that "China produces about 80% of the world's air-conditioners, 70% of its mobile phones and 60% of its shoes."[14] Apple produces over 95% of its iPhones, iPads, Airpods, MacBooks, and Apple Watches in China.[15] Just like most of UK's cotton manufacturing was concentrated in Manchester, China's high-tech manufacturing is concentrated in Shenzhen, a coastal city in southeastern China that connects Hong Kong to China's mainland. Ninety percent of the world's electronics are produced in Shenzhen, which boasts thousands of R&D and design centers and agile factories.[16]

Besides being concentrated geographically, China's manufacturing is also centralized in a handful of massive industrial complexes that would make Henry Ford envious. China's largest private employer is FoxConn, the Taiwanese contract manufacturer that makes iPhones. FoxConn employs 800,000 people across China in a dozen gigantic factories. Its vast factory complex in Zhengzhou employs 200,000 workers, who make half of the world's iPhones, earning the place the nickname *iPhone City*.[17] Today, as the climate crisis worsens, China is scaling up the production of eco-friendly products like electric cars and clean energy like hydrogen. BYD is a Shenzhen-based manufacturer of new energy vehicles (NEVs), which comprise battery electric vehicles (BEVs) and plug-in hybrid electric vehicles (PHEVs). On August 9, 2023, BYD rolled out its 5 millionth NEV, making BYD the first carmaker in the world to achieve this milestone. Barely four months later, on November 24, 2023, BYD announced its cumulative production of NEVs had hit the 6 million mark.[18] In the last quarter of 2023, BYD sold more electric cars than Tesla.[19] Today, BYD operates 30 large-scale industrial parks across six continents. BYD's giant factory in the Chinese city of Xi'an churns out more than 3,600 vehicles per day!

9/11, COVID-19, and the Need for Adaptive Supply Networks

In late 2001, the US witnessed painfully the downside of scaling up manufacturing by concentrating it in a handful of giant factories and suppliers located in far-flung places. Right after the terrorist attacks of September 11, 2001, the US government closed the country's borders, restricting all inbound shipments to the US via air, land, and sea. This sudden border shutdown caught by surprise US companies who ran "lean" assembly lines that had little inventory on-site and were supplied "just-in-time" with materials imported from abroad. For instance, Ford Motor Co. had to slow down its assembly lines in the US because the trucks carrying key auto components were delayed at the Mexican and Canadian borders. As a result, during the fourth quarter in 2001, Ford's industrial output was 13% lower than it had planned.[20] Ford reported a loss of $5.5 billion in 2001, most of it in the fourth quarter. Likewise, Toyota, which pioneered just-in-time manufacturing, almost shut down production at its Sequoia SUV plant in Indiana due to delayed delivery of steering sensors that were air-shipped from Germany.

When 9/11 happened, I was working as a supply chain analyst at Forrester Research, a technology research and advisory firm based in Cambridge, Massachusetts. In 2000, I had written a report titled "Manufacturing Deconstructed" in which I recommended US manufacturers to decentralize their operations by distributing them globally.[21] I encouraged US firms to outsource manufacturing to emerging markets like Mexico, China, and India not just to lower cost but also to leverage innovative local talent. The 9/11 attacks shifted – or rather broadened – my perspective. I still believed in the beneficial power of globalization. But I realized 9/11 has ushered in the era of VUCA (volatility, uncertainty, complexity, ambiguity).

In this VUCA world filled with risks, US and European firms should build global supply chains that are optimized not for *efficiency* but for *agility* and *resilience* – by, for instance, sourcing a critical component from different suppliers or designing "plant-agnostic" products so they can shift their manufacturing from one factory to another around the globe within days. In 2002, I published a Forrester report in which I explained how US and European manufacturers can build "adaptive supply networks" that can sense and respond effectively to unexpected supply disruptions caused by terrorist attacks or pandemics.[22]

During the 18 years that followed the publication of this 2002 report, US and European firms continued to aggressively outsource their manufacturing to low-cost nations – especially China. Their main motivation in globalizing their supply chains was profit (as labor in the "third world" is cheap), not the pursuit of agility and resilience. China benefited handsomely from this trend by scaling up its own manufacturing capabilities to produce in large volume everything the world needed, from shoes and iPhones to drug ingredients and surgical masks. In a letter dated August 6, 2019, Chuck Grassley, who was then US Senate Finance Committee Chairman, warned the Department of Health and Human Services and Food and Drug Administration that 80% of active pharmaceutical ingredients used in drugs consumed in the US are produced mostly in China and India.[23]

In late 2019, China, which had become the center of global manufacturing, also emerged as the epicenter of a global pandemic as the coronavirus (COVID-19) outbreak hit the central Chinese city of Wuhan. In 2020, the COVID-19 virus got out of China, and, as it spread globally, it wrecked global supply chains. Dun & Bradsheet found that 938 of the Fortune 1000 firms had major suppliers located in Wuhan region.[24] Automakers like Ford and GM and consumer electronics giants like Apple that source massively from China were badly affected. In February 2020, Apple reported that it would fail to meet its first-quarter revenue target as the COVID-19 outbreak forced the shutdown of many Chinese factories that produce iPhones and iPads. By early March 2020, COVID-19 had already paralyzed 94% of Fortune companies' supply chains, costing the global economy $2.7 trillion.[25] Between February 19, 2020, and March 23, 2020, the S&P 500 Stock Index lost 34% of its value, erasing three years' worth of gains in just a month.

In March 2020, I was living in New York when COVID-19 engulfed America. New York, the city that never sleeps, came to a standstill. Soon, America's economic capital became the global epicenter of the pandemic and COVID-19 deaths soared. The US, despite its immense wealth, was incapable of swiftly producing vaccines, masks, and ventilators to protect its citizens. The world's most powerful military, which could send mighty drones to kill terrorists anywhere in the world, was unable to defend its own citizens against the lethal attack of a tiny virus just 0.12 micron in diameter. The Wall Street financial wizards who executed trades at lightning speeds and excelled at financial engineering couldn't use basic engineering to rapidly develop face shields to protect health workers in the Big Apple when they were direly needed. I realized that the US was an economic giant with industrial *feet* of clay. Its businesses had optimized their global supply chains for efficiency, but not agility. Unfortunately, money cannot buy agility, especially agility of mind.

I used above the allegory of "industrial feet" to imply that manufacturing is the *foundation* of our modern societies. Despite all the hoopla about the "digital economy," we still live, move, and work in a physical world. To satisfy our basic needs – such as food, shelter, housing, mobility, clothing, and health – we still need to make *stuff*. Since the explosion of the internet in the late 1990s, policymakers and CEOs in the US and other developed economies (except for Germany and Japan) all believed that *bits* (basic units of data in computing) carry more value than *atoms* (basic building blocks of physical matter). COVID-19 proved them all wrong. Atoms do matter. To put it poetically: "Matter matters!" Manufacturing is the art and science of manipulating and combining structures of atoms to create physical products that fulfill our material needs and desires. COVID-19 painfully brought home the point to the Western nations – which massively deindustrialized their economies in recent decades and relied heavily on imported goods made in far-flung places – the vital role of manufacturing and the need to make stuff at home, close to where consumers and citizens live.

The English word *manufacture* comes from the Classic Latin *manū* ("hand") and Middle French *facture* ("making").[26] Literally, manufacturing is about making things by hand. Figuratively, it could mean taking matter(s) into one's own hands and "manufacturing" your own solution to a pressing problem, rather than wait for or depend on others to solve it. This is exactly what happened during 2020. In the three countries I am culturally affiliated with – US, France, and India – national governments and big businesses were like deer caught in the headlights when confronted with the onset of COVID-19. These "big" institutions – despite wielding immense power and resources – appeared incapable to scale up rapidly the production of masks and respirators to meet demand at a national level. The top-down approach to solving a country-wide problem didn't work.

However, at the state and city levels, ingenious entrepreneurs, small and medium businesses, nonprofits, and local officials were able to improvise bottom-up solutions to contain the pandemic. They resourcefully marshaled locally available materials and talent to set up ad hoc manufacturing facilities and rapidly produce medical supplies to meet local demand. On April 17, 2020, 238 seamstresses from across the Brittany region formed a grassroots movement called *Invisible Factory*.[27] Working 24/7 in small shops scattered across Brittany, they produced collectively 172,000 cloth masks in just two months. In India, 300 makers (digitally savvy tinkerers) from 42 cities and villages across India joined forces to set up the M19 Collective on March 29, 2020.[28] Working daily for 16 hours, these M19 makers used the materials and equipment available in each city to produce and hand-deliver facial shields to local hospitals. Altogether, they produced 1 million face shields in just seven weeks! As mentioned in Chapter 2, on April 1, 2020, the Ohio State government teamed up with state-wide industrial and health care organizations to launch the Ohio Manufacturing Alliance to Fight COVID-19 (OMAFC).[29] OMAFC worked with hundreds of regional manufacturers to retool their factories so they could produce personal protective equipment like face shields, isolation gowns, and masks rapidly and cost-effectively and supply them to hospitals across the state without depending on other countries.

These successful grassroots examples of localized production show the great value and deep impact of **distributed manufacturing**, a novel industrial paradigm that enables companies to drastically cut costs, boost agility, and contribute sustainably to local economies. Distributed manufacturing replaces the hierarchical pyramid of centralized production with a distributed network of hundreds or even thousands of micro-factories. These modest-size plants, located close to points of consumption, can produce customized, high-quality goods in low volume using locally sourced materials and leveraging local talent.

Scaling Out Versus Scaling Up

Distributed manufacturing entails a profound mindset shift. Western companies must learn to think and act *horizontally*. Rather than scale up vertically their industrial operations by building a few giga-factories, businesses must *scale out* horizontally using a distributed supply network with many small, hyper-agile factories located near customers (see Figure 5.1). By producing closest to demand, manufacturers can

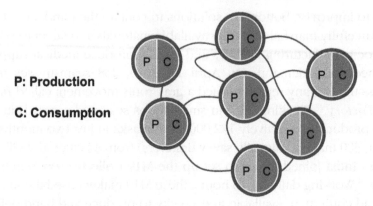

P: Production

C: Consumption

Figure 5.1 Scaling out manufacturing enables firms to produce flexibly closer to customers.

be more agile and cope with huge customer and supplier diversity cost-effectively, as well as leverage this vast diversity constructively.

Let me show you how to scale out manufacturing in two industries where production is highly centralized today: automotive and energy.

Scaling Out Auto Manufacturing to Maximize Local Impact

I met Frédéric Mourier in his "micro-factory," the size of a large garage located in La Rochelle, a coastal city in southwestern France. Mourier is founder of Avatar Mobilité, an industrial startup that aims to democratize not only access to electric cars but also their production.

Named Ulive, the compact electric vehicle (EV) developed by Mourier and his team boasts soft lines and distinguishes itself by its lightness. Thanks to a reduced number of parts and an aerodynamically optimized design, Ulive weighs only 350 kg (771 pounds), whereas a typical EV weighs 1,500 kg (3,306 pounds) or more. The ultra-light Ulive consumes three times less energy than a traditional EV, which gives it a competitive advantage given that 75% of a car's consumption is tied to its weight. Marketed and sold as a "quadricycle," Ulive is both wallet-friendly and planet-friendly. It costs you only €0.80 (US$0.85) to drive 100 km (62 miles). And Ulive emits just 20 grams of CO_2 per kilometer, or 0.62 mile (by comparison, the average passenger vehicle in the US emits about 400 grams of CO_2 per mile).[30] By driving a Ulive, you save 1.1 ton of CO_2 per year.

A mechanical engineer and industrial designer by training, Mourier found it ridiculous that we need a huge volume of natural resources to produce just a single car.[31] The French Commission for Sustainable Development estimates that "the mass of raw materials mobilized to build a car is 7 to 10 times the mass of the vehicle manufactured." To produce a car that weighs 1,300 kg (2,866 pounds), you need 3 to 4 tons of metallic minerals, 2 to 3 tons of nonmetallic minerals, and 2 to 3 tons of fossil fuels.[32] With between 74 and 78 million new cars sold every year worldwide, adding to the global fleet of 1.4 billion cars already in circulation today, you can imagine the ecological impact!

Sensing a growing need among customers to travel sustainably in lighter cars, Mourier set out to design the most frugal vehicle in France that would seamlessly integrate five major qualities: affordability, safety, efficiency, comfort, and sustainability. I took the Ulive for a short test-drive and was impressed by its exceptional maneuverability, stability, and ergonomics. Its roomy interior and slightly reclined seats make long-distance driving restful. Its robust structure made with resilient materials like Arpro (an energy absorbing foam material used to make helmets) confers a great sense of security.

Destined for daily suburban and rural travel, Ulive can transport up to four passengers and carry goods weighing up to 350 kg (771 pounds). It is powered by two 3.5kWh batteries that offer 150 kilometers (93 miles) of autonomy and a maximum speed of 90 km/h. You can recharge the batteries in just four hours using a regular household outlet. Because the batteries are extractable and portable, if you run out of juice while driving the Ulive, you can just swap batteries and keep going. Impressively, the Ulive roof is covered with solar panels that can be charged while you drive and give you an additional autonomy of up to 30 km (19 miles). The Ulive is sold at €15,000 (US$16,000), which is a bargain compared to the EVs sold in the US for an average price of $60,544.[33] Avatar targets the market of businesses and local authorities that want to promote sustainable mobility while curbing the total cost of ownership of their vehicle fleet.

But the real innovation of Ulive – and its application of frugality – does not lie so much in its disruptive product design as in its innovative manufacturing model and its original supply chain. A typical car is made up of 30,000 parts that are assembled by a team of multiple skilled workers in a huge, specialized factory. However, a Ulive is composed of fewer than 250 parts that can be swiftly assembled anywhere in a modest-sized workshop. In principle, a Ulive can be assembled by a single person in three days, or even in one day if it is put together by three people.

Say goodbye to the huge centralized and polluting factories – like Ford's River Rouge complex – of the 20th-century auto industry! Avatar wants to catalyze the emergence of a "distributed production network" with hundreds of micro-factories in the *territoires* (the French term for counties) across France where self-employed people and SMEs can locally assemble Ulives using kits provided by Avatar. The idea is to relocate production as close as possible to customers and recreate qualified jobs locally. The noble mission of Avatar is to replace the complex "value chain" controlled by a single large manufacturer with a simplified "value(s) network," which is facilitated by Avatar in synergistic collaboration with several local players. Mourier believes that by distributing manufacturing we also distribute economic opportunities across an entire country, empowering local communities to create and capture sustainable value.

Avatar has made the design of both its Ulive vehicle and its micro-factory available in open source. In doing so, Avatar seeks to achieve two goals: (1) enable creative entrepreneurs worldwide to build customized vehicles adapted to the local context (hence the name of the startup, Avatar, which means "a new (local) incarnation" in Sanskrit) and (2) accelerate the global deployment of its micro-factories using a franchise model.

Avatar is in discussions with many local government agencies and businesses both in France and abroad to implement this distributed production model. With a prototype already finalized, the startup expects its Ulive vehicle to be approved by the European Union in 2025. Avatar is gearing up to produce and market its first units in 2026. The startup plans to "scale out" a network of micro-assembly sites across France by 2027 and around the world by 2029.

Scaling Out Energy Generation to Build Sustainable Communities

Beyond traditional industrial sectors like automotive, distributed manufacturing can reinvent the dynamics of key sectors such as energy. Since World War II, developed nations have built increasingly larger power-generation units. Today, electricity is generated in a handful of centralized mega plants and transferred over hundreds of miles to clients' homes and offices. This centralized power generation model is asset- and resource-intensive, expensive to maintain, vulnerable to cataclysmic events such as terrorist attacks or blackouts (which occurred in northeastern America in 2003 and in California in 2019), and heavily polluting (electricity generation accounts for 42.5% of global CO_2 emissions).

The good news is we see the emergence of distributed energy systems based on modest-sized power-generation units that can be installed closer to key consumption points. This scaling out of power generation is enabled by innovations in renewable energy technologies, which make small-scale energy production less onerous and more accessible. A classic electricity power plant generates 1 gigawatt (GW), whereas a wind turbine's output is 2 to 3 megawatts and a solar panel's a few kilowatts. As a result, today, it is technically feasible to generate electricity at one millionth of the scale.

These micro power-generation units – which can be grid-connected or off-grid – can be rapidly implemented during an unexpected surge in demand (for instance, during severe winters), a large-scale power outage triggered by natural calamities (like Hurricane Sandy, which ravaged the mid-Atlantic coast of US in 2012, inflicting over $70 billion in damages), or voluntary power shutoffs (like those that took place across California in October 2019 to avoid risk of catastrophic wildfires caused by power lines). Facts and Factors estimates the global distributed energy generation market worth $282 billion in 2022 will grow to $745 billion by 2030.[34]

Sensing a huge market opportunity, big industrial players like ABB, Caterpillar, Eaton, Enel X, ENGIE, GE, Siemens, and Schneider Electric now offer end-to-end solutions to businesses and communities to build and operate distributed power systems.

Schneider Electric has designed and deployed more than 350 advanced microgrid projects in North America alone. After enduring widespread outages caused by a devastating storm, the 1 million people–strong Montgomery County in Maryland used Schneider's services to install microgrids to keep critical facilities up and running in the event of power outages. With these microgrids, the county not only gains in resilience but also can achieve its goal of reducing its greenhouse gas emissions 80% by 2027.[35]

The Italian energy giant Enel is now helping citizens and small businesses who install photovoltaic systems or mini-wind power systems to feed their surplus energy directly into the national grid. As of 2023, Enel has already connected 1.4 million "prosumers" (customers who produce their own energy locally) to its grids, for a total new generation capacity of 5.6 GW.[36] Today, according to Decode39, only 27% of Europe's energy is fed directly into distribution networks. This share will reach 50% by 2034.[37]

With Siemens' help, Blue Lake Rancheria (BLR), a century-old Native American reservation in Northern California, implemented a solar-powered community microgrid to power government offices, local businesses, and key facilities. In addition to creating new jobs, the microgrid will save the community $200,000 and cut 200 tons of CO_2 emissions annually, bringing it closer to its net-zero carbon target by 2030.[38]

When, in October 2019, the utility firm PG&E cut power for several days across California to prevent wildfires, the community relied on its off-grid energy system to keep its people safe and power medical equipment, thus saving four lives. BLR's success could inspire other Native American tribes across the US who never had access to the electric grid to leapfrog straight to a microgrid solution to achieve energy independence and economic resilience.[39]

■ ■ ■

As the two preceding examples demonstrate, by scaling out their manufacturing and producing in small factories located closer to customers, businesses can achieve multiple benefits. Specifically, companies can accomplish the following:

◆ **Save big on fixed costs and operating expenses.** Firms can avoid the huge capital expenditures required to build and operate giant high-volume factories. For instance, Tesla plans to invest $10 billion to build its gigafactory in Mexico, which is nearly twice more than Tesla's Berlin gigafactory, which cost $5.5 billion.[40] In comparison, setting up an Avatar Mobilité's micro-factory in the outskirts of a city will cost much less. Likewise, Scąle Microgrids estimates that its optimized solar, battery storage, and dispatchable generation microgrids save its clients 10% to 15% in annual energy expenses.[41] To date, its customers have saved a total of $420 million in utility costs and avoided 5.6 billion pounds of CO_2e (the equivalent of keeping 562,530 cars off the road for one year). Eaton, a power management company that offers distributed energy solutions, installed a microgrid on its own manufacturing facility and saved 40% on energy cost.[42]

- **Reduce logistics costs.** By sourcing raw materials and components locally companies can save on inbound logistics costs because they don't need to transport raw materials from multiple suppliers in far-flung places to a centralized factory. By selling directly to customers located closer to their micro-factory, firms can get rid of middle operators and save big on distribution costs because they don't need to ship their finished products to remote points of consumption.

- **Gain resilience and agility.** Distributed manufacturing offers greater "supply chain redundancy" compared to centralized production. If a micro-factory X in location A goes down for whatever reason, a micro-factory Y in a nearby location B can pick up the workload and fulfill pending customer orders. Even better, you can dispatch a "factory in a box" in a container that can be deployed rapidly on location A to provide "emergency manufacturing" services while micro-factory X is being fixed. For instance, inspired by Germany's famous bratwurst (sausage) food trucks, the global pharmaceutical and biotech company Bayer, which makes aspirin, piloted a flexible manufacturing project called F3 (flexible, fast, and future) factory. Based on a "plug-and-produce" philosophy, the F3 factory is composed of mobile and modular production units that fit inside a container. This "factory on wheels" can be rapidly deployed at a customer's industrial site to produce and deliver locally in small volume a wide range of custom chemicals. The F3 pilot project showed it can reduce capital investments by 40%, save 30% in energy, cut CO_2 footprint by 30%, and significantly reduce time to market.[43]

You can also gain in agility by using multipurpose micro-factories that can be reprogrammed to produce a variety of goods. Bright Machines (BM) is a San Francisco-based startup that develops fully automated and easily configurable micro-factories that bring the production of a variety of goods from electronics to home appliances closer to the customer, paving the way for agile and sustainable manufacturing. BM's micro-factories, made up of pods the size of a big refrigerator, leverage adaptive robots, machine learning, computer vision, and 3D printing to perform complex and delicate tasks like inserting dozens of $1,000 processors onto a circuit board. As it learns fast, the system's performance goes up swiftly. With BM's tools, clients can make multiple versions of a product – or multiple products – on the same assembly line, which reduces costly changeovers. Using BM's micro-factory, one client was able to do new product introduction 28 times faster than manual assembly. Another customer was able to increase production throughput by 2.5 times.[44]

As BM's micro-factories demonstrate, one major benefit of scaling out manufacturing is that it enables businesses to achieve **economies of scope**. In the 19th and 20th centuries, firms scaled up their production in ever-bigger factories in pursuit of economies of scale. They vied to reduce cost by increasing in *volume* the production of a *single* product that can be sold to the masses (hence the term *mass*-production). In the 21st century, however, customers seek personalized products and services that are produced closer to where they live (I will elaborate on this trend in Chapter 7). As a result, companies must reinvent their industrial model for economies of scope. They must try to realize savings by producing in low volume a wide *variety* of customized products in flexible micro-factories located in proximity to customers. To achieve economies of scale, you need to become more *efficient*. To realize economies of scope, you must increase your *agility*.

♦ **Become more sustainable**. Micro-factories are very sustainable because they consume less energy and raw materials and emit less CO_2 than giant plants. By equipping their micro-factories with digital fabrication technologies (DFTs) like

Computer Numerical Control (CNC) machining and additive manufacturing, also known as 3D printing, companies can reap three benefits: use less raw materials, generate less waste, and reduce transportation costs.

Since the 19th century, products were made in factories using subtractive manufacturing, where you take a large block of material, like hard metal, and cut and hollow it until you achieve the desired form. This subtractive process is best described by Michelangelo who said, "The sculpture is already complete within the marble block before I start my work. It is already there. I just have to chisel away the superfluous material."[45] By contrast, additive manufacturing, or 3D printing, is akin to your grandma's knitting technique. 3D printers create an object in a bottom-up fashion by adding several successive layers of a material until the product is finalized. 3D printing generates 70% to 90% less production waste compared to traditional manufacturing processes.[46] In addition to being very resource efficient, 3D printers are also versatile because they can work with a wide range of materials such as plastic, carbon fiber, ceramics, glass, nylon, stainless steel, and titanium. The market size of additive manufacturing is poised to grow from $17 billion in 2022 to $44 billion in 2027.[47]

A global network of micro-factories powered by DFTs like 3D printers will obliterate the need to ship parts around the world to be assembled in a giant, centralized factory. Instead, you can send electronically the design data of a new product to a micro-factory nearest to your customer, which can 3D print it using locally available materials. Lou Rassey cofounded and led Fast Radius, a cloud manufacturing company that built a large network of micro-factories equipped with 3D printers and CNC machines (Fast Radius was acquired by SyBridge Technologies in 2022). Rassey notes:

Throughout human history, we have moved parts three ways: by ground, by air, and by sea. Now, we have a fourth mode of transportation, which is moving parts through the internet at the speed of light and producing them local to where those parts are needed around the world. The ability to store parts digitally and move parts digitally is profound. It creates a more sustainable global supply chain model. Something the world desperately needs. It also allows us to fulfill the physical products that people need around the world in a more responsible way. And this distributed digital supply chain infrastructure is here today. It works.[48]

♦ **Maximize social impact in local communities.** Raghuram Rajan, a professor of finance at the University of Chicago's Booth School of Business and former governor of the Reserve Bank of India, encourages big businesses to reconnect with and regenerate local communities by embracing "inclusive localism." He writes, "Rather than using antitrust law to keep firms small, which could be a disservice to consumers given the significant scale of production today, it would be better if large corporations decentralized their corporate social responsibility activities. These should be more focused in left-behind communities where they have a significant presence and can aid community revival."[49] Companies can build capacity and revitalize underdeveloped communities by setting up micro-factories that would source from small suppliers in proximity and train and employ local talent.

By scaling out their manufacturing with a distributed network of agile micro-factories anchored in local communities, companies can produce and deliver customized products faster, better, and cheaper. Let me show you how scaling out industrial activities can help, as stated in this book's subtitle, "build a better world with less."

CHAPTER 6

Scaling Out Next-Gen Virtuous Economies

Ingenious startups and visionary firms are leveraging distributed micro-manufacturing to boldly reinvent centuries-old industry models and business paradigms and restructure the way we design, build, sell, and use products. Let's examine how these frugal innovators are shaping new multitrillion-dollar markets and building inclusive and sustainable economies.

Turning Waste into Gold

By adopting the principles of the "circular economy," manufacturers can make their micro-factories even more sustainable. The circular economy replaces the linear value chain – where firms extract raw materials, make products, and customers use and dispose of them – with a circular value network in which businesses and consumers reduce, recycle, and reuse products in a closed loop system. With a global circular economy, we could fulfill all humans' needs with just 70% of the materials we currently extract and use. Sadly, only 7.2% of the current global economy is circular.[1] By accelerating the adoption of circular business models, we can reduce global greenhouse gas emissions by nearly 40%, halt and even restore our natural ecosystems, and create over 6 million new jobs and $4.5 trillion in additional economic output by 2030.[2]

Here is the problem: many CEOs and policymakers are using the old mental models inherited from the linear economy to build a circular economy. These business and political leaders are calling for "scaling up" the circular economy: they want to ship waste across country borders to be processed in large, centralized factories that can deliver "economies of scale." This go-global-and-bigger approach to recycling defeats the go-local-and-smaller ethos of the circular economy. Rather than enlarge the loop by building national or global circular value chains, we must shrink the loop through hyper-local circular value chains that can *valorize* (create value from) waste at a city level.

If you visit Governors Island in New York City (NYC), you can enjoy Manhattan's skyline while sitting on one of the comfy red Adirondack chairs that adorn the island. These red chairs are made from recycled milk jugs. Sitting on one of them in 2018, Chris Graff, a manufacturing entrepreneur, had an epiphany. He realized that, although plastic milk jugs are readily available in NYC, the jugs used to make the Adirondack chairs had to travel thousands of miles worldwide and go through a complex multistep manufacturing process before it was finally transformed into a chair that Graff was sitting on. Graff asked himself, "Why can't we take some of this recyclable trash and manufacture something here (in NYC) instead? We can then sell it into the same market?"[3] Graff felt this would "tighten the loop, save money, save energy, and create local jobs."[4] In 2019, Graff launched the NYC Curb-to-Market Challenge to recognize and reward entrepreneurs who propose innovative ideas for using NYC's recycled waste to locally manufacture a product that could be sold in NYC. One of the challenge winners is Barent Roth, a sustainable designer, who teamed up with Graff to launch Circular Economy Manufacturing (CEM), an industrial design firm. CEM has set up on Governors Island a solar-powered micro-factory that recycles on site postconsumer, single-use plastic waste collected from the streets of NYC into durable goods like compost bins and traffic cones that are put to use in the Big Apple. CEM assembled the micro-factory, which you can watch online, within a repurposed shipping container.

Two billion pairs of jeans are produced each year. From the cotton field to the shop, each pair of jeans travel up to 65,000 kilometers (40,389 miles), which is 1.5 times around the Earth.[5] Most of these jeans are worn for just three to four years and then thrown away, adding to the 92 million tons of textile sent to landfill annually, which cause 10% of all CO_2 emissions.[6] Having these used jeans travel *again* 1.5 times around the planet to be recycled is nonsensical. That's why Re-Fresh Global, a Berlin-based company, has developed micro-factories that use patented technology to upcycle low-value textile waste collected locally into high value raw materials that can be used to make new products in construction, automotive, medical, fashion, cosmetics, and packaging industries. Under a franchise model, Re-Fresh Global can set up its 1,000 m2 (10,763 sq ft) micro-factory in any city.[7] It trains people in local communities how to collect, sort, disassemble, and upcycle mixed textile waste in its facility. By shrinking the loop on textile recycling with its micro-factories, Re-Fresh Global enables community-led circular economy initiatives that both fight climate change and create social and economic impact locally. Re-Fresh Global is growing rapidly in the European Union (EU, where, under new regulations, as of 2025, all member states must collect textile waste separately). By 2030, all textile products sold in the EU must be repairable and recyclable and made mostly from recycled fibers.

Curing Our Fossil Fuel Addiction with the Bioeconomy

The bioeconomy is a sustainable economic system that aims to eliminate our dependence on finite fossil fuel resources as our main primary sources of energy and raw materials. By enabling the equitable use of renewable biological resources and ecosystems, the bioeconomy will replace the toxic and polluting petroleum materials used in our industrial value chains with cleaner bio-based materials. Using nature as a source of inspiration for innovation, the bioeconomy is reinventing agricultural and industrial systems so we can produce healthier food, drugs, and other products for more people using with fewer resources and generating fewer greenhouse emissions.[8]

The bioeconomy holds immense growth potential. The European bioeconomy is worth nearly €2.5 trillion and employs 18 million people (8.2% of total labor force).[9] The US bioeconomy is today valued at over $1 trillion, or 5% of US GDP.[10] In May 2022, China unveiled the country's first five-year bioeconomy plan, aiming to create a $3.3 trillion bioeconomy by 2025, which will be bigger than America's.[11] Globally, the bioeconomy is expected to reach $7.7 trillion by 2030.[12]

AFYREN is a French bioeconomy startup. Its NEOXY factory – essentially a biorefinery – in northeastern France recycles agricultural residues into seven high-value biomolecules, known as organic acids, for various applications ranging from animal and human nutrition to cosmetics and lubricants. By leveraging green chemistry AFYREN optimized NEOXY's industrial processes so they generate five times less CO_2 and greenhouse gas emissions than conventional methods of producing acids of fossil origin. AFYREN estimates there is a global market of $15 billion for its seven bio-based organic acids.[13] The most fascinating thing is that its suppliers are mostly located within a 250 km radius of the factory (see Figure 6.1). This plant is serving its global customers via their Western European industrial sites for further product transformation.

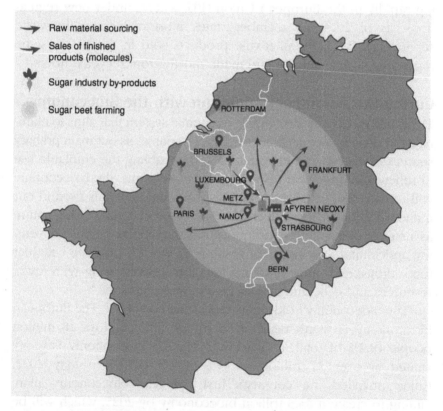

Figure 6.1 AFYREN's biorefinery is located close to suppliers and customers.
Source: With permission of AFYREN.

In early 2023, AFYREN announced a partnership with Mitr Phol, a global leader in the sugar industry based in Bangkok, Thailand. AFYREN intends to set up its second biorefinery in Thailand that will upcycle sugarcane by-products sourced from local suppliers into high-value-added and low-carbon, bio-based products destined for Asian markets, which represent 25% of the world market for carboxylic acids.

AFYREN is exploring the possibility of setting up its third biorefinery in a US state that will turn agricultural waste – like corn by-products – sourced from local US farmers into high-value solutions for the North American market.

As you can see, rather than scale up its production by running a single giant factory that would supply all global markets, AFYREN has "scaled out" its bio-manufacturing by operating modestly sized factories located in two major regional markets: Europe and Asia.

Each of its biorefineries uses only locally available raw materials to supply mostly regional clients. AFYREN's hyper-local and circular bioeconomy value chains have a very limited carbon footprint and improve the livelihoods of local farmers who earn more by selling their agricultural waste.

Enhancing Lives Through Personalized Medicine

Let's now look at how to scale out manufacturing in a complex, regulated sector like *health care*. Let's explore how hyper-local biopharmaceutical value chains can not only save but also enhance billions of lives worldwide.

Life-saving vaccines are usually manufactured in big, centralized factories with large-scale production and purification capacities, necessitating substantial capital investments and long lead times for construction and process engineering. These giant factories churn out large numbers of clinical-grade doses of a single product by following strictly good manufacturing practices guidelines from the US Food and Drug Administration or other national regulatory agencies. Final products are then stored and shipped to various markets via complex and time-consuming global logistics networks.

Centralized manufacturing, however, lacks the agility needed to produce vaccines to cope with regional endemic infections that involve lower numbers of doses or local genetic variants. In other words, today's vaccine manufacturing model is optimized for high-volume, low-variety mass production and for global markets and not for low-volume, high-variety production tailored to regional markets.

For instance, African countries import 99% of their vaccines.[14] Although Africa has 10 vaccine manufacturers, these local companies do not make a vaccine's active ingredients; they just "fill and finish" imported products. This lack of domestic manufacturing capabilities explains why *only 10% of people in the African continent* have been fully vaccinated against COVID-19.

What if we could scale out (decentralize) vaccine and drug manufacturing by using mobile micro-factories that can be deployed quickly in areas where patients need them most? These "on-demand" micro-factories can produce faster, better, and cheaper drugs and vaccines that are tailored to local demand. This ideal scenario is now a reality thanks to breakthroughs in biopharma manufacturing.

In late 2023, the German biotech firm BioNTech inaugurated its first mRNA vaccine production facility in Rwanda.[15] This micro-factory, called BioNTainer, is a flexible container solution. It offers turn-key manufacturing capabilities. The whole micro-factory can be shipped via air or sea in six containers and deployed rapidly anywhere.[16]

Compared to large, centralized pharma factories, the smaller and flexible BioNTainer offers two major advantages. First, BioNTainer is versatile and can manufacture *multiple* products. In Rwanda, the BioNTainer will produce various mRNA-based vaccines to fight COVID-19 but also malaria and tuberculosis. Second, it makes *personalized* products that are tailored to specific local needs. For instance, the vaccines produced by the Rwandan micro-factory will work better for local African populations than imported ones because they were formulated considering the genetic makeup of local people.

BioNTech envisions its Rwanda-based BioNTainers to become the first node in a decentralized and resilient end-to-end biotech manufacturing network across Africa. In 2025, its Rwandan micro-factory will start producing the first mRNA vaccines entirely made in Africa.

BionNTech is not the only biotech firm that has found a way to scale out vaccine manufacturing. The South African biotech firm

Afrigen (mentioned in Chapter 4) is collaborating with drug manufacturers in many developing nations to build capacity to produce mRNA vaccines locally.

BioWin is a world-class health cluster in the Wallonia region in Belgium that has fostered amazing biotech firms like Univercells, Orgenesis, and SalamanderU. These startups have all developed modular bio-manufacturing units that can be easily set up in resource-constrained settings and can rapidly churn out personalized therapeutic vaccines to treat serious ailments like cancers and genetic diseases.[17] Orgenesis decentralizes cell therapy manufacturing. Its innovative platform enables the development of personalized cell therapies at the point of care. This transforms hospitals into smart micro-manufacturing units that can produce on-site cell therapies. SalamanderU is developing a compact isolator that will decentralize vaccine production by bringing manufacturing closer to the clinical centers. Univercells' modular and automated platforms decentralize biomanufacturing faster and empower developing nations to locally produce vaccines and other biologics to treat diabetes, cancer, and other diseases.[18]

These micro-factories promise to revolutionize health care. Responsive and flexible, they will be able to quickly produce a wide variety of personalized medicine on a small scale and in a sustainable manner by using only locally available resources. This would be the antithesis of the 20th-century global industrial pharmaceutical model based on large-scale, hyper-polluting standardized drug manufacturing. Welcome to the era of "micro health care": a decentralized approach to producing and delivering personalized therapies that will enable billions to live longer and healthier.

Capturing and Using CO_2 to Create Local Value

To reverse climate change, we need to achieve two goals simultaneously:

1. Decarbonize our industrial value chains so they emit less or no CO_2 *today* and *in the future*.
2. Remove billions of tons of *already* emitted, or historic, CO_2 from the atmosphere.

We can realize goal number 1 through two techniques: carbon capture and storage (CCS) and carbon capture and utilization (CCU). CCS reduces emissions from industrial sources by first capturing CO_2 from large point sources of pollution such as power plants, refineries, and steel and cement factories.[19] Then, the captured carbon is transported, via ships or pipelines, to a permanent storage site where the carbon is injected deep underground in geological formations. CCU is like CCS except that the captured carbon is not stored away, but rather used as a raw material to make valuable new products such as fuels and building materials.[20]

Achieving goal number 1 with CCS and CCU, two methods that avoid releasing "new" CO_2 in the air, is necessary but not sufficient. We must also pursue goal number 2 to remove the "old" carbon already in the atmosphere. According to the UN Intergovernmental Panel on Climate Change, we need to remove at least 6 to 10 billion tons of CO_2 per year by 2050, and another 20 billion tons each year thereafter, to stick to a 1.5°C warming pathway.[21] Carbon dioxide removal (CDR) aims to realize this goal number 2. CDR is a wide range of methods and technologies that remove historic CO_2 that exists already in the atmosphere and then store it durably, hence achieving "negative emissions."[22] CDR technologies like enhanced rock weathering (ERW) and direct air capture (DAC) can lock away permanently (over 100 years) the CO_2 captured from the atmosphere. Short-term CDR methods like afforestation and reforestation, which increase soil carbon sequestration, can only store CO_2 for 25 to 100 years. DAC technologies use chemical or physical processes to extract carbon dioxide directly from the ambient air at a particular location for CO_2 storage or use on site.[23]

Despite climate urgency, we are not aggressively pursuing either goal. In a landmark 2023 report that assesses the current state of global carbon removal, scientists at the University of Oxford estimate that, each year and worldwide, only 2.2 billion tons of *old* CO_2 are being removed from the atmosphere.[24] This is tiny compared to the 36.6 billion tons of *new* CO_2 being released in the air annually from fossil fuels and cement.[25] These Oxford scientists are calling to increase carbon removal 1,300 times – by leveraging novel technologies and methods like bioenergy with CCS, DAC, ERW, and biochar – to keep global warming below 2°C by 2050.[26]

I share these scientists' concern. But I believe that instead of scaling up carbon removal and storage, we need to scale it out. Rather than *look up* at the polluted sky and strive to remove excess carbon in the air, let's *look down* to figure out how we can best *use* the captured carbon *locally* on the ground. Let's complement CDR with another acronym, **CLV: carbon local valorization**. If CDR aims to capture carbon, CLV aims to capture economic and social *value* from that captured carbon and do so for the benefit of local communities. This entails building end-to-end CDRLV (carbon direct removal and local valorization) ecosystems within a county or city (I will show how this can be done in Chapters 7 and 12).

Concrete is the world's most-used building material (after water) but also one of the most destructive for the planet because it is responsible for 8% of global emissions.[27] And yet, concrete can also be the *solution* to climate change. With the global building stock poised to double by 2060 – the equivalent of building another New York City each month – concrete offers a strategic opportunity to permanently store vast quantities of CO_2 in our built environment.

CarbonCure is a Canadian startup whose mission is to reduce embodied carbon in the construction industry by 500 million tons annually by 2030 (the construction sector accounts for 40% of global emissions). CarbonCure's technology injects captured CO_2 directly into fresh concrete (during mixing) where it is permanently stored. This helps significantly lower the carbon footprint of concrete while boosting its performance (by increasing its strength).

Heirloom is a San Francisco-based DAC tech startup that aims to remove 1 billion tons of CO_2 from the atmosphere by 2035. In February 2023, CarbonCure teamed up with Heirloom and Central Concrete (a concrete supplier in the Bay Area in California) to successfully run a demonstration project in the Bay Area that shows how to decarbonize the construction sector faster and better by leveraging *hyper-local value chains* that capture and use CO_2 closer to customers.

Here is how CarbonCure and Heirloom describe this pilot project[28]:

Heirloom captured CO_2 from the atmosphere using their DAC technology at their headquarters in Brisbane, California. CarbonCure's reclaimed water technology injected the captured CO_2 into the process wastewater at a Central Concrete batch plant in San Jose, California. Central Concrete used the CO_2-treated wastewater to make fresh concrete, which was produced for a range of construction projects across the Bay Area. The CO_2 is durably sequestered in the concrete as calcium carbonate, and will not be returned to the atmosphere, even if the concrete is demolished.

Amazingly, this *entire* value chain – from carbon capture to CO_2 injection in concrete mixing to the construction sites using this decarbonized concrete – is located end-to-end within the Bay Area. This perfectly illustrates the value and impact of a *hyper-local value network*, a new paradigm explored in the next chapter.

This is *concrete* evidence that (1) we can scale out CO_2 capture, removal, and use, and (2) we can leverage hyper-local value networks to decarbonize rapidly sectors like construction that massively contribute to climate change.

By leveraging their carbon capture and use technologies, Heirloom and CarbonCure are shaping the *carbontech* industry, which vies to upcycle CO_2 waste into high-value products that benefit local communities. The carbontech market is expected to reach $6 trillion globally.[29]

Carbontech startups like Heirloom and CarbonCure are modern-day alchemists who transmute "low-value" carbon in the atmosphere into "high-value" solutions that create positive socioeconomic value on the ground (see Figure 6.2). In doing so, these innovators perfectly embody the spirit of a frugal economy, which aims to do *better* with *less*.

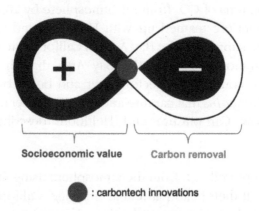

Socioeconomic value   Carbon removal

● : carbontech innovations

Figure 6.2 Carbontech firms create more social and economic value while removing carbon.

■ ■ ■

We've explored the *supply side* of scaling out manufacturing by showing how companies can shift their production from a handful of centralized mega-factories to a distributed network of agile micro-factories anchored in local communities. Now let's explore the demand side drivers that in fact are the main catalyst for scaling out manufacturing and, by extension, co-building hyper-local value networks.

CHAPTER 7

Hyper-Local Value Networks

Today, Western manufacturers no longer "make" anything. Instead, they orchestrate globally distributed supply chains. Raw materials sourced in one continent are shipped to another to make individual parts. These are shipped to another corner of the world for final assembly. The finished product is again transported via sea or air to the end user markets. These global supply chains are not only geographically dispersed but also very complex due to the multiple steps involved in making a car or an airplane.

As we witnessed painfully during COVID-19, today's globally dispersed supply chains lack agility and resilience due to two reasons. First, there exists a massive distance between where a product is manufactured (say, facial masks made in Guangzhou, China) and where it is consumed (panicky New York at the outset of COVID-19). This *geographic* gap makes it hard for companies to rapidly respond to a sudden spike or shift in demand. Second, due to the hyper-specialization of tasks within multitiered supply chains, there are huge delays in how vital information – like sudden shifts in customer needs or a shortage of a critical component – is shared along the supply chain. To compensate for this *time* gap in supply chain communication, companies carry extra inventory as a "protective buffer" against shortages. These inventory outlays cost billions of dollars to electronics brands and automakers who manage multitiered supply chains.

Together, these two shortcomings constitute a **value gap** (measured in *distance* and *time*) between supply and demand.[1] This value gap hampers firms' agility and prevent them from responding to changes in demand faster, better, and cheaper (see Figure 7.1).

There is, however, also a gnawing **values gap** between brands and customers, who increasingly make buying decisions based on deep aspirations rather than just material needs. Socially conscious and eco-aware Gen Y and Gen Z consumers are turning away from brands that merely "push" cookie-cutter products to them rather than cocreate personalized solutions with clients, do not produce their goods using local suppliers, and indulge in greenwashing rather than genuinely fight climate change.

Many studies confirm this values gap. McKinsey & Company reports that 71% of consumers want personalization but are upset when businesses fail to deliver it.[2] According to Participation Brand Index, four out of five brands do not connect emotionally with customers. Three-quarters of buyers no longer trust brands.[3] Bain reports that only 28% of consumers trust large companies to create authentically sustainable offerings.[4] According to Morning Consult, two-thirds of US consumers favor "Made in America" products but find their high prices off-putting.[5] As a result of this multidimensional disconnect, firms see their brands losing their *relevance* and *trust* among values-driven customers.

The good news is that businesses in the US and in European countries are starting to bridge the value(s) gap between supply and

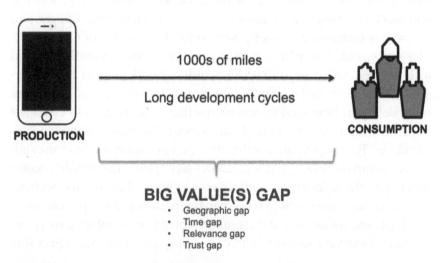

PRODUCTION   1000s of miles   Long development cycles   CONSUMPTION

BIG VALUE(S) GAP
- Geographic gap
- Time gap
- Relevance gap
- Trust gap

Figure 7.1 The growing value(s) gap between supply and demand.

demand. Having massively relocated their industrial activities to lower-cost countries like China, Western firms are now bringing manufacturing back to their home countries from overseas. This trend, called *reshoring*, has accelerated since 2020 due to COVID-19 but also because of growing geopolitical tensions with China, the world's factory. According to Kearney, 96% of US CEOs are now looking to reshore their manufacturing operations, or have already done so, an increase from 78% in 2022.[6] Companies spent $114.7 billion in 2022 to build new manufacturing facilities in the US, a 62% increase over the previous five years.[7] Reshoring Initiative estimates that during 2023, reshoring created 365,000 manufacturing jobs in the US.[8]

Western governments are keen to accelerate reshoring. On August 16, 2022, US President Biden signed the Inflation Reduction Act into law, which will encourage the sustainable production of critical goods like drugs and energy on US soil and help fight climate change. In 2022, the US Congress passed the CHIPS Act, which invests $280 billion to bolster domestic R&D and manufacturing of semiconductors in the US.[9] In May 2023, the French government unveiled a major plan to "reindustrialize" France and strengthen national sovereignty by supporting domestic manufacturing of essential goods.[10] In July 2023, the European Union approved its own €43 billion ($47.5 billion) plan to increase semiconductor production in Europe, hence curbing its total dependence on Taiwanese microchips.[11]

But just replacing a factory in China or Taiwan with a factory in Ohio or northern France isn't enough to regain industrial autonomy and achieve global competitiveness. Why did European and US companies – especially the big ones – offshore our manufacturing to low-cost countries in the first place? The obvious answer is because it's *cheaper* to produce in China or Vietnam than in the US. And economists will argue you should produce goods where it's cheapest. But that's the *objective* reason. There is, however, a subjective reason: Western CEOs today no longer *value* manufacturing. It would have never occurred to Henry Ford, Thomas Edison (founder of GE), or Thomas J. Watson (founder of IBM) to offshore the production of their cars, light bulbs, and computers to Mexico or China. These visionary founders of whole new industries – automotive, electric power, and information technology – were tinkerers who loved getting their hands dirty (literally). They had an emotional attachment to manufacturing. They believed they were not just building cars, power stations, or computers, but building an entire nation. Ford, Edison, and Watson were all excellent at R&D and marketing, but they considered these corporate functions as being *equal* in value to manufacturing. Sadly, today's MBA-minted CEOs of big businesses prefer building Excel models on their laptop than building cars in a US factory. They value R&D, product design, and marketing way higher than manufacturing, which is viewed as a "cost center." By offshoring their production to low-cost countries, these profit-seeking CEOs "lightened" the company's balance sheet and were treated like heroes by investors. And they still proudly proclaimed that their products are "Made in China, (but) Designed in the USA"!

Figure 7.2 offers a simplified view of a value chain, a key management concept introduced by Harvard Business School professor Michael Porter.[12] A value chain is "a progression of activities that a firm operating in a specific industry performs in order to deliver a valuable product (i.e., good and/or service) to the end customer." Note that production (manufacturing) occupies a central role in the value chain. Until the 1960s and 1970s, the CEOs of US and European industrial firms valued highly and equally all activities in the value chain. Hence, they kept the entire value chain, including production, localized in their domestic markets.

Sadly, as I mentioned previously, in recent decades, Western CEOs no longer viewed production as a strategic *value-adding* activity and offshored it to countries where it's cheaper to make their goods. As a result of this poor value judgment, or rather a new hierarchization of *values*, the linear value chain has devolved into a curved *values* chain called the *smile curve* (see Figure 7.3). Today, Western firms concentrate their in-house resources on "high-value-added" functions like R&D, design, sourcing, sales, marketing, and service, and relegate production – judged as a "low-value-added"

Figure 7.2 A value chain is a linked set of activities to create and bring a product to customers.

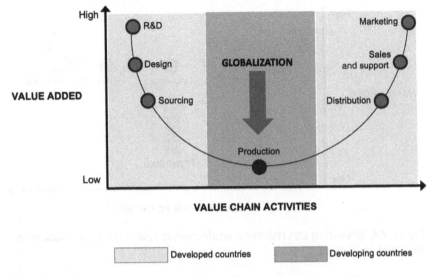

Figure 7.3 Globalization devalued manufacturing in the eyes of the Western world.

Source: Adapted from Stan Shih's smile curve.

activity – to developing countries. This smile curve reminds me of the Indian caste system, in which the upper-caste Brahmins control the intellectual work and deal with the "intangibles" (hence keeping their hands clean), while the lowest-caste Shudras, confined to physically demanding manual labor, produce "material" stuff.

Reshoring is not just about opening a new factory in Tennessee or Bavaria. It should also be about opening the *minds* of business leaders. Western CEOs should use reshoring as an opportunity to reset their own values system and elevate public perception of manufacturing as a noble activity that can deliver as much value to society as "smart" R&D and "sexy" marketing (see Figure 7.4). If done right, reshoring can bridge the previously mentioned *values gap* between brands and customers who want to buy personalized eco-friendly products made locally.

In November 2023, American Compass teamed up with YouGov to survey 1,000 Americans to assess their views on globalization and manufacturing.[13] The results are revealing (I must confess, they *really* challenged my own cynical view of American values). Forty-one percent of Americans acknowledge they personally benefited from

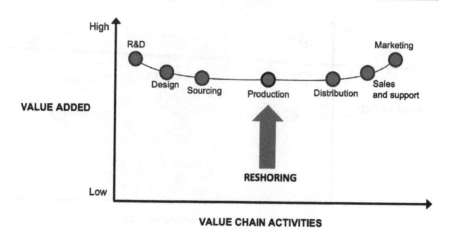

Figure 7.4 Reshoring can redeem manufacturing and make it as valuable as R&D and marketing.

globalization and trade with China, but 47% recognize that the nation suffered from it. Seventy percent of respondents want policymakers to focus on "helping struggling areas (that lost jobs due to offshore manufacturing) to recover" and only 30% prefer policies that help people move to more prosperous areas. For Americans, not only "place matters," "making things matter," too. When asked why America needs a strong industrial sector, 42% answered "manufacturing is important to a healthy, growing, innovative economy," whereas "good jobs" (25%) and "national security" (16%) – two arguments touted by politicians – were not perceived as big drivers. Only 3% believe – as economists do – that "the goal should be producing things where it can be done at the lowest cost." But here is the bad news: 62% to 38%, Americans would rather pay steeper prices to bolster US manufacturing than pay higher prices to fight climate change. Fifty-two percent of Americans want policymakers to prioritize strengthening the US industrial sector over improving the environment, and for 47% Americans it's the other way around.

From this American Compass-YouGov survey, you can see how Americans are torn between three conflicting aspirations: they want to regenerate economically disadvantaged communities, revive and support domestic manufacturing, and fight climate change. They believe it is hard to balance and reconcile these three seemingly divergent priorities. It is true that traditional industrial value chains are optimized to address at most two of these three objectives. For instance, building a mega-factory in California or in Texas creates good-paying manufacturing jobs in that individual state, but what about the other 49 US states? Likewise, if a company decides to "scale out" its manufacturing across all 50 US states by building a micro-factory in each to serve the local market, it needs to ensure its 50 micro-factories are not only operationally efficient but also eco-logically sound.

But what if we take advantage of the reshoring movement in the US and Europe to fundamentally reinvent manufacturing value chains in a way to reconcile the three mentioned conflicting priorities? To realize that Holy Grail – reconciling economic development, social harmony, and ecological preservation – we need to rethink and rein-vent value chains.

The traditional value chain – as depicted in Figure 7.2 – suffers from three major limitations in today's customer-driven, collabora-tive, and fast-paced economy.

The Value Chain Fails to Engage "Prosumers"

Today customers are treated as passive recipients of the output (products and services) of the value chain: they don't contribute actively to R&D, production, or marketing activities. But the internet, social media, digital tools like 3D printing, and creative hubs like makerspaces and FabLabs are turning passive customers into active "prosumers" who are leading a do-it-yourself (DIY) revolution.[14] In his 1980 book *The Third Wave*, futurist Alvin Toffler coined the term *prosumers* to describe people who produce their own personalized goods and services, blurring the line between production and con-sumption. All of us are already prosumers on social networks because we both produce and consume our own content on X (formerly Twitter), Facebook, and LinkedIn.[15]

MacGyver is a US television series that aired in the 1980s and 1990s that follows the global adventures of a very resourceful secret agent named MacGyver who can solve any problem with the resour-ces at hand. In *Jugaad Innovation*, my coauthors and I highlighted many resourceful MacGyvers in emerging economies like Africa, India, and Brazil who develop ingenious solutions using limited means to address local community needs.[16] This grassroots innovation movement is now spreading across the US and Europe thanks to Fab-Labs and makerspaces, which are digital fabrication workshops that offer wannabe inventors and entrepreneurs the training, tools, and support to design, rapidly prototype, and build physical products. In *Makers*, Chris Anderson, a former *Wired* magazine editor, narrates this MacGyverization of the US economy, which is accelerating due to the democratization of digital fabrication tools such as 3D printers and popular events such as the Maker Faire that showcase the DIY inventiveness of ordinary citizens.[17] At the Fab Summit 2013, the mayor of Barcelona proclaimed boldly that his city would make locally all that it consumes within four decades. Tomas Diez, the executive director at Fab City Foundation, believes FabLabs could radically transform our economies. Diez notes, "Our systems of production and consumption are incrementally producing social conflicts and environmental devastation, but what if we can create a shortcut by bringing production back to the city? It won't happen in one day. We have to work within the current system to transform it. But it's going to create new business opportunities and a new economy based on a reorganization of our resources."[18] All major US cities now host makerspaces and FabLabs. NextFab is a network of makerspaces in Philadelphia that offer inventive artists, engineers, and scientists the tools, collaborative space, and resources to turn a product idea into a reality or even a startup.

This "prosumation" megatrend, which blurs the line between production and consumption, is forcing companies to rethink how they engage with their customers all along the value chain. As my coauthor Jaideep Prabhu and I explain in our book *Frugal Innovation*,

> Many customers no longer want to be treated as passive buyers or "wallets on feet"; they want to actively participate in the design, production and even distribution of goods and services. Furthermore, customers want to contribute to the life cycle of the brands they consume. In sum, customers are becoming both consumers and producers, or prosumers. As a result, branded product and service suppliers as well as retailers must find ways to engage these prosumers and co-create value with them. By doing so, firms can lower the

overall cost of innovation, develop and market products and services faster and better, delight customers with tailored experiences and boost customer loyalty.[19]

The Value Chain Doesn't Favor External Collaboration

The traditional value chain is inward-looking. It depicts a linear and sequential set of interconnected activities that are performed by a single company using its own assets and capabilities to transform an idea into a finished product or a service delivered to the customer. In his 1985 global bestseller *Competitive Advantage*, Harvard management guru Michael Porter introduced the value chain as a strategic tool that firms can use to identify and analyze their various activities, study their connections, and optimize their value to achieve a competitive advantage within a particular industry.

In today's interdependent business world, however, industry lines are blurring. Rather than compete for a small share in a crowded and shrinking market, visionary businesses are seeking a "cooperative advantage." They want to work with other firms, including rivals, to cocreate new and bigger "blue ocean" markets that benefit everyone.[20] With the rise of business-to-business sharing, explored in Part I of this book, companies no longer need to *own* R&D, production, and marketing assets to create value to customers. Multiple firms within and across industries can pool and share their physical and intellectual resources to synergistically create greater value and jointly shape new lucrative markets. As a result, the firm-specific value chain must evolve into a *collaborative ecosystem* where a company can combine its internal capabilities with those of its partners to cocreate value for all stakeholders.

The Value Chain Is Optimized for Efficiency and Not Adaptability

Companies have optimized their value chain for efficiency, but not for agility and resilience. Using their well-oiled value chain, firms can today build and get their products faster and cheaper to customers. But what happens if customers overnight change their minds and want whole different products? Firms can't rapidly adapt their static value chain to respond to sudden market shifts. Likewise, when unforeseen events like pandemics and natural disasters strike, most firms struggle to quickly reconfigure their rigid value chain processes to avoid disruptions. As we enter a VUCA (volatile, uncertain, complex, and ambiguous) world, companies must engage with its suppliers and partners to co-build highly adaptive and resilient value chains that can both anticipate and react effectively to unexpected changes in supply and demand.

The Value Chain Is Too Complex to Decarbonize and Reach Net Zero

The Greenhouse Gas Protocol Corporate Standard places a company's greenhouse gas (GHG) emissions into three categories, known as *scopes*. Scope 1 emissions are direct emissions from sources owned or controlled by a company. Scope 2 emissions are indirect emissions from the generation of purchased energy such as electricity, cooling, and heating. Scope 3 emissions are all indirect emissions that are not included in scope 2 and occur all along the value chain of the reporting company, including emissions resulting from both upstream and downstream activities.[21] Scope 3 emissions, also known as *corporate value chain emissions*, are related to activities that a company doesn't directly control. And yet, these indirect emissions generated by suppliers and contract manufacturers account for up 65% to 95% of many companies' total carbon impact.[22] In the case of Apple, 99% of its emissions fall under scope 3, with 76% emanating from its outsourced product manufacturing operations.[23]

Companies have a hard time collecting reliable data on their scope 3 emissions due to a lack of visibility into their value chains, which have become too big and complex in recent decades as a result of unbridled globalization and mindless outsourcing.[24] Hence, scope 3 has become a stumbling block even for highly motivated firms that want to lead their industry in sustainability. For instance, 54% of the companies surveyed by the Science Based Targets initiative cite scope 3 as the biggest challenge they face in setting net-zero (emissions) targets.[25]

Even if miraculously overnight companies' complex value chains were to become totally transparent and their emissions can be tracked and reported accurately, getting all partners in the supply chain to decarbonize their operations will require a lot of money and time.[26] This explains why, in its final rule issued on March 6, 2024, the Securities and Exchange Commission decided to scrap the requirement for publicly traded US companies to divulge their scope 3 GHG emissions as part of their climate-related disclosures.[27] Instead of seeking better ways to measure and track scope 3 emissions, I believe companies should first reinvent their opaque and complex global value chains to make them transparent and simpler to manage. Once simplified, these end-to-end value chains will be easier to decarbonize, hence enabling companies to reach their net-zero targets rapidly.

Bottom line: to bridge the supply and demand value(s) gap, it's not enough to scale out manufacturing by building micro-factories distributed across a country closer to local markets. Businesses, especially in the US and European nations who want to reshore manufacturing and reindustrialize their countries, must *scale out their entire value chains*. Specifically, firms must stop managing hyper-global value chains that are static and insular. Instead, they need to learn to facilitate **hyper-local value networks (HYLOVANs)** that are agile and resilient, maximize local socioeconomic impact, and minimize ecological impact.

A HYLOVAN is an open and dynamic ecosystem that engages diverse stakeholders within a locality – a city or a county – to co-innovate personalized solutions tailored to local market and social needs. Let's examine each word in HYLOVAN to understand what makes it, by its inherent nature, so unique and very impactful.

Hyper-local means that a HYLOVAN's geographical scope can be as small as a neighborhood or cover an entire city. But it doesn't stretch beyond the county level in the US (there are 3,143 counties spread across 50 US states), a *département* in France (the Metropolitan France, the part of France attached to Europe, is geographically divided into 101 départements), or a German *(Land)Kreis* (in Germany, a *Kreis*, or district, is an intermediate level of administration between a *Länder* (a state), and the *Gemeinden* (municipalities) in it; there are 294 *Landkreise* (rural districts) and 107 *Stadtkreise* (urban districts) in Germany).

To reduce supply chain costs and ecological impact, a HYLOVAN sources most of its inputs – the human resources and raw materials – locally. And much of its output – products and services – is consumed locally, even if a modest portion can be distributed using sustainable logistics to neighboring localities. This is already the case for HYLOVANs specialized in recycling or producing energy and food locally close to customers. For instance, the Brooklyn Microgrid in New York is a blockchain-based, peer-to-peer renewable energy marketplace that empowers Brooklyn residents with solar panels to sell their excess energy to other residents and business owners in their neighborhood, hence boosting community resilience and interdependence.

The term *hyper-local* may sound backward in today's globalized digital economy. You may wonder, why reason at a small village level when, thanks to the internet, we live today in a global village? Hyper-localism is not a jingoistic or regionalist reaction to unbridled globalization. Rather, hyper-local networks can be construed as the letter T: they are globally connected (top horizontal line) and yet they are deeply anchored and act locally (middle vertical line).

Today, we are witnessing *glocalization,* which is the "simultaneous occurrence of both universalizing and particularizing tendencies in contemporary social, political, and economic systems."[28] Irrespective of where we live, we are all facing growing social inequalities, worsening climate change, and dwindling natural resources. But these globally shared issues have different effects in different parts of the world, and even within the same country or state. Some regions and cities are suffering from heavier rainfalls while others grapple with extreme heatwaves and severe droughts. And yet, each locality has unique natural resources and capabilities that a HYLOVAN can leverage to decarbonize the local economy and transition to a sustainable future. As such, the best way to solve big "problems without borders" such as climate change is, paradoxically, by innovating *within* the borders of our state or even county and cocreating local solutions using resources around us.

In December 2023, researchers at Lawrence Livermore National Laboratory (LLNL) and scientists at more than a dozen other institutions published a landmark report titled "Roads to Removals" that identifies different carbon dioxide removal (CDR) pathways to remove CO_2 from the atmosphere cost-effectively at the gigaton scale (at least a billion metric tons per year) and store it safely.[29] CDR is a key enabler to help the US achieve its goal of net-zero emissions by

2050. The report shows how to scale out carbon removal across the nation by forming HYLOVANs. It highlights specific opportunities for carbon removal in all 3,143 counties across the US, hence generating 440,0000 long-term jobs nationwide (see Figure 7.5).[30]

For each county, the report identifies the top CDR method that can optimally leverage local resources and capabilities and yield maximum benefits. The four major CDR methods proposed are forests, soils, biomass carbon removal and storage, and direct air capture and storage. "Every geographical region has a unique story, as well as an opportunity to help take enough CO_2 out of the air and meet our net-zero emissions goal by 2050," notes LLNL scientist Jennifer Pett-Ridge, the lead author of the report.[31] In Figure 7.5, darker-shaded counties designate substantial CO_2 removal opportunities with potential environmental and socioeconomic benefits.

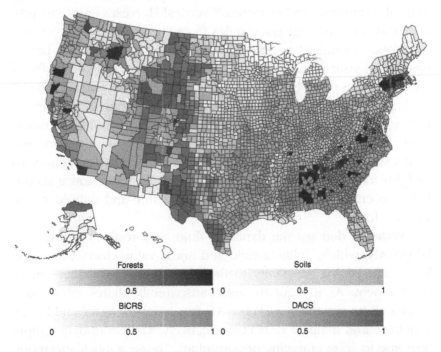

Figure 7.5 Options and opportunities for carbon dioxide removal (CDR) in all 3,143 counties in the US. The options are based on capacity and/or cost, weighted by the EEEJ (Energy Equity and Environmental Justice) index and Center for Disease Control's SVI (Social Vulnerability Index) scores.

Source: Roads to Removal: https://roads2removal.org.

Value(s) implies three things. First, a HYLOVAN strives to *valorize* – that is, bring out the full value of – the natural, intellectual, cultural, and social assets that, for economic or historic reasons, have been underused and/or devalued in a local context. Second, the firms embedded within a HYLOVAN cocreate *long-term* socioeconomic value that stays locally. This durable value is the exact opposite of the short-term value created by a capitalist business that opens a factory or shop in a rural area, exploits the local resources for a while, and then abandons the community overnight when it's no longer profitable to do business there. Third, a HYLOVAN fosters positive *values* – like solidarity, trust, sustainability, and equity – in a community by embodying them.

For instance, Vertical Harvest's three-story-tall vertical farm occupies just 1/10 of an acre plot in Jackson, Wyoming, but can supply 100,000 pounds of fresh leafy greens year-round exclusively to local restaurants and groceries.[32] Vertical Harvest's nutritious produce travel on average just 6 miles from farm to fork (by comparison, food consumed in America travels up to 2,500 miles before landing on your plate).[33] Vertical Harvest's hydroponic urban farms minimize water use by 85% but maximize human potential 100%. Its flagship farm in Jackson, Wyoming, a city where 78% of people with disabilities are without a job, employs community members with developmental disabilities such as people with autism and Down syndrome. By vertically growing greens and offering upward mobility to the disadvantaged, Vertical Harvest shows how a HYLOVAN can create economic and ecological value and uphold strong social values.

Network denotes the dynamic, fluid, and resilient nature of a HYLOVAN, which, unlike a rigid and linear value chain, can adapt, learn, and evolve constantly to flexibly respond to changes in its environment. As it regularly and transparently shares information among all its members, a HYLOVAN can innovate faster and better, anticipate and mitigate risks cost-effectively, and coordinate a rapid response to seize emerging opportunities. To use a music metaphor, a value chain is like a giant orchestra that is led by a single conductor in a top-down manner, whereas a HYLOVAN is like a modest jazz band with a horizontal and flexible structure that supports bottom-up improvisation and free-flow creativity.

Since the new millennium, I have advocated and consulted dozens of businesses, especially large firms, on how to replace their vertically integrated R&D-to-market value chains with *innovation networks*. Innovation networks are open and dynamic ecosystems that fluidly weave and synergize internal and external ideas, talents, and capital to codevelop disruptive products and services. This collaborative approach to creating value is also called *open innovation*.[34] During the 2000s, with the rise of Africa, Mexico, India, and China, I advised Western companies on how to build "global innovation networks" that combine the science and technology-led R&D capabilities in the US and Europe with the frugal ingenuity of entrepreneurs in emerging economies.[35]

As globalization, however, takes a back seat to localization, businesses in both developed and emerging economies must learn today to build innovation networks within their home country. By building *hyper-local innovation networks,* manufacturers can develop and harness local talent and resources, especially in rural areas and historically disadvantaged regions, to codevelop sustainable products and services that deliver great economic social and economic impact for local communities. Eschewing the linear and sequential product development approach, which is inflexible and resource-intensive, a HYLOVAN relies on open, agile and frugal innovation processes that support continuous experimentation and learning.

Instead of being constrained by the sequential "design-build-deliver" workflow in a traditional value chain, companies in HYLOVANs engage with local prosumers and partners in an iterative process to (see Figure 7.6):

1. Co-discover local capabilities and socially relevant market opportunities.
2. Codevelop personalized products and services iteratively.
3. Co-deploy high-impact solutions quickly and cost-effectively.

In *Jugaad Innovation* and *Frugal Innovation,* my coauthors and I offer companies many proven tools and techniques on how to adopt this dynamic co-discover–codevelop–co-deploy process to design, build, and launch new products and services faster, better,

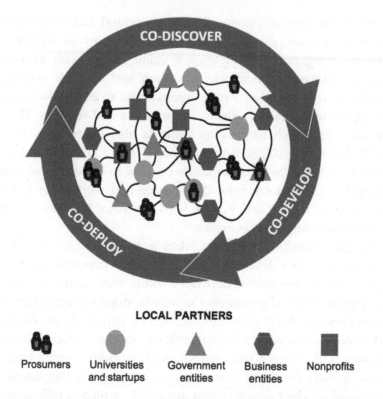

LOCAL PARTNERS

Prosumers   Universities and startups   Government entities   Business entities   Nonprofits

Figure 7.6 A HYLOVAN uses open and agile processes to engage with a diverse set of local stakeholders to innovate faster and better.

cheaper, and with more sustainability. I believe, however, that businesses can apply this dynamic approach not just to develop new products more effectively but also to reinvent their *entire* organization so it *operates* more effectively as a HYLOVAN.

Let me walk you through a case study to show how companies can use HYLOVANs to evolve from a monolithic organization into a "decentralized" and agile organization that can cocreate sustainable value(s) with local communities.

GRDF, France's leading natural gas distribution operator, has set up a network of Living Labs deeply anchored in the *territoires* (the French equivalent of US counties) that aim to put local citizens back at the heart of the energy transition. Conceptualized in the late 1990s at MIT Media Lab, the Living Lab "represents a user-centric research methodology for sensing, prototyping, validating and refining complex solutions in multiple and evolving real-life contexts."[36] In practical terms, a Living Lab is a collaborative innovation space set up in a city or a rural area that brings together local stakeholders – citizens, entrepreneurs, businesses, nonprofits, government agencies – to codevelop meaningful products and services that contribute to and enhance the common good. GRDF's Living Labs engage local communities to experiment with and catalyze disruptive solutions – such as the development of green gas and agroecology – which are tailored to the local context but can be replicated elsewhere.[37]

Specifically, GRDF is using these Living Labs to create awareness and gain support in local communities for projects involving methanation, the process of producing biogas and bio-methane from locally sourced organic waste such as livestock effluents, agricultural residues, and food waste. By producing bio-methane locally and injecting it into GRDF's distribution network, communities gain energy independence, reduce GHGs, improve soil quality, preserve water tables, and create new jobs. By building these Living Labs across France, GRDF is proactively scaling out its own operating model to facilitate and lead the decentralized production of renewable gases, which, in turn, will enable the decarbonization of local communities.

As of late 2023, 547 methanization units located across France were injecting directly into GRDF's distribution network. "The production of green gas in France already represents more than the power of a nuclear reactor and we will be able to make up for Russian gas imports by 2027–2028. One day we will even be able to export from decentralized production," predicts enthusiastically Laurence Poirier-Dietz, CEO of GRDF.[38] ADEME (the French Environment and Energy Management Agency) projects that bio-methane, injected by 1,400 sites from all over France, will account for 16% of the gas in the national distribution network by 2030.[39] According to GRDF's best-case scenario, 73% of the gas circulating in the distribution grid in France could be green gas by 2050. The European Union wants to fully decarbonize its energy system by 2050 by leveraging, among other things, renewable gases like bio-methane.

GRDF's Living Labs hold a critical lesson for Western CEOs and policymakers who are so eager to reshore manufacturing to US and European countries. In a *MIT Sloan Management Review* article titled "A Reshoring Renaissance Is Underway," Erin McLaughlin and Dana

M. Peterson, respectively a senior economist and the chief economist at The Conference Board, write, "Reshoring is now driving a dramatic rise in manufacturing construction activity. Companies are constructing U.S. manufacturing facilities at a higher rate than any other property type. Such spending rose to an annual rate of $114.7 billion in 2022, according to the U.S. Census Bureau – a 40% increase year over year and a 62% increase over the past five years."[40] I am not against building a lot of factories in America. But let's also build HYLOVANs around these factories that yield maximum economic and social benefits to local communities.

Here is my warning: manufacturers shouldn't build HYLOVANs in the 21st century with the *old mindset*. Today, US and European firms are reshoring manufacturing with the same old if-you-build-it-they-will-come mindset of the 20th century. Essentially, they pick a location in the US or Europe and build a factory there with a clear idea of what specific product(s) they want to make there. Unlike this top-down, preplanned approach to implementing a manufacturing value chain that pushes standard products to passive customers, a HYLOVAN – like GRDF's Living Lab – emerges gradually and organically from the bottom up by pulling inputs actively from various local stakeholders. A HYLOVAN engages a diverse set of local partners – prosumers, universities, startups, government bodies, trade groups, SMEs, and nonprofits – to identify the why (the social purpose of building a local manufacturing ecosystem), how (the unique processes and local resources used as production inputs), and what (the specific products and services manufactured locally). Working together, these stakeholders first craft a bold and optimistic vision of what they want their community to look like in 10 to 15 years. Then they identify the readily available local assets and resources that can be harnessed as well as the talents that can be cultivated for productive use to turn their societal vision into an economic reality. Finally, the HYLOVAN members decide which innovative goods and services they need to produce in priority that will (1) yield maximum social, economic, and ecological *value* for the local community and (2) support its rapid transition to a more inclusive and sustainable future.

In French, *renaissance* means "rebirth." A century ago, megafactories and globally distributed value chains gave birth to the capitalist industrial system. As we enter the third millennium, manufacturing is not going away, but is being reborn as the "perma-industry," that is, an industrial ecosystem rooted in a local community that coevolves symbiotically and synergistically with its sociocultural environment.[41] HYLOVANs – anchored by agile and sustainable micro-factories – are ushering this virtuous manufacturing renaissance. As Kevin O'Marah, cofounder of Zero100, a community research platform working toward zero carbon, 100% digital supply chains, optimistically predicts, "In coming decades, I foresee across the US and Europe, the emergence of regionalized value chains in fairly small catchment areas that boast agile micro-factories powered by advanced robotics that source a variety of materials available in proximity. Brands in fast-moving sectors like fashion, health, food, and beauty will leverage these sustainable and hyper-local value networks to cocreate mass-customized products with cohorts of consumers that are tailored to their specific genetic makeup and optimized for local climatic conditions."[42]

HYLOVANs will drive not only an industrial renaissance but also an organizational revolution in the 21st century. Visionary firms like GRDF are using HYLOVANs to ditch their monolithic corporate structures and reinvent themselves as a nimble *hyper-local enterprise* (HLE). An HLE, according to leading French sustainability expert Elisabeth Laville, is an agile business that operates as a decentralized network with fully empowered regional hubs.[43] These hubs innovate and operate autonomously to better leverage physical and human resources that exist as close as possible to markets and create a sustainable impact locally.

An HLE leverages HYLOVANs to cocreate value (and values!) with diverse partners in local communities, a value with a certain stickiness (staying power), which remains in the community. It's the antithesis of a capitalist business driven by opportunism that exploits local resources and suppliers just because they are cheap but can shift its operations elsewhere overnight.

An HLE *coevolves* in a symbiotic manner with each community in which it operates, sharing – even forging – a common destiny. It actively contributes to the cocreation of the local ecosystem and nurtures it by continually increasing its value and expanding its skill set.

■ ■ ■

"Not your grandfather's manufacturing" is what you may have thought as you read Chapters 5, 6, and this one, which showcase next-generation factories and industrial value networks. And yet, believe it or not, the manufacturing revolution chronicled in these three chapters is merely a return to our modest industrial roots as Americans. Ben Franklin, one of the (and my favorite) founding fathers of the United States, famously said, "The way to wealth is as plain as the way to market. It depends chiefly on two words, industry and frugality; that is, waste neither time nor money, but make the best use of both. Without industry and frugality nothing will do; with them, everything."[44] Ben Franklin was himself a *frugal manufacturer*. Using sheer ingenuity and his bare hands, he tinkered using limited resources and yet developed useful products like the Franklin stove that delivered twice more heat than traditional stoves while using 75% less wood. Franklin never patented his valuable inventions such as the lightning rod, bifocals, or the carriage odometer, arguing that "as we enjoy great advantages from the inventions of others, we should be glad of an opportunity to serve others by any invention of ours; and this we should do freely and generously."[45]

Sadly, during the 20th century, America – as well as Europe – lost touch with both industry and frugality. US and European businesses massively offshored their industrial activities and scaled up their operations, favoring gigantism over parsimony. Profligate, their global industrial value chains devoured natural resources and heavily pol-luted our air, water, and land, plunging us into a climate pandemo-nium. It's not too late. Let's bring back not only manufacturing but also frugality in the US and Europe. By scaling out manufacturing and co-building HYLOVANs, the West can rebuild its industrial foun-dation on a sustainable ground. Even better: we shall use frugal manufacturing to make our economies not just sustainable but regenerative.

PART III

Regenerating People, Places, and the Planet

CHAPTER 8

The Rise of Regenerative Businesses

In recent years, aware of the worsening climate crisis, companies have multiplied efforts to make their business activities more sustainable. Eager to act "less badly" for the planet, they are focused on *lessening their negative impact* on the environment by reducing two things: waste and emissions.

To reduce waste, many businesses have embraced the principles of the *circular economy*. Unlike the linear "take-make-use-dispose" economy, which is resource-intensive and wasteful, the circular economy aims to reduce and reuse resources and recycle waste materials into new products. The circular economy can have a significant impact in resource-hungry and waste-prone sectors like consumer-packaged goods, automotive, and fast fashion.

The Ellen MacArthur Foundation, which conceptualized the circular economy, estimates that the fast-moving consumer goods sector represents 35% of material inputs in the economy, devours 90% of agricultural output, but also produces a staggering 75% of municipal waste, in particular plastic packaging.[1] The foundation believes that by adopting the three tenets of the circular economy – that is, reduce, reuse, and recycle resources – the consumer goods sector can save more than $700 billion annually while considerably reducing emissions.[2] This explains why all consumer-packaged goods giants like Coca-Coca, PepsiCo, Procter & Gamble, Nestlé, and Unilever are racing to make their value chains and products less material-intensive and less wasteful. For instance, since 2015, Unilever operates globally zero-waste factories, ensuring that no hazardous manufacturing waste is sent to landfills. By 2025, Unilever aims to curb by 50% the use of virgin plastic in packaging and boost the use of recycled plastic by 25%. All its plastic packaging will be totally reusable, recyclable, and compostable by 2025. Unilever also plans to halve food waste in its global operations by 2025.[3]

The automotive sector accounts for 10% of plastics, 17% of steel, and 42% of aluminum consumed in Europe.[4] To produce a single car weighing 1,300 kg (2,866 pounds), you need 3 to 4 tons of metallic minerals and 2 to 3 tons of nonmetallic minerals.[5] These inputs are *virgin* raw materials, such as rare earths, sourced directly from nature as opposed to recycled materials that are generated by processing existing resources. For instance, by weight, a passenger car on average is made of 65% steel and iron, but only 25% of the steel used in car bodies is recycled steel. Under the European Commission's proposed new regulation, 30% of plastics from end-of-life vehicles (ELVs) should be recycled, up from 19% today, and new vehicles should include at least 25% of recycled plastic.[6] Some carmakers are racing ahead in recycling without waiting for new circular economy regulations. In 2014, Jaguar Land Rover (JLR) launched Jaguar XE whose body panels are made with the aluminum alloy RC5754, which contains up to 75% recycled aluminum. Buoyed by this success, JLR launched REALITY, a bold enterprise-wide initiative to recover a maximum of aluminum from ELVs to build next-generation vehicles, including all-electric cars.[7] In late 2022, French carmaker Renault set up The Future is NEUTRAL, a dedicated business unit that offers recycling solutions to the entire auto industry at every stage of a vehicle's life, from supply to production to use and end of life.

Companies are also multiplying efforts to *decarbonize* their supply chains to reduce their CO_2 and greenhouse gas emissions – the main culprits of climate degradation. For instance, apparel maker Levi Strauss aims to achieve 90% reduction in greenhouse gas emissions and 100% renewable electricity in all its facilities by 2025. By then, Levi Strauss also aims to reduce freshwater use in manufacturing by 50% in areas of high-water stress areas.[8] Likewise, Apple and Google have committed to achieving zero carbon for their supply chain and all products and power all their operations with clean energy by 2030. Finally, aware that the built environment accounts for 42% of annual global CO_2 emissions, over 1,300 members of the

American Institute of Architects have committed to reaching carbon neutrality for all new buildings, developments, and major renovations by 2030.[9]

All these virtuous sustainability strategies – curbing waste and emissions and shifting to renewable energy – aim to "do more with less," that is, produce more economic value by polluting less and consuming fewer natural resources like water, and is called *decoupling*. See Figure 8.1.

But this "**do less harm**" (to the environment) stance is not enough, for six key reasons:

◆ **Worsening climate change.** Climate change is accelerating. It is a known fact that unless global warming is kept below 1.5°C by 2100, the planet and humanity will suffer grave consequences. In its 2015 report, the Intergovernmental Panel on Climate Change estimated the risk of exceeding 1.5°C to be zero. But that turned out a rosy forecast. Summer 2023 was the hottest on record globally by a wide margin, according to Copernicus Climate Change Service.[10] The World Meteorological Organization projects there is a 66% chance that the world will breach the 1.5°C threshold before 2027.[11] We are *already* paying a heavy price for our inaction on climate change, whose worst effects have yet to come.

◆ **Draining of natural resources.** We are rapidly running out of natural resources. In 2023, Earth Overshoot Day – the point in the

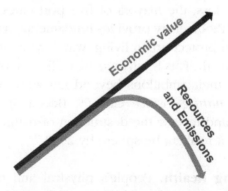

Figure 8.1 Sustainable development, also known as *decoupling*, aims to create more economic value using fewer resources and polluting less.

year when humanity's natural resources consumption exceeds the planet's ability to regenerate – was on August 2, earlier than ever.[12] At the current rate, by 2030, humanity would need two planets to supply the resources we need and to absorb our waste. If every citizen in the world consumed like an average American does, five Earths will be required to sustain them![13] Sadly, we only have one. With 700 million people joining the global middle class by 2030, demand for energy, food, water, and materials will jack up prices for natural resources and land. Global freshwater demand will exceed supply by 40% by 2030.[14] Already today, 2 billion people around the world lack access to clean and safe drinking water. According to McKinsey & Company, unless we boost land-use efficiency, the world will need 70 to 80 million hectares (Mha) of additional cropland – the equivalent to the total cropland of Brazil today – by 2030 to satisfy our rising demand for fuel, food, and natural capital.[15] The UK is expected to run out of farmland by 2030 as food must compete with housing and energy for the limited space available.

♦ **Dwindling biodiversity.** Our biodiversity is shrinking at an alarming pace. The World Wildlife Fund's Living Planet Report 2022 found that wildlife populations have declined almost 70% since 1970. A 2023 study of 71,000 existing animal species worldwide found that nearly 50% are declining.[16] Rising sea surface temperatures have caused the loss of 14% of the world's coral reefs between 2009 and 2018, exposing islands and coastlines to damaging waves, storms, and floods.[17] Noting that half of the GDP in cities worldwide is threatened by nature loss, the mayors of five port cities across different regions wrote, "Biodiversity provides fundamental natural 'dividends' that nourish and protect urban living, way beyond its intrinsic – and incalculable – worth. This is why we are calling on other global leaders to re-frame their ambitions beyond net zero and align actions towards more *nature-positive* cities."[18] Becoming nature positive means "to halt and reverse the destruction of nature by 2030 with a full recovery of a resilient biosphere by 2050."[19]

♦ **Declining health.** People's physical and mental health is declining rapidly. Americans are getting sicker. A 2017 RAND study shows that 60% US adults suffer from a chronic illness and 40% have two or more. Since 2015, the US GDP has kept growing but Americans' life expectancy has been declining (compared to other developed nations, the US decline has been longer and steeper). American longevity plunged from nearly 79 years in 2019 to 77 years in 2020, and then to 76 years, 5 months in 2021. In 2022, US life expectancy was only back to 77 years, 6 months.[20] "We basically have lost 20 years of gains," notes Elizabeth Arias, a health scientist at CDC.[21] Americans' mental health is more worrisome. Major depression diagnoses in the US have jumped 33% since 2013. In 2022, the number of suicides in the US was the highest since 1941.[22] According to a Lancet Commission report, the economic cost of mental illness globally would surpass $16 trillion by 2030.

◆ **Rising social inequality and poverty.** Poverty and social inequalities are exploding. Poverty, viewed by many as a "third-world scourge" now plagues the developed world too. Today, 95 million Europeans live below the relative poverty line.[23] In France, 14.5% of the population – mostly women and children – live in poverty. According to a 2024 Oxfam report, between 2020 and 2021, 63% of all new wealth created globally filled the pockets of the richest 1% of humanity, with the remaining 99% receiving just 37% of new global revenue.[24] In 2020, a study by Financial Health Network, which tracks Americans' financial health from year to year, found that more over two-thirds of Americans – 167 million people – experienced financial hardship. After improving slightly in 2021, the situation has gotten even worse in recent years. In 2023, the share of financially vulnerable Americans grew to 17%, up from 15% in 2022, with the Black, Latinx, and younger Americans being affected disproportionally.[25]

◆ **Increasing expectations.** Next-gen consumers and employees favor businesses that go beyond the basics. Gen X consumers like me were impressed when a beverage firm began selling a zero-calorie and sugar-free soda or a car company launched new vehicles that were 25% more fuel efficient. Millennials want more from brands. They expect a beverage company to offer organic drinks with botanical herbs that enhance vitality. Gen Ys, who pioneered carsharing, want automakers to become solution providers that deliver end-to-end clean mobility services for entire cities. Generations Z and Alpha – who will account for nearly 50% of the global population by 2030 – demand that brands go far beyond doing less harm to people, communities, and the planet. These values-driven consumers and employees want to buy from, and work for, brands that sell only eco-friendly products but also actively restore biodiversity and revitalize local communities as part of their *core business model* and not just their corporate social responsibility (CSR). They prefer working in office buildings that are not just carbon-neutral but net-positive by generating free clean electricity for local communities.

For these six reasons, businesses need to go beyond sustainability and CSR, which merely strive to do less harm to society and the planet. Conscious consumers, employees, and investors demand businesses to actively help build healthy, fair, and equitable societies and restore and revitalize natural ecosystems. It's high time for businesses to become regenerative.

Regenerative Businesses Do More Good

According to national surveys conducted by ReGenFriends in 2019 and again in 2020, nearly 80% of US consumers prefer regenerative brands to sustainable brands.[26] Nils-Michael Langenborg, cofounder of ReGenFriends, explained to me why: "Aware of the climate emergency, buyers, especially young people, want companies to go well beyond sustainability. They find the term 'sustainable' too passive. They demand that businesses take inspiration from nature and build a virtuous regenerative economy based on *renewal*, *restoration* and *growth* (the three essential qualities of all living systems)."[27]

To become regenerative, businesses should learn from nature.

In her inspiring TED Talk "How Trees Talk to Each Other," Suzanne Simard, a forest ecology professor at University of British Columbia, demonstrates how nature is generous – a virtue you don't attribute to the hyper-competitive and cutthroat corporate world.[28] Forest trees magnanimously share information and nutrients with each other using a deep network of soil fungi.

What if companies reinvented their value chains and business models so they operate altruistically like a forest? Then they will think, feel, and act as **regenerative businesses** that give back 10 times and even 100 times more to society and the planet than what they take from it. To use organizational psychologist Adam Grant's analogy, businesses can evolve from "takers" to *"givers."*[29] Regenerative businesses are "net-positive" – a concept developed by Paul Polman and Andrew Winston to designate companies that venture beyond sustainability.[30] A net-positive company "improves well-being for everyone it impacts and at all scales – every product, every operation, every region and country, and for every stakeholder, including employees, suppliers, communities, customers, and even future generations and the planet itself."[31] A net-positive business profits by solving the world's biggest problems instead of creating or amplifying them.

A sustainable business strives just to reduce its ecological footprint. A regenerative business, however, boldly vies to enlarge its socio-ecological *handprint* – as Gregory Norris, director of SHINE, a joint MIT/Harvard project, describes it – by boosting the health and the vitality of communities (people and places) and the planet.[32] In doing so, regenerative businesses can achieve superior financial performance and customer loyalty than their sustainability-focused counterparts. See Figure 8.2.

The stacking of the Plus ⊕ above Minus ⊖ in Figure 8.2 does not imply a hierarchy. Regeneration is in no way *superior* to sustainability. Sustainability and regeneration are not two opposing concepts. Rather, they are complementary and mutually reinforcing.

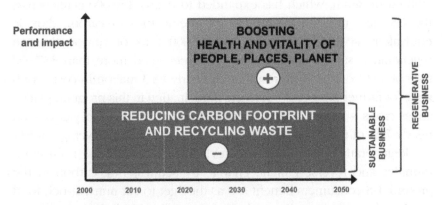

Figure 8.2 A regenerative business increases its social and ecological handprint while reducing its ecological footprint.

Indeed, a regenerative business does **better with less**: it revitalizes people, places, and the planet (⊕) while *also* engaging in sustainability by recycling and reducing waste and use of scarce resources (⊖). In doing so, regenerative businesses can realize greater financial performance and affect than their sustainability-focused peers.

Through a series of short case studies, I want to introduce you to vanguard regenerative businesses across different sectors and highlight their *diverse* approaches to profitably renew, restore, and grow natural ecosystems and communities.

REGENERATING THE LAND AND THE FARMERS WHO FEED US: DANONE NORTH AMERICA

Since 2017, Danone North America, the US-based business unit of the French food and beverage multinational Danone, has been enabling its US and Canadian farming suppliers to adopt **regenerative agriculture**. This rigorous approach uses science-based techniques and natural methods like crop rotation to enrich the soil, preserve and foster biodiversity, and enhance animal welfare while reducing emissions (especially methane).

By adopting these practices, financially challenged US farmers can do better with less: they can boost yields – hence their revenues – and the long-term value of their land while minimizing emissions and use of toxic fertilizers and precious irrigation water.

In 2022, Danone North America reported that its regenerative agricultural program, which has expanded to nearly 150,000 acres across the US, has "reduced nearly 119,000 metric tons of carbon dioxide equivalent, sequestered more than 31,000 tons of carbon through regenerative soil health practices, and prevented more than 337,000 tons of soil from erosion, resulting in nearly $3.3 million in cost avoidance for farmer partners."[33] Farmers participating in this program placed cover crops – which offer soil protection and boost crop yields – on nearly 70% of the program's acreage versus the national average of 5%.

Regenerative agriculture can revitalize vulnerable US rural communities and reverse climate change by sequestering carbon in the ground. US consumers benefit too as they get to eat nutrient-rich food produced by high-vitality soil. Danone calls this holistic approach "One Planet. One Health," which is based on its conviction that the health of people and the health of our planet are interconnected.

In 2023, Danone ranked number 3 in the Food and Agriculture Benchmark, which ranks the sustainability performance of the 350 most influential firms in the entire agrifood value chain based on their ecological, nutritional, and social impact. Since 2018, Danone North America has operated as the world's largest certified B Corp, a demanding label which recognizes a new type of company that solves major social and ecological problems as part of its business goals.

REGENERATING THE AMAZON'S NATURAL AND CULTURAL BIODIVERSITY: NATURA

In the Amazonian Forest grows a palm tree called *murumuru*. Amazon Indians cut down these palm trees and used their wood to make commodity products like brooms.

It turns out that we can extract from the seeds of this palm tree an ultra-hydrating butter that repairs and regenerates damaged hair very effectively. These seeds are seven times more valuable than the wood of this palm tree. It is therefore *seven times* more profitable for the Amazon Indians to keep this exceptional palm tree alive than to cut it down!

Natura, a Brazilian cosmetics brand, is working with Amazon Indians to use their ancestral agricultural practices to sustainably extract this murumuru butter to make a range of hair care products.[34]

Through this win-win partnership, Natura is regenerating Indigenous communities simultaneously on three levels: *economically* (by enabling them to earn more), *culturally* (by maintaining and leveraging their traditional farming knowledge), and *ecologically* (by preserving the Amazon biodiversity and its forest – the ancestral home of Indigenous people).

REGENERATING LOCAL COMMUNITIES WITH FACTORIES AS FORESTS: INTERFACE

Interface, the world's leading modular carpet producer, piloted a "Factory as a Forest" project in Australia as part of its Climate Take Back (CTB) strategy. With CTB, Interface aims to not just fight but *reverse* global warming and go well beyond net zero (which Interface became in 2019) by becoming a regenerative business that gives back more to society and the planet than it takes from them.[35]

In principle, a Factory as a Forest would freely supply the local community with many valuable "ecosystem services" (benefits) that the surrounding healthy ecosystems near the factory provide, such as air cleaning, biodiversity support, water storage, pollination, carbon sequestration, and nutrient cycling.[36] All these beneficial services enhance the well-being of the local community. "The new civic gesture is not a stadium; it's a healthy ecoregion," notes Janine Benyus, cofounder of Biomimicry 3.8, the world's leading bio-inspired consultancy that Interface partnered with to design and implement the Factory as a Forest project.[37]

Interface collaborated with Biomimicry 3.8 to apply design interventions based on the knowledge gained from this pilot project in Australia in order to transform its US facility outside of Atlanta, Georgia, into a high-performing ecosystem. Interface is now looking to replicate this successful regenerative model across the company globally.

Interface is working toward making all its products regenerative, too. The firm achieved carbon neutrality for all of its products by 2018. It is now setting a much higher standard. The world's first *carbon-negative* carpet tiles were introduced by Interface in late 2020; these carpet tiles capture more carbon than they emit from "cradle to gate," that is, from the sourcing of raw materials through manufacturing, without the need for offsets. These tiles are made with more than 90% recycled and bio-based materials like plants that store more carbon than they emit during their manufacturing cycle, hence making them carbon-negative. Interface aims to make its entire company carbon-negative and regenerative by 2040.

REGENERATING RURAL AMERICA WITH KNOWLEDGE-BASED WORK: SPARQ

Sparq (previously named *Rural Sourcing*) views small towns across America as a great untapped pool of creative talent that can benefit the entire country, contrary to the belief held by coastal elites that rural areas in the US are destined for collapse. Today, instead of *offshoring* their IT work to far-flung places like Romania and India, Fortune 500 firms, big tech vendors, and US startups outsource their application development and product engineering to Sparq's experienced IT engineers located in 10 locations across the US, situated mostly in rural areas.

Monty Hamilton, CEO of Sparq, told me that his IT engineers in rural and small-town America have a lot of fire in their bellies and are

very adaptable, creative, and have strong work ethics.[38] By tapping
into these rural IT workers' grit and ingenuity, Sparq's corporate clients gain in business agility and productivity, save costs, and accelerate their digital transformation. Hamilton estimates that his skillful
engineers in small-town America can execute tech projects up to two
to four times faster than offshore IT workers, cost clients 30% less
than big IT service firms in the US, and work up to 25% more pro-
ductively than freelancers.

Sparq regenerates rural communities and small towns in America
by creating well-paid local jobs, but also by increasing the long-term
employability of engineers, particularly young talent from minority
groups, in the US hinterland. These talented tech workers choose to
stay in their rural hometowns rather than flee to San Francisco or
New York seeking better job opportunities.

In Chapter 12, I will elaborate on the great revival of America's
hinterland, which is leading to the emergence of a frugal economy
in the US.

■ ■ ■

These examples of regenerative businesses listed are all inspiring. Yet, the sheer variety of ways in which these vanguard firms
practice regeneration point to the fact that regeneration is still an
emerging paradigm. As of today, there is no standard definition of
what regeneration actually is. As a result, regeneration remains *poly-
semic* as a concept (it has multiple meanings), *polymorphous* in its
practice (it is applied in different forms), and *polyvalent* in its impact
(it yields different results).

Let me highlight four pioneering scholars and practitioners who
have done a great job at conceptualizing and promoting the notion
of regeneration as it pertains to the economy and businesses since
the new millennium:

◆ **Carol Sanford**, a business educator and consultant, has written extensively and advised Fortune 500 firms on how to
   become a "regenerative business," an enlightened organization that ignites the genius lying dormant within each employee
   so they can reconnect with their true essence, develop her

fullest psycho-mental capacity, and authentically and mean-
ingfully contribute to the company, society, and nature. In her
book *The Regenerative Life*, Sanford explains that Gandhi's
exhortation "Be the change" is not to change and improve our
behavior as individuals, but rather evolve our beliefs and
thought patterns so we can become conscious agents of social
change. Sanford calls *regenerative change* the "non-heroic
approach" to becoming more alive.[39] For Sanford, the purpose
of regeneration is not to keep an individual, an organization,
or a society merely alive, but to maximize its *aliveness* (I will
elaborate on this distinction in Chapter 10). As I wrote this
paragraph, I was inspired to learn that Sanford is practicing
what she preached all her life by regenerating her spirit and
joyfully expressing her aliveness even as her body and mind
are degenerating rapidly due to amyotrophic lateral sclerosis
(ALS or Lou Gehrig's disease).[40]

♦ After a successful 20-year career on Wall Street at JP Morgan,
John Fullerton left the financial firm in 2001. His first-hand
experience with 9/11 shifted his perspective. He decided to
apply his financial background to reinvent capitalism and economics, so they serve life rather than destroy it. In 2010, Fullerton set up Capital Institute, which brings together 1,000+
change makers from around the world to build a pathway for
our societies to evolve an extractive economy into a regenerative economy that enhances the long-term well-being of people, planet, and business. Inspired by the qualities (generosity,
cooperation, robustness) and the dynamics (self-organization,
self-sustained oscillations) of living systems, Capital Institute
created the *regenerative economics* framework.[41] This framework is based on eight core operating principles that enable
businesses and markets to sustain and regenerate themselves
constantly by operating in dynamic balance within a "window
of vitality" that makes them both efficient and resilient.[42]

♦ In 2005, while working on his PhD thesis on design for sustainability, **Daniel Christian Wahl** realized that sustainability
was too modest a goal. Being both a humanist and an ecologist at heart, Wahl advocates the design of a "regenerative
human culture" that is "healthy, resilient, and adaptable, cares

for the planet and cares for life in the awareness that this is the most effective way to create a thriving future for all humanity."[43] Just like in Chapters 5 through 7, where I emphasized the need to scale out production by localizing value networks, Wahl emphasizes the importance of scaling out regeneration through local ecosystems. "The local and regional scale is not only the scale at which we can act most effectively to preserve biological diversity, but also the scale at which we can preserve cultural diversity and indigenous local wisdom," notes Wahl.[44] I will expand on this critical idea of *place-based regeneration* and how to cultivate it in Chapter 10.

- ◆ **Isabelle Delannoy**, who is an agriculture engineer by training, notes, "In a finite world, there is no sustainability without regeneration of resources. And there is no regeneration possible without (human) cooperation with living things."[45] In her book *The Symbiotic Economy*, Delannoy shows how businesses and communities can leverage three types of resources – technological, sociocultural, and natural resources – to "regenerate the fertility of the environment on which they depend." By adopting symbiotic development principles, Delannoy believes we can reduce the need for physical materials by 90% in our economy and develop the productive capacities of local communities, making them autonomous and resilient. "We [only]have ten years to [innovate and] move towards a new economy . . . that is no longer destructive, but regenerative," predicts Delannoy.[46]

In addition to Sanford, Fullerton, Wahl, and Delannoy, other top business thinkers and environmental activists have also developed frameworks, tools, best practices, and communities to build regenerative businesses and enable our transition to regenerative economies. For instance, **John Elkington**, a world-renown expert in corporate responsibility dubbed as the *godfather of sustainability*, published in 2017 *Green Swans: The Coming Boom in Regenerative Capitalism*. In this optimistic manifesto, Elkington shows how we could embrace breakthrough innovations that will "steer us toward regeneration instead of pulling us down into a world ridden with Black Swan characteristics."[47] In 2021, building off his book

Regeneration: Ending the Climate Crisis in One Generation, leading environmental activist **Paul Hawken** launched Project Regeneration, a global movement to identify, host, and connect learning communities worldwide that are trailblazing innovative practices to reverse global warming and regenerate planetary ecosystems.[48]

I applaud the efforts of these pioneering scholars and consultants who promote the regenerative economy as a virtuous alternative to our extractive economy and help businesses go beyond sustainability and become regenerative. Yet, I feel something is missing in articles being published, conferences being hosted, and consulting services being offered on regenerative businesses or regenerative economy. Most discussions and (best) practices today are centered on the how and what of regeneration, that is, how to leverage new technologies like AI and novel approaches like biomimicry to develop regenerative products, processes, and business models that will "do good" to the planet, and to some extent to society. That is fine. But few thought leaders and practitioners are answering *why* do we regenerate our ecosystems and, more important, *who* is doing the regeneration ?

Einstein famously said something along the lines of "You cannot solve a problem with the same mindset that created it." I would push this statement further by saying "You can't transform a dysfunctional system with the same *consciousness* that created it." As I wrote in a Fast Company article titled "Before We Reinvent the Economy, We Must Reinvent Ourselves," "Before we transform our agricultural and industrial systems, we must transform ourselves as human beings. To preserve nature, we must first change our inner nature. If we build the (regenerative) bioeconomy with the same mindset that built our existing economic system – characterized by resource-hungry mass production and individualistic mass consumption – we will end up producing, consuming, and doing the wrong things faster, better, cheaper, and more sustainably (and more regeneratively)."[49] And I gave the following example to back my argument: "What's the point of using a self-driving car built with biomaterials and powered by biofuel that runs on solar-powered highways to get us to work faster when 87% of employees feel disengaged or worked to death (literally, as Stanford professor Jeffrey Pfeffer shows in his scary book, *Dying for a Paycheck*)?"[50]

You get my point. Unless we raise and expand human consciousness, we risk re-creating a regenerative economy that could well reverse climate change and restore depleted natural ecosystems but, sadly, would sustain (no pun intended) "bullshit jobs" and wasteful lifestyles that plague our existing economy and social lives. This is what happened to the *circular economy*, a popular sustainability concept that aims to "reduce, reuse, and recycle" (3R) resources and materials. Most companies, however, who claim to be *circular businesses* are practicing circularity selectively by focusing exclusively on recycling their waste to make *more* new products and sell *more*, but not on incenting people to reduce consumption and reuse the products they already have (by, for instance, sharing them, as discussed in Chapters 2 through 4). In other words, businesses today (ab)use the notion of *circularity* to just "do *more* with less (waste)." The same fate awaits *regeneration* – a promising concept that risks being "hijacked" by the profit-hungry capitalist system to keep selling more useless stuff and alienating workers stuck in meaningless jobs. If we want to avoid that, we need to figure out how regeneration can be applied wisely to fulfill the noble purpose of a frugal economy, which is to "do *better* with less." What do I mean by *better*? The answer lies in the very definition of *regeneration*. The French dictionary Larousse defines *regeneration* as follows:[51]

1. Reconstruction of damaged organic tissues in living beings.
2. Moral renewal, amendment of what was corrupt, altered (as in): *The regeneration of society.*

The first definition, borrowed from biology, applies to the body and mind (at least the *brain*). A new promising field called *regenerative medicine* is specialized in the "process of replacing, engineering or regenerating human or animal cells, tissues or organs to restore or establish normal function."[52] For instance, researchers at Whitehead Institute are studying certain species with the amazing capabilities to regenerate rapidly damaged or lost limbs and even their entire bodies. For instance, a planarian (*Schmidtea mediterranea*), a type of flatworm, "can be cut into many pieces and each piece will regrow into a full worm within about two weeks."[53] By researching how planarians pull this off "could lead to a better understanding of the necessary factors for regeneration, both in planarians and more broadly," including in humans.[54]

What interests me is the second definition ("moral renewal"), which pertains to the *soul* of not just an individual, but an entire society. What if we can regenerate the *soul* of communities world-wide and transmute people's fear and anger into positive energies to create a *better* society? What if we can apply **regenerative development** as a new socioeconomic growth paradigm to build a *conscious society* that maximizes well-being and unleashes the potential of all citizens? What if companies evolved from sustainable businesses to *regenerative enterprises* that can boost the health and vitality of employees, customers, and all stakeholders in local markets?

This is no utopia.

In Chapter 9, using a spiritual perspective, we'll explore the regeneration of the soul and how it contributes to the evolution of human consciousness. I will walk you through an inspiring case study on regenerative development undertaken in a small town in France that successfully reinvented its ailing economy and reinvigor-ated its people's floundering soul. You will learn how enlightened political leaders can raise citizens' consciousness, ignite their resilient spirit, and channel their creative energies to regenerate our econo-mies and communities.

In Chapter 10, I will show how businesses can apply systemic thinking and adopt a holistic approach to regenerating people, places, and the planet simultaneously and synergically. In doing so, companies can evolve into *regenerative businesses* that not only "do good" but "*are* good."

CHAPTER 9

Regenerative Development

CERN, the European Organization for Nuclear Research in Geneva, Switzerland, is the world's largest physics laboratory. Within the grounds of CERN stands a 2-meter-tall (6.6 feet) statue of the Hindu god Shiva (see Figure 9.1). In 2014, the Indian government gifted this statue of Shiva to CERN to celebrate their long-standing scientific

Figure 9.1 A statue of Shiva performing the cosmic dance stands majestically at CERN.
Source: Kenneth Lu / Wikimedia Commons / CC BY 2.0.

collaboration.[1] This majestic statue depicts Shiva as Nataraja, or "Lord of the Dance" in Sanskrit, blissfully performing *tandava*, the "cosmic dance" of creation and destruction.[2] In this dynamic pose, Shiva symbolizes and expresses Shakti, the life force or the primal energy that animates everything in our universe down to the subatomic particles.[3]

Astronomer Carl Sagan noted, "The Hindu religion is the only one of the world's great faiths dedicated to the idea that the Cosmos itself undergoes an immense, indeed an infinite, number of deaths and rebirths."[4] Physicist Fritjof Capra, author of *The Tao of Physics*, explains why the Nataraja statue is an apt metaphor for CERN's study of particles, tiny pieces of matter that make up everything in our universe: "Modern physics has shown that the rhythm of creation and destruction is not only manifest in the turn of the seasons and in the birth and death of all living creatures, but is also the very essence of inorganic matter . . . For the modern physicists, then, Shiva's dance is the dance of subatomic matter."[5]

This rhythm of creation and destruction is symbolized by the *damaru,* a two-headed hand drum in the shape of a horizontal hourglass (ᛗ) that you see Shiva carrying in his upper right hand in this statue. The drum's two heads symbolize the outward duality in nature and the handle signifies the underlying unity of existence. CERN is home to the Large Hadron Collider, the world's largest and highest-energy particle collider. A collider accelerates charged particles to nearly the speed of light and smashes them with other particles traveling in the opposite direction. The intense energy of the collision is turned into matter, generating new particles, such as the Higgs boson, also known as the God particle, that scientists analyze to understand the subatomic world and the origin of the universe. In the same spirit, by vibrating the damaru, you harness the *creative tension* between its two heads, which produce dissimilar sounds, to generate a unified sound, which echoes "Aum," the primordial sound that created and sustains the universe. This vibrant pulsation, called *spanda*, has two alternating phases: expansion and contraction. *Spanda* is the pulse of life: we inhale and exhale and our heart beats rhythmically.[6]

The *tandava* that Shiva performs attuned to *spanda* symbolizes the spiritual essence of regeneration.

Let me unpack this for you. The word *regeneration* is composed of *re*, which means "again," and *generation*, which means "bringing to life." As such, regeneration means rebirth or re-creation. This implies that what existed before must *die* first so it can be reborn anew. This is a key point: death is a prerequisite to life. I don't mean physical death, but something deeper. In the West, Shiva is misconstrued as "the Destroyer" and the "God of Death." This is a gross misunderstanding of the deeper symbolism of Shiva. First, if Shiva destroys, it is to create space for something else to emerge *organically*. As such, Shiva is a *disruptive creator* (not be confused with the *creative disruptors* in Silicon Valley who create innovative new stuff with the sole intent of destroying the "old" world order and replace it with their "better" version). Second, what Shiva destroys is your insecure ego, symbolized by that dwarflike demon he crushes with his right feet, so you can realize your true divine nature.

Hence, regeneration is a *spiritual rebirth*. The true purpose of regeneration is to dissolve your limited sense of self so you can "at once reveal and revel in your light."[7] Carl Sagan famously said, "The cosmos is within us. We are made of star-stuff. We are a way for the universe to know itself."[8] If so, regeneration is a conscious self-development process to experience the *spanda* of the universe within our own selves, so we become fully alive and shine like bright stars.

Expanding Awareness and Acting Consciously

Figure 9.2 captures the spirit of what I just explained. Carried out properly, **regenerative development** – at an individual, organizational, or community level – can gradually (1) heighten your awareness of your authentic self and reveal your unique talents and gifts and (2) enable you to creatively and wisely apply your distinctive capabilities to serve others.

Although the shape in Figure 9.2 could remind readers of other well-known frameworks, like spiral dynamics, I use the spiral image intentionally to convey three key points.

First, regenerative development is not a smooth linear path akin to a ladder you can climb effortlessly. It is more like the challenging Indian board game *Moksha Patam* known in the West as Snakes and Ladders or Chutes and Ladders. A rapid increase in awareness (ladder) can be followed by a drastic drop (chute). For instance, a country can elect a president who hails from a minority group, making

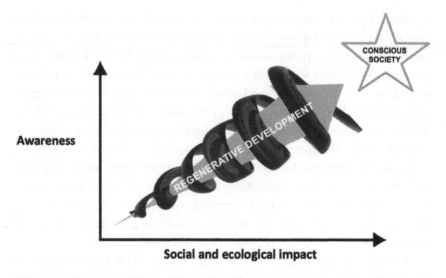

Figure 9.2 Regenerative development gradually raises human awareness and expands social and ecological impact by involving all citizens in co-building a conscious society.

you believe that nation has elevated its consciousness and irrevocably entered a post-racial era. Eight years later, however, that same country can retrograde in consciousness and elect a racist president. These ups and downs in awareness during the regenerative journey are normal as they mirror the ebbs and flows of life itself. So, enjoy the roller coaster ride . . . consciously!

Second, heightened awareness, which represents just one facet of regenerative development (the Y axis), is utterly useless unless it leads to meaningful *action* that creates social and ecological impact (the X axis). For example, most people today in the world are aware of the climate crisis, yet they feel powerless as they don't know how they could act at their level to make an impact. This gnawing "awareness action gap" leads to *eco-anxiety*.

Third, and this is a crucial point, when the level of awareness in an organization, a community, or a nation drops drastically due to fear or anger, and its *spanda* (life force) severely contracts, a wise leader would detect it. They will respond by crafting a noble purpose for their company or community that can uplift the employees or citizens and raise their consciousness. This enlightened leader will act as an alchemist and transmute the negative emotions of fear and anger surrounding them into expansive positive energies that can regenerate their organization or community.

Let me show you how a visionary political leader revitalized his dying town by first expanding its citizens' contracted consciousness and then accompanying the local community in a spiral journey of regenerative development.

Regenerating the Spirit of a Broken Town

The situation was dire when, in 2001, Jean-François Caron was elected mayor of Loos-en-Gohelle, a small town of 7,000 residents situated in a mining basin in Northern France. The last coal mine was shut down in 1986, leaving this historic mining town severely hurt by deindustrialization in the 1970s and 1980s. The soil was contaminated, unemployment was at an all-time high, and morale was at an all-time low. Caron, who belongs to the green political party Europe Écologie Les Verts, saw this crisis as a once-in-a-lifetime opportunity. He asked himself, "What if I could inspire my voters to regain self-confidence and work with me to transform Loos-en-Gohelle from one of the least sustainable places in Europe to a city that is a world-class reference in *regenerative development*? And what if we could achieve this feat within a single generation?"[9]

To implement his bold long-term vision, Caron embarked his city on what he calls a **systemic transition** that integrates five complementary dimensions: social, cultural, economic, ecological, and democratic.[10] The social and cultural aspects of this transition are just as significant as the environmental aspects, making these five dimensions work in concert. In fact, one of Caron's very first initiatives as mayor was to persuade UNESCO to officially recognize, in 2012, the mining basin where Loos-en-Gohelle was situated as a UNESCO World Heritage Site.[11] By getting the slag heaps in his town (the tallest in Europe) the same recognition and status given to the pyramids in Egypt, Caron wanted the people in this town to feel proud of their cultural past, no matter how traumatic it was. Caron believes that any city must "own" its *entire* past to confidently build its future.[12]

Then, Caron set out to regenerate the wounded spirit of his fatalistic voters. To restore the self-confidence of his voters, Caron decided to involve them as committed actors in the reinvention of their own town.

This is the "democratic" aspect of the systemic transition, what Caron calls *citizen self-empowerment*.[13.] I would call it a *psycho-democratic* process: by rebuilding their shattered town from the bottom up, the citizens also rebuild their own (broken) selves.

For instance, the town started a "Citizen Solar Plan" to produce locally all the renewable energy to address 100% of its electricity needs (Loos-en-Gohelle aims to be powered 100% by renewable energies by 2050). This plan incentivizes residents to drive the installation of solar panels throughout the town by acting as both investors and advocates. Furthermore, the municipality established France's first green business incubator, which creates innovative solutions to fight climate change. The incubator is located on the site of a former mining pit, a symbolic nod to the city's industrial heritage and its capacity to boldly transition from an extractive economy that damaged the planet toward a regenerative economy that heals the environment.

During the 22 years (2001–2023) that he served as its mayor, Caron boldly and wisely led Loos-en-Gohelle in its regenerative development journey. This journey had its ups and downs, but its citizens have remained steadfastly committed to the systemic transition in their town. France is a country (infamously) known for top-down, centralized political governance. In Loos-en-Gohelle, however, participative democracy rules: all local redevelopment projects are coled with, by, and for the people. For instance, under the "50–50 program" initiated by Caron, citizen groups and community organizations can submit a plan for economic, social, cultural, or ecological development and the municipality will finance 50% of the project while its proposers finance the other 50%.[14]

In the past 15 years, dozens of 50–50 projects have been successfully implemented, like installing solar panels on the rooftop of the local church (Let there be *solar* light!), schools, and municipal and commercial buildings; renovating and improving the energy efficiency of homes that were poorly insulated and heated with coal; and engaging local farmers and their equipment to fix rural roads (which saves the municipality 70% in maintenance costs). The 50–50 program has elevated citizens' self-awareness: rather than view themselves as powerless victims, they gained trust in their capacity to initiate and lead change in their town. By improving their town, these citizens also boosted their "agency" (the power to make conscious choices) and expanded their "capability" to lead a good life.[15] Today, the French environmental agency ADEME acknowledges Loos-en-Gohelle as an exemplar model for undertaking sustainable and regenerative development at a city level with active participation of local citizens.[16] In November 2018, French President Emmanuel Macron visited Loos-en-Gohelle and discussed with Caron, as they climbed together a steep slag heap, how to replicate the success of the local regenerative development model in other ailing towns across France struggling to reinvent themselves.

I interviewed Caron for this book in Loos-en-Gohelle in early 2023, a few weeks before he left his office. I asked him whether, drawing on his 20 years of leadership experience, he could provide other cities with Loos-en-Gohelle's "recipe" for success so they might speed up their own systemic transition. According to Caron, there is no one-size-fits-all formula; instead, each *territoire* (county or city) must develop and implement its own regenerative development model with creative input from all relevant local stakeholders. However, based on his experience, Caron listed five key ingredients that are crucial for the success of any regenerative development journey:[17]

- ◆ All stakeholders in the city must first accept that the world of yesterday is truly "dead and buried." We must counter any nostalgic impulse to re-create a "glorious past" or make the count(r)y "great again." If you regenerate a dead body, you will end up with a zombie! It is said that Shiva performs his regenerative (cosmic) dance in cremation grounds, implying that the old (systems and worldviews) must die so the new can arise. If the terms *death* and *dying* frighten you, here is a reassuring metaphor: a talented jeweler melts golden jewelry and uses the molten gold to craft a more beautiful piece of jewelry. Here, the gold didn't "die"; it just lost its old "form" and gained a better one. When a place – or a person – is regenerated, their unique "essence" is preserved; they find a new, better way to "express" authentically that essence and share it with others.

  In physics, the first law of thermodynamics, also known as the *law of conservation of energy*, states that energy is neither created nor destroyed. Rather, energy changes from one form to another. In the same vein, a city's *genius loci,* or life energy, can never be destroyed, but its embodiment can evolve from one form to another form. Sadly, when that life energy gets "stuck" in a system (like in the aftermath of a trauma in a human body or even an entire society), the system "freezes" and loses its capacity to change form and evolve. Jean-Francois Caron was trained as a *kinésithera-peute,* French for chiropractor. *Kiné* means movement. Without movement, life atrophies. When a chiropractor releases your stuck joints, your innate life energy flows freely through your body, and you experience greater vitality and your mobility improves. Caron wanted to liberate that frozen life energy trapped in the collective subconsciousness of his traumatized city so it can regain its freedom of movement and willingly transition to a better form.

◆ Today the word *transition* is very popular (even in the US, which long resisted the term), but it is still interpreted too narrowly through an exclusively environmental lens. Most people think of "*energy* transition," that is shifting our energy system from fossil fuels to renewable energy sources to reduce emissions. To have a broad and deep impact at a local level, however, a transition can't be just ecological. Rather, it must be *systemic* and integrate five interrelated dimensions: social, cultural, economic, ecological, and democratic. This final component is essential because, as Caron is fond of saying, "there is no ecological transition possible without a democratic transition." The success of the 50–50 program mentioned previously, which marries citizen empowerment with ecological transition, is proof of that.

Caron also believes that economy and ecology can be harmonized in a systemic transition that contributes to "fair growth," a middle ground between inequitable growth (defended by die-hard capitalists) and degrowth (advocated by hard-core environmentalists). Caron explains, "I am an elected environmentalist, but I don't just defend the environment. In a mining town with a record unemployment rate and a total loss of self-confidence, I must also reinvent the local economy and restore the dignity of all citizens. We must help financially challenged citizens reconcile 'end of the world' and 'end of the month.' The systemic transition that I am leading aims to simultaneously regenerate the human psyche, the social foundation, the cultural roots, and the natural ecosystem."[18]

♦ Making the collective decision to leave the old world is a positive step, but we still need to choose the destination ("Where to land?" as the social scientist Bruno Latour put it) in thick fog. Instead of relying on cold logic, we must invite local stakeholders to use their imagination and intuition to codesign a *fictional world* that will enable them to project themselves into the future.

Next, we have to craft an inspiring *narrative* that (1) depicts vividly the course of a city's systemic transition to a bright future while honoring and "appropriating" its past, no matter how painful it was (as Loos-en-Gohelle did), and (2) offers a compelling vision of a conscious society that awaits local citizens at the final destination: this the North Star (see Figure 9.2) that confers meaning to the regenerative transition.

♦ Then, and then only, we must codevelop a *transition road map* with citizens and other stakeholders in the city.

♦ Finally, for bottom-up change to be facilitated with courage and humility at the local level, *enlightened political leadership* is required. We need servant leaders who can subordinate and sublimate their ego for the greater good.

It is very challenging and even unproductive to mobilize these five components at a national level to undertake the systemic transition of an entire country. A "national regenerative development plan" designed and implemented in a top-down manner will fail because it doesn't heed the vast diversity of resources, constraints, needs, and aspirations that exist across regions and cities. As such, it's only at a *local* level that one can best harness the five ingredients previously mentioned and carry out a systemic transition effectively.[19]

This is why Caron founded and leads *La Fabrique des Transitions* (The Transitions Workshop), an alliance of elected officials, associations, and community leaders from 400 *territoires* (counties) all over

France.[20] The alliance members meet regularly and share best practices and failures in undertaking a systemic transition at a local level. By learning collectively, they hone their change management strategies and identify ways to remove the material and psychological roadblocks on the regenerative development journey. Of particular interest to alliance members is figuring out how to synergize ecological and democratic transition and how to create inspiring narratives that mobilize local citizens to join and colead the regenerative movement.

I am aware that I've already introduced in this chapter many new concepts such as regenerative development, systemic transition, and consciousness. You might wonder what all these concepts have to do with a frugal economy, which aims to do better with less. Let me show you explicitly the connections.

First, *systemic* sounds like a fancy word, but actually it's synonymous with *frugal*. Likewise, *transition* simply means "making something better." Say you are a city mayor, and you want to make your city better. You could invest in five distinct "transition" projects to improve five areas: social cohesion, cultural renewal, economic development, environmental sustainability, and democratic governance. Assume each project costs $1 million. Then the municipality must spend $5 million in total to implement these five projects (which, by the way, have no synergies). Or, as Loos-en-Gohelle did, you can involve citizens in coinvesting in small-scale "systemic transition" projects that each cost only $100,000 to $200,000 and yet deliver benefits *simultaneously* in all five domains: social, cultural, economic, ecological, and democratic. Wouldn't that be more frugal? By coleading systemic transition, be it within a city or in a big company, mayors and CEOs can do "better with less," that is, deliver greater benefits to multiple stakeholders with less investment.

Second, most citizens associate *sustainable* with *unfrugal* and believe doing good for the planet by buying "sustainable products" may hurt their wallet. They are right. Ashley Nunes, a senior research associate at Harvard Law School, notes that electric vehicle (EV) prices in the US over the past 13 years have gone up, not down. "The median income for a US family of four is somewhere around $70,000. The average electric car in 2022 cost more than $60,000. So, think about that: the near equivalent of what you're pulling in for the year," notes Nunes.[21] Climate-conscious European cities are demanding real estate firms to construct residential buildings that are eco-friendly. Yet, complying with this demand jacks up the construction cost, which in turn hikes the price of units sold, making them unaffordable for low-income and even middle-class home buyers.

For instance, in 2021, inspired by the LEED certification of "green buildings," the city of Bordeaux, led by a green party mayor, created a "Frugal Building" label to certify new eco-friendly buildings that do "better with less," that is, deliver more comfort to residents while using less energy. These "frugal buildings" are supposed to be built using biomaterials like earth, which offer higher thermal comfort during hot summers and better insulation during cold winters, hence reducing by 80% the energy costs related to air conditioning and heating. Sadly, this "frugal building" is not frugal to build because adhering to its 42 stringent sustainability criteria increases the construction budget by at least 10%, which dissuades developers from undertaking such a costly "frugal building" project. In 2024, three years after the Frugal Building label was introduced by the municipality of Bordeaux, not a *single* construction project in the city has yet earned that lofty certification, which is deemed "inapplicable and unapplied."[22]

By contrast, rather than *impose* any sustainability standards in Loos-en-Gohelle, Caron encouraged citizen-driven and holistic approaches to sustainability. A great communicator, Caron was able to convince his citizens that (1) becoming sustainable is not a costly affair, (2) the city can leapfrog from unsustainability straight to regeneration and bypass sustainability altogether, and (3) by *investing* their own money in local regenerative development projects, and *coleading* them hands-on, citizen groups would realize not only how frugal these projects are but also how *profitable* and *impactful* they can be.

For instance, the Loos-en-Gohelle municipality bought 15 hectares of land and offered them at no cost to a group of local farmers on condition that (1) they learn and apply regenerative and organic agriculture techniques to improve the quality and yield of the land and (2) for each hectare of the "public" land they exploit, they also commit to transitioning one hectare of their own private land to organic farming. The schools and elderly homes in the county supported this project by committing to buy the organic food produced by local farmers. This hyper-local value network, described in Chapter 7, is not only ecologically sustainable but also creates additional revenue for farmers and improves the health of citizens. In the same vein, *Solar Mine*, the nonprofit citizen group that installs and maintains solar panels on buildings across Loos-en-Gohelle, not only helps inhabitants save big on energy bills but also, by selling the surplus solar energy back to the grid, the nonprofit *generates* revenue that it reinvests in community development projects.

■ ■ ■

Loos-en-Gohelle is living proof of what French chemist Antoine Lavoisier said, "Nothing is lost, nothing is created, everything is transformed." A town or a nation can never "lose" its spirit, which is eternal. When their city or country face severe socioeconomic difficulties, its political leaders launch a redevelopment project aimed at creating a "new and better" version of their town or nation, just like you upgrade your iPhone. Such top-down schemes may reboot the economy but fail to revive the ailing spirit of people.

In Loos-en-Gohelle, however, Jean-Francois Caron did something better. Rather than cut ties with the past and build a version 2.0 of his town, he first healed the broken spirit of citizens and made them feel proud of their history. And then, as an alchemist, he *transformed* their negative energies such as fear and anger into positive vibrations, which raised their awareness and restored a sense of agency. These conscious citizens felt empowered to colead with Caron the systemic transition of their beloved town from an extractive economy to a regenerative economy. This bottom-up approach to regenerative development in Loos-en-Gohelle did work because it revitalized people, places, and the planet altogether in an integrated and synergistic manner. How businesses can lead such *triple regeneration* is the focus of the next chapter.

CHAPTER 10

How Businesses Can Lead Triple Regeneration

At 37, at the peak of my career, I experienced a debilitating burn-out. I had lost a lot of weight, felt depressed and overanxious, and my mind was in overdrive, causing insomnia. No Western doctor was able to diagnose, let alone treat what ailed me. Thankfully, I found my salvation in Ayurveda, the traditional Indian medicine, Yoga, and Vipassana (mindfulness meditation).

Ayurveda is a natural system of medicine that emerged in India 5,000 years ago. The term *Ayurveda* is made up of the Sanskrit words *ayur* (life) and *veda* (science or knowledge). Hence, Ayurveda means "science of life" or "knowledge of longevity."[1] Predicated on the belief that "disease is due to an imbalance or stress in a person's consciousness, Ayurveda encourages certain lifestyle interventions and natural therapies (based on herbs and oils) to regain a balance between the body, mind, spirit, and the environment."[2] In contrast to Western medicine, Ayurvedic rejuvenation treatments, such as the three-week *Panchakarma* regimen, are highly customized; treat the body, mind, and soul holistically; and emphasize prevention over cure. After completing my very first Panchakarma program in 2007, I felt physically revitalized and spiritually awakened. It was like a rebirth. I was *regenerated*.[3]

I say "I was *regenerated*" and not "I was *cured*." Curing a disease is getting rid of its symptoms, often in a forceful manner. Western medicine adopts a warrior-like attitude to *fight* an illness (just like the current calling to *fight* climate change). In Ayurveda, a disease is not a *problem* to be fought and eliminated with brute force (like using chemotherapy to "kill" cancerous cells). Rather, Ayurveda views a disease first and foremost as a *malaise*, a lack of ease that results from an *imbalance* in your *prakriti*, your natural state of being. As such, Ayurveda goes to the root cause of an ailment and *regenerates* (restores) your body and mind to their natural state of ease, which makes all symptoms go away. Let me unpack this for you.

According to the Ayurvedic perspective, every human being has a unique pattern of energy known as *prakriti* (your constitution, or natural state, determined at the time of conception), which is a particular blend of physical, mental, and emotional attributes. Every person's constitution is made up of three vital energies known as *doshas*.[4]

Vata is the cinetic energy that regulates motion-related body processes like breathing, heartbeat, blinking, and blood circulation. Dry, mobile, cold, and light in nature, vata is made of the air and ether (space) elements. A balanced vata energy makes you creative and boosts your vitality. Imbalanced, vata causes fear and restlessness.

Pitta is the transformative energy responsible for controlling the body's metabolic processes, such as regulation of body temperature and digestion and assimilation of food. Composed of the fire and water elements, Pitta is hot, liquid, and oily in nature. When balanced, pitta sharpens your intellect and promotes contentment. A pitta imbalance can make you angry and even cause ulcers.

Kapha is the cohering energy that stabilizes and nurtures the body, supporting its growth. Kapha hydrates the skin (the largest organ in the body), lubricates the joints and bones, keeps the immune system strong, and delivers water to every tissue of the body. Love, forgiveness, and steadiness are the expressions of kapha in harmony. When kapha is out of equilibrium, jealousy, lethargy, and sadness result.

Everyone has vata, pitta, and kapha in their constitution. But usually, one or two are dominant in a particular person. My constitution is predominantly vata and pita. Many things can disturb the energy balance, such as stress, an unhealthy diet, inclement weather, and strained relationships. The disturbance shows up first as disease (a vague sense that something is off) and then evolves into a full-blown disease. Ayurvedic practitioners prescribe customized holistic treatments to bring the three doshas back into balance and reconnect with your inborn vitality. Unlike Western medicine which aims to "cure" a disease, viewing it as a "problem" that must be "fixed," Ayurveda strives to "regenerate" a person, by activating and tapping into their self-healing capacity to restore the natural equilibrium in their vital energies.

According to Ayurveda, our stressful lifestyles deplete the vital essence of our *dhatus* (body tissues) and trim years off your life expectancy. The deep rejuvenation treatments known as *Rasayana chikitsa* in Ayurveda revitalize our body at a cellular level by restoring our *ojas*, which means vigor or essence of vitality. Ojas are your "mojo."[5] Originating from our heart, the ojas is the vital energy that circulates throughout our body to boost our immunity, strengthen our weakened *dhatus*, and uplift our spirit. Rasayana is "the path of juicing up."[6]

In Ayurveda the notion of "longevity" has a larger meaning beyond the number of years in life. "Ayurveda is the science aimed at enhancing the quality *and* quantity of life. Quality of life means physical strength, physical balance; mental strength, mental balance; peace, harmony, and balance. Enhancing the quantity of life is about longevity. Following the principles of Ayurveda can help us to live longer and live with the optimal quality of health," explains Dr Jayarajan Kodikannath, one of the Ayurvedic doctors who treated me in California.[7] Ayurveda believes that if you live your *best* life by staying aligned with your *dharma* (purpose) and realizing your full potential, a *long* life will ensue.

I want to show why and how businesses could adopt this holistic Ayurvedic perspective on life and strive to regenerate not only the planet (by, for instance, restoring the biodiversity) but also the people (customers, employees) and the places (communities) where we live to maximize their *aliveness*.

Humanizing Regeneration and Anchoring It in Places

In the Introduction of this book, I explained why "decoupling" economic growth from resource consumption and emissions is not enough to address the *triple urgency* facing humanity: the disintegration of the human psyche (due to existential angst), the breakdown of social structures (due to rising inequalities and political polarization), and the impending biosphere collapse (due to climate change). Throughout this book, I have showed how to "recouple" or tightly reconnect economic activity with people, the environment, and local communities. A *regenerative development* paradigm made possible by such close recoupling, as discussed in Chapter 9, will advance human growth, foster greater social and ecological harmony, and move use closer to a conscious civilization.

I want to briefly explain why I insist on the *human* dimension of regeneration. In *Collapse: How Societies Choose to Fail or Succeed*, Jared Diamond identified five factors that historically caused human civilizations to collapse, namely, "climate change, hostile neighbors, collapse of essential trading partners, environmental problems, and the society's response to the foregoing four factors."[8] All these factors are exogenous to human beings. I fear, however, in today's hyperconnected and hyperactive world that pressurizes our mind, our overtaxed nervous system risks collapsing well before the overstretched ecological or social systems. We already live in "the burnout society," to cite the Korean-German philosopher Byung-Chul Han, who believes that in our achievement-extolling and performance-driven culture, "we actually exploit ourselves passionately until we collapse. We realize ourselves, optimize ourselves unto death. The insidious logic of achievement permanently forces us to get ahead of ourselves."[9] Hence, before we stop exploiting dwindling natural resources, we must end overexploiting (voluntarily!) our own mind, body, and psyche to death. And rather than bridge the wealth gap between the rich and poor in our society, we must first bridge the gnawing inner gap between our gratification-seeking ego and our alienated soul.

I have often asserted that I am a humanist first, then only an ecologist. In all my previous books, I showed how we can unleash and harness our abundant inner resources – ingenuity, empathy, and wisdom – to build inclusive and sustainable economies. This book is no different. I want to follow in the footsteps of German-born British economist E. F. Schumacher who, in his global bestseller *Small Is Beautiful*, invited us to rethink "economics as if people mattered."[10] We need to humanize the field of economics and ensure that emerging paradigms like the regenerative economy truly contribute to the flourishing of people.

People, however, don't exist in a vacuum. They work and live in a specific physical place. Unfortunately, in dualistic Western civilizations, just like we believe we humans exist separately from nature, we also view ourselves as distinct from the physical space – the city and the land – that we inhabit. This is not true in many nondualist Eastern cultures and animistic Indigenous traditions that believe that humans, animals, plants, the land, oceans, the sky, the stars, as well as objects and places, are all alive with spirit and form an interconnected and interdependent web of life. For instance, in Australia, songlines are the "aboriginal walking routes that crossed the country, linking important sites and locations. Before colonization they were maintained by regular use, burning off and clearing."[11] Songlines, also called *dreaming pathways*, were memorized and used by travelers to navigate the vast landscape in Australia and locate waterholes, food sources, natural shelters, and sacred sites along the journey. For more than 80,000 years, songlines have played a significant role in First Nations societies in Australia. Songlines convey the laws and legends that First Nations people follow.

Regenerative Songlines Australia (RSA) is an Indigenous-led grassroots movement that aims to establish dialogues, relationships, and projects across the Australian continent that empower people to construct regenerative economies and communities and to "Care for their Country." As RSA members explain, "In the Dreaming, as in Country, there is no separation between the animate and inanimate. Everything is living – people, animals, plants, earth, water, and air. We speak of Sea, Land and Sky country. Creator ancestors created the Country and its interface, the Dreaming. In turn, Dreaming speaks for Country, which holds the law and knowledge, Country has Dreaming, Country is Dreaming."[12] Add RSA members, "Songlines, related to Dreamings or Dreaming tracks, connect sites of knowledge embodied in the features of the land. It is along these routes that people traveled to learn from Country. Songlines are foundational to our being – to what we know, how we know it and when we know it. They are our knowledge system, our library, our architect from which all subjects are derived."[13] Recognizing that diversity is the key to resilience, the RSA network promotes and strengthens a wide variety of *bioregional regeneration* projects that enable the flourishing of human and nonhuman life while having a positive social and environmental impact – all at a local level.

Bioregionalism is "a philosophy that suggests that political, cultural, and economic systems are more sustainable and just if they are organized around naturally defined areas called bioregions."[14] A *bioregion* "re-connects us with living systems, and each other, through the places where we live. It acknowledges that we live among watersheds, foodsheds, fibersheds, and food systems – not just in cities, towns, or the countryside. A bioregion is shaped by characteristics of the natural environment rather than by man-made divisions – its geology; topography; climate; soils; hydrology and watersheds; agriculture; biodiversity, flora and fauna, vegetation."[15] Rather than divide the world in 195 countries, the One Earth Foundation has created an interactive map that delineates the Earth's 185 discrete bioregions. A bioregion is a "life-place" that invites us to first ask the fundamental question "*where* am I?" – the answer to which will lead us to discover the answers to two other existential questions "who am I?" and "what is my life purpose?" *Bioregioning* is a set of collective and experiential practices that "re-connect people with natural systems, and each other, through the places where they live, enabling deeper understanding of the interdependence between them and human flourishing."[16] By continually regenerating these deeper connections, bioregioning projects like Regenerative Songlines in Australia, Bioregioning Tayside in Scotland, and Bioregional Learning Centre in South Devon in England offer a "place-based response to the climate and biodiversity crises."[17]

A place-based response to economic crises is also being sought out to regenerate the distressed regions in Europe and the US that failed to adapt to globalization in the 1990s and then to the internet-based tech revolution since 2000. In a November 2018 report titled "Countering the Geography of Discontent: Strategies for Left-Behind Places," researchers at the Brookings Institution noted how large, tech-driven coastal metros like San Francisco, Boston, and New York had bounced back quickly from the Great Recession of 2008–2009, creating 72% of all new jobs in the US since the financial crisis. Conversely, small metropolitan areas accounted for less than 6% of the increase in employment in the US since 2010, and "micro" towns and rural areas had yet to match the pre-recession employment levels. The report notes that "the 2016 election of Donald Trump represented the revenge of the places left behind in a changing economy."[18]

To counter uneven development, the Brookings researchers call for radically new economic thinking and policies that bolster growth opportunities in left-behind places in America, given that "orthodox economics has few answers to the problem of regional inequality." As they explain, "Traditionally, regional development policies have taken two distinct forms: spatially blind, 'people-based' policies that seek to maximize economic efficiency by supporting the natural emergence of dynamic high-value, big-city economic activity, and 'place-based' policies that try to achieve regional equity to ensure more regionally inclusive economic growth. What is actually needed, by contrast, is a mixed strategy that respects the efficiency of hubs of concentrated economic activity but seeks to extend this kind of dynamism to more regions by ensuring access to the basic prerequisites of high-quality growth."[19] This new hybrid approach to regional development is called "place-sensitive distributed development policies" (PSDDP), or what I would like to call "**scaling out development**" (akin to the scaling out of manufacturing discussed in Part II).

PSDDP was conceptualized by Simona Iammarino, Andrés Rodríguez-Pose, and Michael Storper, three academics at London School of Economics and Political Science.[20] PSDDP goes beyond place-based policies in that the objective is not just to distribute economic growth across as many regions as possible within a country (like the US) or a geographical zone (like the European Union) but do so by identifying and leveraging the *unique* capacities and resources available within each region. As the PSDDP theoreticians explain, "The ultimate goal of place-sensitive development is to maximize the potential for economic development and well-being across a large group of heterogeneous territories, as those found in Europe and in most other parts of the world. This implies combatting the under-utilization of cities' and regions' people and resources, so as to distribute development more widely and exploit a territory's full development potential."[21] PSDDP enable left-behind places to *frugally* regenerate themselves by identifying, mobilizing, and better exploiting the physical and intangible resources and capabilities that *already* exist locally. For instance, Heartland Forward has developed a PSDDP guide that enables "left behind" places in American hinterland to "translate local expertise, found in existing small and medium sized firms and their skilled workforce, academic research, and nascent stage entrepreneurial companies, into great economic opportunity."[22] The guide helps regions identify their existing strengths – such as community capacity, firm and industry capacity, entrepreneurial capacity, and innovation support capacity – that they can leverage to build local innovation and industrial ecosystems, which in turn will regenerate the local economy. PSDDP's true value and merit lies not as much in enabling lagging regions to enkindle economic growth as in encouraging these lagging places to cultivate a *growth mindset*, the belief that human qualities and abilities are not carved in stone but can be developed and improved over time through perseverant effort and grit.[23]

Throughout 2023, the Organisation for Economic Co-operation and Development (OECD), an intergovernmental organization with 38 member countries, organized a series of expert workshops on PSDDP as part of a joint project between OECD and the European Commission (EC) titled "Placed-Based Policies for the Future."[24] The scholars and policymakers who partook in these workshops agreed that a place-based approach is key to tackling the two biggest challenges of the 21st century: social inequalities and climate change. For instance, they noted, "Reaching the objectives of the Paris Agreement on Climate Change will require tailoring actions and investments to the needs and realities of different regions, cities, and rural areas, as mitigation and adaptation challenges and opportunities differ sharply across places."[25]

Ayurveda recognizes that each person has a unique *prakriti* (psycho-physiological constitution) which, when it becomes imbalanced, can lead to poor health. Likewise, each place has a unique energy pattern, which when disturbed can cause a degradation in local socioeconomic conditions and the well-being of its residents. The Romans believed in *genius loci,* the protective spirit of a place. Literally, *genius loci* means the genius of a place. Just like Ayurvedic treatments reconnect patients with their body's in-born wisdom to self-heal, consciously designed policies can rejoin distressed places with their *genii locorum*, hence enkindling their innate capacity for self-renewal. Akin to Ayurvedic rejuvenation procedures that restore a weak person's depleted vitality (the *ojas*), economic regeneration projects could rebuild the *vitalism* and *dynamism* of a waning place.

Nobel Prize–winning economist Edmund Phelps believes that an individual or a place (be it a city or a nation) can maintain its dynamism and vitality, and thus keep flourishing, as long as it is adheres to three modern values: "individualism (thinking for yourself, working for yourself, willingness to break from one's group and from convention), vitalism (relishing challenges and overcoming obstacles, taking initiative, acting on the world), and self-expression (imagining and creating, demonstrating a unique insight by testing it, voyaging into the unknown in hopes of making a mark on the world)."[26] When these values are no longer upheld and actively practiced, people and places decline – as it is happening now worldwide. I believe businesses can play a crucial role in reviving these dynamic values of individualism, vitalism, and self-expression both within their own organizations and in the communities they serve.

Boosting Corporate Vitality and Longevity Through Triple Regeneration

In Chapter 8, I explained why companies must go beyond sustainability and become *regenerative businesses*. In Chapter 9, I showed how cities and regions can consciously transition from an extractive economy to a *regenerative economy*, and how *regenerative development*, if done right, can elevate human awareness and create a deeper and wider social and ecological impact. In this chapter, so far, I articulated why we need to broaden the scope and practice of regeneration beyond the purely ecological dimension and incorporate the people and place dimensions. I call it **triple regeneration**, a holistic approach to boosting the health and vitality of people, places, and the planet (3Ps) altogether synergistically. See Figure 10.1.

Note that the 3Ps I am referring to is different from the 3Ps (people-profit-planet) mentioned in the sustainability-focused accounting framework known as the triple bottom line.[27] I de-emphasize profit because I believe that if companies were to reinvent their business models and their corporate cultures around the notion of "care" – that is, caring for people, places, and the planet – they will become *better* organizations, and profit will automatically follow. As Luigina Mortari points out, "Care is the most important ontological phenomenon because we *are* what we care *for*."[28] If so, the Figure 10.1 conveys something profound: it depicts not only what a regenerative business *does* (i.e., regenerate the 3Ps), but *who*

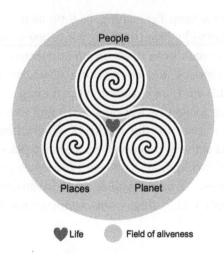

Figure 10.1 By revitalizing people, places, and the planet, triple regeneration fosters a field of aliveness.

Source: Adapted from original graphic by AnonMoos, Public domain, via Wikimedia Commons.

it is, which is a life-centric *organism*, rather than a profit-centric organization. Triple regeneration is the raison d'être, the true purpose, of corporate existence.

Let's analyze the content in Figure 10.1 and apprehend its deep meaning. A *triskelion*, or triskele, is "an ancient motif of a triple spiral exhibiting rotational symmetry or of other patterns in triplicate that emanate from a common center."[29] Many ancient cultures used the triple spiral sign, also known as the three-spiral volute, first appearing in Malta (4400–3600 BCE) and in the astronomical calendar of the well-known megalithic monument of Newgrange in Ireland, which was constructed in 3200 BCE. In Celtic civilizations, a triskele is a venerated spiritual symbol that represents *simultaneously* balance and harmony as well as movement and constant change. It indicates the continuous, dynamic, and cyclical flow of life (birth, death, rebirth) outpouring from the stable center, the life source. It also represents the harmony that results from balancing the three interdependent elements: body, mind, and spirit (*triskele* comes from the Greek τρισκελής [triskelés], meaning "three-legged"). The spiral is a symbol of fertility as it is spiritually associated with the *generative* power of the womb. Hence a triskele signifies triple (re)generation. The *triquetra*, or the trinity knot, another Celtic symbol of three interlaced arcs, represents the immutable trinity in unity (one God as three distinct and unchanging persons: the Father, son, and holy spirit). The triskele, however, is the *dynamic* expression of the unity *as* trinity. The triskele speaks to my soul. As a tricultural person (Indian, French, American), the triskele invites me to joyfully express my unified life essence *through* three distinct cultures, rather than let my core identity be narrowly defined *by* these three cultures.

I placed life as a beating heart at the center of this triskele in Figure 10.1 to highlight the right spirit in which businesses must undertake triple regeneration, especially in the performance-driven Western societies that seek to "optimize" everything. As Pierre Moniz-Barreto and Myriam Maestroni, coauthors of the excellent book *Régénération!,* warn us, "If the Western regenerative approach ends up reducing the regenerative phenomenon to functionalized, criterion-based, standardized approaches or programs, it will once again miss what is most profound and more vital, more buoyant and stronger, and which is the only one capable of being up to the historical challenge and the civilizational turning point which accompanies this crisis: the essential depth (which relates to Being) and the cosmic magnitude (which relates to the Universe) of the vital phenomenon of regeneration!" Moniz-Barreto and Maestroni add, "An ersatz of well-programmed and packaged regenerative solutions cannot be able to fully respond to the profound vital challenge posed to us. Regeneration invites us to contemplate it as a miracle of Life, and to integrate it as such into our activities."[30]

Moniz-Barreto and Maestroni use the term *buoyant* to describe the *qualia* (subjective quality) of life. In physics, buoyance is a force applied on an object that makes it rise or move upward. Love is such an uplifting force: when we feel loved, we feel buoyant, that is cheerful and optimistic. The purpose of triple regeneration is to cocreate a loving *field of aliveness* that can uplift people and places and make them buoyant. And vice versa: the more life there is in people, places, and the planet, the more buoyant they become, hence enlarging and reinforcing the field of aliveness in which they all exist. As Duane Elgin, author of *The Living Universe,* explains,

> Because we share the same matrix of existence, the totality of
> life is already touching each of us and co-creating the *field of*

aliveness within which we exist. We can each tune into the non-local field of life and sense what is in harmony with the wellbeing of the whole. In seeing the Universe as alive, we naturally shift our priorities from an "ego economy" based upon consuming deadness to a "living economy" based upon growing aliveness. An aliveness economy seeks to touch life more lightly while generating an abundance of meaning and satisfaction. Aliveness is the only true wealth.[31]

Let me show you how a business can regenerate people and places by enabling them to experience, grow, and express their aliveness.

Meiji Yasuda Boosts Your Vitality Rather Than Insuring Against Mortality

Meiji Yasuda, Japan's oldest and third-biggest life insurance business, was established in 1881. Meiji Yasuda stated in 2017 that it aspires to become "a long-respected life insurance company that cares about people first" whose core mission and management philosophy is to provide "peace of mind, forever."[32] By concentrating on its clients, the business followed its purpose and carried out its vision for the ensuing three years.

When COVID-19 struck Japan severely at the beginning of 2020, Meiji Yasuda's employees hurried to help the communities where they lived. They remotely counseled clients on how to maintain their health. At that moment, Meiji Yasuda realized that its true mission should be to maintain and even increase people's *vitality* rather than shield them from death. It also understood that it needs to extend its focus beyond serving its clientele and learn to engage with empathy with *local communities* and its own staff. This new awareness led the company in April 2020 to unveil MY Mutual Way 2030, a 10-year strategy aimed at making Meiji Yasuda "the most accessible, industry-leading life insurer in its industry capable of (delivering) wellness for people (and) vitality for communities" by 2030.[33] Drawing on the 17 Sustainable Development Goals of the UN, this bold strategy calls to actively engage clients, local communities, employees, and future generations to co-build a caring and sustainable society that "places great value on mutual aid, which is the fundamental concept and value of life insurance."[34]

To carry out its commitment to prolong the healthy life expectancy of its clients, Meiji Yasuda is encouraging clients to embrace a new health paradigm that emphasizes illness *prevention* above treatment. For instance, to help its clients anticipate and prevent cardiovascular problems, the company collaborated with the National Cerebral and Cardiovascular Center in Japan to create new digital tools. The business also broadened the responsibilities of its agents in April 2022 to include duties typically performed by social workers. Clients are matched with locally accessible public social support services via agents. "We've seen elderly customers living alone in Japan. These people might have drugs prescribed to improve sleep and mood, but in that kind of situation, non-medical support has tremendous potential in helping these people lead healthier lives," observes Hideki Nagashima, CEO of Meiji Yasuda. He adds, "Technology can help, but it's people with empathy who can create value."[35]

Meiji Yasuda has signed extensive collaboration agreements with 800 municipalities across Japan to make public resources and local health services available to its clients. Additionally, as part of its "community vitalization" project, the company has teamed up with J League, the Japanese professional football league, to host in-person or online physical exercise sessions in several locations.

Compared to other countries, Japan's population is aging more quickly, with 30% of its population already over 65. Japan has the highest number of centenarians worldwide and the average life expectancy of its citizens is 84 years.[36] However, longevity doesn't guarantee vitality. "It's not the years in your life that count. It's the life in your years," noted Abraham Lincoln. Meiji Yasuda offered life insurance to millions of Japanese citizens during the first 143 years of its existence. Over the next 100 years, the company aims to increase the vitality of clients and foster fields of aliveness in local communities throughout Japan. A person who is 110 years or older is called a supercentenarian. As a supercentenarian organization, Meiji Yasuda "strives to excel as a young and vibrant life insurance company that constantly takes on new challenges while also stewarding history and tradition."[37]

Sadly, not many companies get to celebrate their centenary. Many don't even reach their 20s. According to a Credit Suisse report, the average lifespan of a company listed on the S&P 500 fell dramatically from 60 years in the 1950s to under 20 years today.[38] A study by researchers at Santa Fe Institute of 25,000 publicly traded North American companies, from 1950 to 2009, reveals that a publicly traded firm survives on average just 10 years before it gets acquired, goes bankrupt, or is disrupted by nimble rivals.[39] Why are companies dying younger? The popular answer since the late 1990s, with the surge of the internet, has been, "Businesses fail to keep up with technological changes." That may be partially true, especially today with the AI revolution that is sweeping across the world, upending business models in all industries. I studied computer science and worked for nearly a decade as an analyst at Forrester, a market research firm that believes that "technology changes everything." Hence, I don't deny the transformative power of new technologies and their disruptive effect on businesses.

I believe, however, that over the next 20 years, the biggest cause of death of companies will not be their inability to harness the value of digital tools like AI and quantum computing but their failure to adapt to new *values* embodied by next-gen customers, employees, and investors. By 2035, as socially conscious and purpose-driven Generations Z and Alpha come to dominate the workforce and the consumer base and climate change, left unattended, ravages our planet, businesses will be pressured by markets, employees, and governments to evolve and step into new roles as caretakers of communities and natural ecosystems. The long-lasting firms in the 21st century will be enlightened businesses that continually regenerate people inside and outside their organization, places where they operate, and the planet that sustains us.

Part III of this book is titled "Regenerating People, Places, and the Planet." Hence, it is appropriate to conclude it with an inspiring case study on how a visionary company in one of the most climate-unfriendly and the least frugal industries – fashion – is going beyond sustainability and is regenerating people, places, and the planet, and in the process is leading a revolution in consciousness in its sector.

Beyond Sustainable Fashion: Eileen Fisher Leads Triple Regeneration

The apparel sector – led by fast fashion – is the world's largest polluter, right after oil. Today, we throw out 92 million tons of clothes every year, enough to fill one and a half Empire State buildings *daily*.[40]

Worried that fast fashion is destroying the planet, the women's clothing brand Eileen Fisher (EF) is trailblazing "slow fashion" by launching fewer but more durable clothes every year.[41]

A staunch feminist, social activist, and environmental advocate, Eileen Fisher, who founded her eponymous firm in 1984, has built and led a frugal apparel industry that can do better with less – that is, launch *fewer* clothes of *higher* quality that last longer and damage *less* the planet. Designed with elegant simplicity, EF clothes are easy to mix and match.[42]

A certified B Corporation, her brand is a quadruple bottom line enterprise that values equally the environment, human rights, employee well-being, and financial interests as part of doing business.

Heeding Gandhi's motto "Be the change," Fisher implemented conscious business principles first within her own organization. She has created a safe and supportive work environment that empowers all its employees, the majority of whom are women.

In addition to offering a competitive salary and many onsite wellness services, the brand invests heavily in its employees' personal growth through a wide array of programs that boost their self-awareness and confidence and hone their relational skills and leadership capabilities.

In 1992, Fisher boldly moved her fledging firm from the neurotic Manhattan – the global epicenter of fashion – to the quaint Irvington, a suburb of New York, right next to the Hudson River, enabling her employees to feel grounded and creative.

In 1984, Eileen Fisher launched her namesake brand with just $350. In 2022, it generated $267 million in global revenue, up from $207 million in 2020. Fisher owns 60% of the firm and employees own the remaining 40%. As Fisher wisely notes, "Once we started having extra profit, the first thought was share it with the employees. They do all the work, it's only fair to share, which I think all companies should have to do."[43]

As early as 1997, Eileen Fisher activated the heart chakra of her employees and external partners by setting up a Social Consciousness group (a world first!). For more than two decades, this group has created industry-wide awareness and invested in social initiatives that enhance women's well-being and catalyze gender and racial diversity and pay parity.

Leading by example, the clothing brand pays wages above industry average to its subcontractors in developing countries and offers them social benefits like health care and education that improve their livelihood and support their families.

Starting in 2015, aspiring to become one of the world's most sustainable apparel firms, EF has boosted efforts to sustainably source organic and regenerative fibers, is phasing out chemical dyes, and has drastically reduced the use of water and energy in production and curbed emissions in transportation.

As part of its "Renew" program, EF incentivizes its clients to bring back their old clothes, which are then upcycled into gorgeous new products using the talent of young designers. It has taken back nearly 2 million garments since 2009.

In 2020, EF decided to set the bar even higher on sustainability. With its Horizon 2030 vision, the brand has ambitions to become *a regenerative business* that has a notable positive impact on people, places, and the planet.

For example, through its Supporting Women in Environmental Justice grants, it empowers women to become climate leaders in their communities. It is investing in regenerative farming (to produce responsible wool and cotton) and building transparent supply chains that offer full traceability. It aims to curb greenhouse gas emissions in its own operations by 100% by 2025 (against a 2017 baseline).

Eileen Fisher's frugal mantra is "Just do less: Buy less, consume less, produce less."[44]

In September 2022, Eileen Fisher stepped down after 40 years as CEO and passed the reins to Lisa Williams, who was previously the chief product officer at Patagonia. Like Eileen Fisher, Patagonia is not only a pioneer in sustainability (87% of its products are made with recycled materials) but also an early adopter and supporter of regenerative organic farming practices.[45] In 2001, on Black Friday, Patagonia ran a daring full-page ad in *The New York Times* featuring a fleece jacket and a bold title "Don't buy this jacket" to dissuade customers from buying unnecessary clothes.

"The most environmentally sustainable jacket is the one that's already in your closet," noted Williams when she was Patagonia's head of products.[46] Now, at the helm of Eileen Fisher, Williams is trying to convince younger consumers to buy less and keep their clothes longer.[47] It seems to be working. A 2023 *Wall Street Journal* article wrote, "Once gently jibed for its earth-grandmother spirit, the classic brand (Eileen Fisher) is a hit with Gen Z fans, now in thrall to its sustainable minimalism."[48]

PART IV

Frugal America

CHAPTER 11

The US Must Lead by Example

If there is one country in the world that desperately needs to foster a frugal economy and master the ingenious art of doing better with less, it is America. The US must learn rapidly how to do *better* – by delivering better health care, education, and financial support to all – as well as do *less* – by reducing its overconsumption and its gargantuan (CO_2) emissions.

Let's begin with the US imperative to "do *less*." We Americans consume way too much. With our bulimic demand for resources, we overshoot Earth's carrying capacity. If everyone in the world lived and consumed like an American, we would need five Earths to live, which is just not sustainable (whereas if all humanity lived like an Indian, only 0.8 of an Earth is required to sustain us, which is within our planet's annual regenerative biocapacity).[1] The US accounts for less than 5% of the global population but consumes 16% of the world's energy (however, China comprises 18% of the world's population and consumes 27% of the world's energy).[2] Between 1973 and 2015, the average US household size shrunk from 3.01 persons to 2.54 persons but the square footage of living space per individual in a new US house nearly *doubled* during that same period![3] According to the National Mining Association, "each American needs more than 39,000 pounds (17,700 kg) of minerals and fossil fuels annually to maintain their standard of living."[4]

In America, we also generate a lot of waste. Each year, the US produces 268 million tons of trash, over half of which goes into landfills. The item that Americans throw away the most is food, which represents nearly 22% of all stuff dumped in landfills.[5] According to the EPA, Americans waste 1 trillion gallons of water each year. Only 32% of all US waste is today recycled or composted. The US recycles only 5% of its plastic waste. And just 13% of the 81 pounds of clothes that each American throws away every year is recycled.[6]

As the global warming accelerates, the US needs to drastically reduce its carbon emissions. Today, the Western media carries headlines blaming China and India – with a combined population of 3 billion and rapidly growing giant economies – for polluting the planet. It is true that *today*, as the 2022 data shows, China and India collectively account for a whopping 40% of global CO_2 emissions, whereas the US is responsible "only" for 14%.[7] Although the 3 billion Chinese and Indians can be blamed today (in 2024) for their *collective* responsibility for warming our planet, what about their *individual* responsibility (emissions per capita) and their *historical* responsibility in the past 250 years – the period since industrial revolution that contributed the most to global warming? Here, the data show unambiguously that it is not the Chinese or Indians but rather Americans who hold the greatest individual *and* historical responsibility for polluting Earth. In 2021, per person CO_2 emissions in the US were twice greater than China's and eight times as large as India's.[8] And because the US emitted over a quarter of all CO_2 since 1751, more than any other country in the world, America bears the greatest historical responsibility for climate change (Figure 11.1).[9]

Rather than blame others, it is time for America to grow up and assume its individual, collective, and historical responsibility for global warming and lead the world in reversing climate change. Morally speaking, it is not good enough for a great nation like the US to only decarbonize its economy *in the future* and achieve its net-zero emissions goal by 2050. The US must also show ethical leadership by "owning" *all* its history – the good, the bad, and the ugly – and find innovative solutions *now* to rapidly remove, store, and/or use the CO_2 that it had put into the atmosphere *in the past*. A February 2024 report by National Wildlife Federation shows that citizens even in politically conservative US states like Wyoming and Texas who are skeptical of alternative energy industries are surprisingly in favor of carbon removal solutions, especially if they help create local jobs and improve the quality of air.[10]

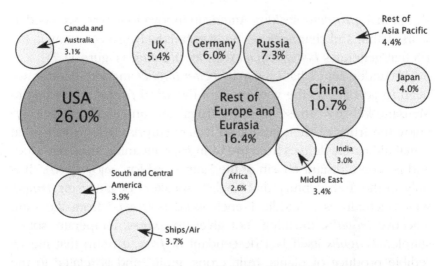

Figure 11.1 This bubble diagram highlights the percentage share of global cumulative energy-related carbon dioxide emissions between 1751 and 2012 across various regions (Hansen, J., et al. (2013). Assessing "dangerous climate change": Required reduction of carbon emissions to protect young people, future generations and nature. *PLoS ONE*, *8*(12), 17). The area and coloring of the circles is proportional to the share of emissions. The radius of the circles equals the square root of (area/π;).

Source: Enescot / Wikimedia Commons / CC BY 1.0.

All this means that the US must learn to consume *less*, waste *less*, and pollute *less*. But that's not enough.

The American ethos is all about *progress*. That progressive and pioneering spirit animates me as a scholar in innovation. The American mind is wired to push the frontiers of knowledge, break boundaries, and make things *better*. As such, telling Americans to "do less" is akin to telling them to "*be* less." They resent being asked to "play it small." And yet, as natural resources like water dwindle and global warming worsens, threatening our very civilization, US businesses and communities will have no choice but to consume less and pollute less. So how do we reconcile the American aspiration (and obsession) for *better* and the ecological reality that calls for *less*? Legendary management guru Peter Drucker famously said, "Company cultures are like country cultures. Never try to change one. Try instead to work with what you've got." The American national and corporate culture is all about *bigness*. Rather than change or, worse, shrink that *grandeur*-seeking American innovation spirit, we need to work with it and channel it properly to build a frugal economy in the US that generates *better impact* with *less wastage* (Figure 11.2).

To understand what I mean by *better impact* and *less wastage*, we need to go back to the very roots of the word *frugal*. According to Merriam-Webster, "those who are frugal are unwilling to (lavishly) enjoy the fruits of their labors, so it may surprise you to learn that frugal ultimately derives from the Latin *frux*, meaning 'fruit' or 'value,' and is even a distant cousin of the Latin word for 'enjoy' (*frui*)." It is only in the 16th century that English speakers began using *frugal*, which actually is a Middle French word borrowed from the Latin adjective *frugalis*, meaning "not given to excess, temperate, sober, simple." *Frugalis* itself is a descendant of *frux*, a noun that means "edible produce of plants, fruit, crops, grain" and is related to the verb *fruor* or *fruī*, which translates as "to enjoy the produce or proceeds of, derive advantage from."[11]

Fructify means "to produce a good or useful result" or "to make something fertile." Unless you cultivate a land, which requires effort, it will not produce anything and will go to waste. A frugal economy aims to *fructify* the seeds (unique talents and capabilities) planted in each one of us so we can bear "good and useful" fruits and share them generously with others, rather than hoard them. In the US

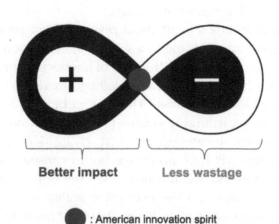

Better impact   Less wastage

⬤ : American innovation spirit

Figure 11.2 A frugal economy in the US will leverage the American innovation spirit to create better and greater social and economic impact for all while wasting less of our natural resources and human talent.

context, this means leveraging the resilient American innovation spirit to "fructify" the God-given graces lying dormant in each citizen so they are not wasted but rather produce a "good or useful result." Note these last four words: we are not talking about generating "*more* result" but "*better* result." Rather than obsess with *efficiency* – creating *more* financial value with *fewer* physical resources – a frugal economy aims for *effectiveness*: creating greater social and ecological *impact* by "fructifying" (making better use of) all available resources.

Enough with abstractions. Let me show you how we can apply the frugal mindset to create better impact and reduce waste in two vital US sectors that are notoriously *un*frugal: health care and finance.

A Pioneer in Frugal Health Care

The US spends more on health care per capita than any other developed nations. Yet infant mortality in the US is the highest among rich nations. Life expectancy in the US – already the lowest among advanced economies – declined in 2021, for the second year in a row.

According to a paper published by Halsted Holman, a professor of medicine at Stanford University, "in the last 20 years, the prevalence of chronic disease in the US has grown by a steady 7–8 million people every five years. Today, chronic disease affects 50% of the population, and its care consumes more than 85% of health care costs. It has become an epidemic."[12] Mental health of Americans is also deteriorating. According to a Gallup survey done in May 2023, nearly 30% US adults have been diagnosed with depression at some point in their lifetime, which is 10% higher than in 2015.[13] Ninety percent of the $4.1 trillion that the US spends in annual health care is to treat people with chronic and mental health conditions.[14]

Meanwhile the cost of paying for health care remains doggedly high in the US. In 2022, 38% Americans skipped medical treatment due to high cost, a 12% increase from 2021.[15] Sadly, in 2024, health insurance costs are poised to increase by over 6% – the highest jump in years.[16]

Between 2022 and 2031, national health care expenditures (NHE) in the US are projected to grow 5.4%, outpacing average GDP growth (4.6%) during that period. NHE as a share of US GDP will increase from 18.3% in 2021 to nearly 20% in 2031.[17] Sadly, increasing health care spending in the US is like pouring more water into a bucket with many holes. A 2012 article in the *Journal of the American Medical Association* identified six major areas of waste in the US health system that account for 20% (about $600 billion) of the system's annual expenditure. The article concluded, "Reducing waste is by far the largest, and most humane, and smartest opportunity for evolving an affordable healthcare system."[18] By US doctors' own recognition, up to 30% of medical services are unnecessary.[19] A 2019 study estimates annual wasteful spending on health care at a staggering $935 billion, or 25% of total US health care expenditure.[20]

Bottom line: the US keeps spending more and more on health care, but citizens are getting less and less in terms of positive health outcomes. We need to reverse this dysfunctional dynamic by creating a *frugal health care* system that delivers better impact for all Americans while reducing waste. Penn Medicine is showing us the way.

Founded in 1751 by Benjamin Franklin and Dr. Thomas Bond, Penn Medicine is America's oldest hospital. The Center for Health Care Transformation & Innovation (CHCTI), set up at Penn Medicine in 2012, is pioneering patient-centric frugal health care. CHCTI's multidisciplinary team includes experts with diverse backgrounds: medicine, health policy, behavioral economics, business development, design, IT, biostatistics, communications, marketing, and operations management. CHCTI's mission is to develop new breakthrough strategies "to reimagine health care delivery for dramatically better value, patient outcomes, and experience."[21]

As Roy Rosin, Penn Medicine's chief innovation officer, explains, "We want to systemically deconstruct each aspect of our care delivery – be it a procedure or a service – and reconstruct it to make it faster, better, and cheaper."[22] Previously, Roy worked as the first vice president of innovation for Intuit, the Silicon Valley firm that pioneered affordable, easy-to-use accounting software. Penn Medicine hired Rosin to infuse Silicon Valley's customer-centric and agile innovation culture into a venerable medical institution with a 273-year history.

CHCTI has tested and implemented at scale several frugal solutions that are simple but deliver high value to patients. Here are two of them that really stand out:[23]

♦ **Reimagining patient experience.** Rather than ask breast cancer patients to get to the clinic for postoperative visits, and try to make these visits faster and better, Dr. Kathleen Lee and Lauren Hahn at CHCTI worked with Dr. Mike Tecce, a plastic surgeon, to shift 80% of follow-up visits from the clinic to the home, thus saving patients 20 hours and increasing convenience. Clinical teams stay in touch with patients via text messages to address concerns. This solution frees up significant capacity at the clinic to accept more new patients and treat them faster. According to Penn researchers, breast reconstruction patients who receive home care need nearly 60% fewer clinic visits in the 30 days after discharge. A 2018 study by *American Journal of Medicine* shows that, across specialties, home health care saved $15,233 per patient in the first year following hospital release.[24] In Part II, I explained how we can bridge the vast distance between a manufacturer and consumer by producing goods locally in places where users live. Taking a cue from the industrial sector, the health care sector must follow Penn Medicine's lead and "hyper-localize" the delivery of care at patients' homes.

◆ **Improving patient follow-up.** Philadelphia, home of Penn Medicine, has had one of the highest number of opioid-related deaths among major US cities. Every year, 2,100 patients with opioid addiction are admitted to Penn Medicine's three downtown emergency departments (EDs). Once an opioid overdose patient is treated in the ED, doctors historically have discharged them with inadequate follow-up, leading to fatal relapses (relapse rate after opioid detoxification can be up to 88% after one to three years). The Center for Opioid Recovery and Engagement (CORE) found a frugal way to deliver better value to opioid use disorder (OUD) patients by leveraging other patients. Today, CORE relies on certified recovery specialists (CRSs), people who are in long-term addiction recovery, to convince other opioid users to get treatment and support them during their recovery process. Thanks to the empathetic involvement of CRSs, the number of OUD patients who stuck with appropriate treatment for at least 30 days after leaving the ED has shot up from 2% to 3% in 2018 to 68% today.[25]

Next, let's look at finance – especially personal finance. America claims to be the richest country in the world. But the reality on the ground doesn't corroborate that claim. Wall Street financial engineering has no impact on main street living. Nearly 12% of Americans – almost 40 million people – live in poverty. One in eight women in the US live in poverty. Only 4% of all small business loans are granted to women. One nonprofit is trying to change that by financially empowering women micro-entrepreneurs across the US.[26]

Empowering Women Through Grassroots Entrepreneurship

Grameen America (GA) is a microfinance organization that was founded in New York in 2008 by Nobel Peace Prize recipient Muhammad Yunus, who successfully pioneered and scaled microfinance in Bangladesh. Yunus believes that, with a little financial support, people can pull themselves out of poverty using their own entrepreneurial spirit. Present in 27 US cities, GA offers small loans to women living below the poverty line, especially in minority groups, to start or expand their own business. GA doesn't require credit score, collateral, or guarantors. Instead, it leverages *social capital* to maximize the viability and impact of its loans.

Here is how it works: women first self-organize into a group of 5 who all want to launch or grow their business. They then join a larger group of 20 women in their community and partake in a five-day financial training program led by a GA center. At the end of training, each member opens a free savings account and receives an initial loan of up to $1,500. Thereafter, the members attend compulsory weekly group meetings, led by a GA loan officer, during which they make repayment and receive knowledge, tools, and peer support to succeed in their business (the peer help encourages members to pay back each loan).[27] Each repayment helps build their credit score. At the end of a six-month loan cycle, each woman repays her loan in full. She can apply and get a larger loan if she regularly attended the weekly training and is approved by her lending group.

What's unique about GA is that, in striking contrast with traditional banks, most of its loan officers are women. Studies show that female loan officers are "more likely to take part in loans requested by riskier members" and "have better information processing skills with respect to unobservable, soft-information factors pertaining to the character and nature of the loan applicant." In addition, "loans screened and monitored by female loan lenders tend to perform better, being 4.5% less likely to be problematic."[28]

Since 2008, GA has given over $4 billion in total loans to over 190,000 women in 27 US cities to help set up and scale their small businesses, which have created or maintained more than 200,000 jobs. As of 2024, GA members have been able to boost their income by an additional $2,101 and achieve an average credit score of 653.[29] Thanks to GA, these women have moved above the poverty line and enjoy steady income and savings that secures their financial future. Most impressively, GA's loan repayment rate is an astounding 99.8%. While millions of Americans strain to make credit card and mortgage payments, low-income women have repaid their GA micro loans at a rate of nearly 100%, which leads GA to conclude, "Most banks believe that low-income women are among the riskiest borrowers. However, Grameen America has proven time and time again that this is not the case. We have found that low-income women are highly dependable and trustworthy. They are in fact one of the wisest investments we can make."[30]

GA's operating model perfectly embodies the frugal economy spirit of "doing *better* with less." Rather than offer "jumbo loans" to clients and saddle them with debt – as big banks do – GA offers minimum loans to women but gives them maximum support by giving them the tools, knowledge, and peer support they need to succeed as entrepreneurs. In doing so, GA increases women's social capital as well as their psychological capital, defined as "an individual's positive psychological state of development, characterized by having high levels of HERO: Hope, (Self-)Efficacy, Resilience, and Optimism."[31] GA turns low-income women into frugal heroes that inspire many others in their local community.

As GA explains,

> We see immense value in women's social capital. Our group-lending model is built not on traditional collateral, but rather on trust and a social contract that holds the members accountable to each other. There is joint responsibility. Moreover, the relationships the women form with each other and their shared values – and often their shared sense of identity – strengthens

them individually. They have a sense of belonging, and because they are part of this social network, they have access to information that they wouldn't have otherwise. And by being a member of the group and getting and repaying their loans, their social capital grows as does their financial independence. They gain support and build greater confidence through the group model. This model itself is a form of social collateral."[32]

GA's success has led big banks such as Bank of America, Wells Fargo, Bank of the West, and Citi to team up with GA to enhance its services, expand its reach, and empower more women entrepreneurs with its grassroots impact across the US. A 36-month study using a rigorous randomized controlled trial done by MDRC on GA's microfinance model shows that women entrepreneurs who received microloans from GA had less material hardship and experienced greater agency and feelings of well-being compared to women in the control group.[33] According to the World Economic Forum, prioritizing and addressing women's financial needs – with microloan programs like GA's – could unlock $10 trillion in additional economic value globally by 2030.[34]

GA's microlending model perfectly captures the essence of Figure 11.2. As I explained in my first coauthored book *Jugaad Innovation,* underprivileged communities are overflowing with entrepreneurial spirit. As such, GA doesn't view low-income women across America as "poor" people, but "creatively rich" entrepreneurs. GA unleashes these women's innovation spirit and "fructifies" their potential by giving them a hand up, not a handout. In turn, these women use frugally the small loans they receive from GA to create better impact in their own communities, hence creating a virtuous cycle that uplifts everyone. The "less wastage" in Figure 11.2 applies to women's' creative talent, which remains undervalued and underused even in so-called advanced economies like the US.

I showed how we can use the frugal spirit to reinvent health care and finance in the US so we can offer better care at lower cost to more Americans and uplift hundreds of thousands of women who have historically been denied economic opportunities. Both Penn Medicine and GA are creating better impact at a *local* level. Penn Medicine is enhancing the physical and mental health of residents in and around Philadelphia. GA is increasing the financial well-being of low-income women located in 27 cities across America. What does this tell us? The best way to create *optimal impact* in any field is at a local level. If so, it won't be fruitful to try to build a frugal economy in America at a national level given the social, cultural, economic, political, and geological diversity of our vast nation. Rather, we must build from the bottom up a diverse set of *frugal economies* across America that heed and leverage the unique resources and respond to the specific needs of each of the 3,143 US counties.

CHAPTER 12

Let 3,143 Frugal Economies Blossom

Here is the good news: across America, a diverse set of stakeholders – visionary entrepreneurs; big and small companies; federal, regional, and local government agencies; think tanks; nonprofits; universities; and citizen groups – are joining forces to build frugal economies across the 50 states. These innovators are unleashing socioeconomic opportunities in each of the 3,143 US counties while fighting climate change at a local level. These pioneers are using the three virtues of a frugal economy – *sharing*, *distributing*, and *regenerating* – as the three foundational pillars to construct a new and better society that benefits people, communities, and the planet.

B2B Sharing: Replacing Competition with Cooperation

Just like Airbnb and Uber pioneered the consumer-to-consumer (C2C) sharing economy, next-gen US startups have developed digital platforms that facilitate and optimize the business-to-business (B2B) sharing of resources among companies.

For instance, Seattle-based Flexe aspires to become the Airbnb for warehouses; its cloud-based, peer-to-peer marketplace enables companies to share their excess warehouse capacity with other businesses seeking storage space. Flexe reports that its clients saved $19 million in capital costs over three years and increased their revenue by $47.5 million in just one year.[1]

LiquidSpace, based in Silicon Valley, enables companies to monetize their excess office space by renting it to other businesses on a short-term or a long-term basis. With LiquidSpace, Gen Z workers seeking a better work-life balance can easily find a place to work closer to their home.

Boston-based Cohealo and Chicago-based Rheaply have built digital platforms that enable hospitals to share their medical equipment and services, thus maximizing their asset use and boosting patient care quality. Likewise, as mentioned previously, 55 health systems representing more than 1,550 hospitals across the US have formed Civica Rx, a nonprofit organization that pools the buying power of 55 health systems across the US to sign long-term agreements with generic drug manufacturers to produce more than 80 essential drugs at low cost. To date, 60 million patients across the US have been treated with Civica's affordable medications.

While doing research for this chapter, I was surprised that although American startups like Uber and Airbnb initiated and led the C2C sharing revolution, European startups are the ones now shaping and leading the B2B sharing economy. This may be because in capitalist America, US businesses inured to competition have a hard time learning to cooperate and share resources with each other. Thankfully, counties and regions across the US and even federal government agencies are now pooling and sharing their physical, financial, and intellectual resources to maximize impact at a local level.

On August 17, 2022, Governors Kevin Stitt and Asa Hutchinson signed an agreement to transform the Oklahoma-Arkansas region into a national hub for advanced mobility and establish a "Silicon Valley for transportation and logistics" by combining their two states' workforce and R&D and manufacturing capabilities.[2] In the same spirit of sharing, the Tulsa Innovation Labs and the Northwest Arkansas Council proposed a joint project named Future Logistics and Advanced Mobility Engine (FLAME) as part of their application for the National Science Foundation (NSF)'s Regional Innovation Engines (RIE) program.[3] The RIE program was authorized in the CHIPS and Science Act of 2022, which aims to strengthen domestic semiconductor manufacturing, boost cutting-edge R&D, and foster regional tech hubs. Each NSF Engine "can receive up to $160 million to support the development of diverse regional coalitions of researchers, institutions, companies and civil society to conduct research and development that engages people in the process of creating solutions with economic and societal impacts."[4] NSF Engines aim to train and upskill local workforce and develop regional innovation ecosystems across the US. Leading by example, the NSF itself signed an agreement with the Economic Development Agency (EDA) to share their facilities, centers, and data infrastructure to create synergies between NSF Engines and EDA Tech Hubs and jointly boost regional innovation capacity and jobs growth.[5]

I would suggest that the EDA offers financial and technology assistance to all 3,143 counties across the US so they can set up their own personalized B2B sharing platform. Local companies within each county can use this platform to share their physical and intangible resources, hence cocreating value that stays within their community. This will make local economies across the US less wasteful and more innovative and efficient.

Distributed Manufacturing: Unleashing Hyper-Local Opportunities

In an insightful report titled "Breaking Down an $80 Billion Surge in Place-Based Industrial Policy," The Brooking Institution explains how three major laws – the American Rescue Plan Act (ARP), the Infrastructure Investment and Jobs Act (IIJA), and the CHIPS and Science Act – passed in just two years (2021–2022) are marshaling $80 billion in public investment to bolster regional innovation and growth through "place-based industrial policy."[6]

In Chapter 10, I explained how place-sensitive distributed development policies (PSDDP) can leverage the "indigenous innovation" capabilities available within US regions to regenerate left-behind places in a "bottom-up" fashion. Place-based industrial policy (PBIP) is a key enabler of PSDDP. PBIP programs engage with "the local needs of individuals and industries" within individual regions or counties and "leverage the 'bottom-up' energy of local talent, networks, clusters, institutions, and ecosystems" to build the hyper-local value networks explored in Chapter 7. By financially bolstering PBIP, the US government is acknowledging "the nation's economy is itself place-based – shaped by a network of 'distinct regional economies, each with its own history and opportunities.'"[7]

The good news is not that we are bringing manufacturing back to the US. Rather, it's the fact that – thanks to public investments in PBIP programs – the reindustrialization of America in the 21st century is done *inclusively* and *sustainably*. Indeed, US manufacturers are *scaling out* their operations by building nimble micro-factories that can produce closer to where consumers live using locally available resources, hence (re)generating and capturing economic value locally. Second, US companies are using clean and renewable energy to power their next-gen manufacturing, hence massively reducing America's industrial carbon footprint. For instance, Canoo and Arrival are two electric vehicle startups that enable companies and communities to set up micro-factories anywhere in the US to build locally customized delivery vans and buses. Arrival has set up two micro-factories in South Carolina to produce 10,000 delivery vans for UPS.[8]

Distributed manufacturing in the US will accelerate in coming years thanks to the Biden administration's push to decentralize energy production as well. For instance, the US is investing up to $7 billion to set up 6 to 10 regional clean hydrogen hubs (H2Hubs) across America. These H2Hubs, in addition to stimulating $40 billion in private investment and creating tens of thousands of jobs in multiple regions, will create the foundation of a national clean hydrogen network. This distributed network will create regional hydrogen-based energy ecosystems that can power heavy industries (steel and cement production) and heavy-duty transportation in individual regions across the US.[9] This will enable US states to substantially decarbonize their local manufacturing and logistics. In late 2023, the US government announced the selection of seven H2Hubs that span Appalachia, the American heartland, California, the Gulf Coast, Mid-Atlantic, the Midwest, and the Pacific Northwest. Each H2Hub will harness locally available abundant energy sources to generate hydrogen. The H2Hubs in California and Pacific Northwest will use exclusively locally sourced renewable energy to generate "green" hydrogen, whereas the H2Hubs in the Gulf Coast and the Appalachia will leverage natural gas, abundantly available in those regions, to produce hydrogen.[10]

Furthermore, the US Department of Energy is funding several regional initiatives to accelerate both carbon capture, use, and storage and carbon dioxide removal across US states. As I mentioned in

Chapter 7, this will enable each of the 3,143 US counties to locally remove, capture, and store CO_2, or use it as a low-cost resource to manufacture products locally.

I am cautiously optimistic that the US could become a world leader in distributed clean manufacturing. One main reason is that there is broad bipartisan support for it. A *Financial Times* study found that "more than 80% of investment in large-scale clean energy and semiconductor manufacturing pledged since (the) passage of the Inflation Reduction Act and the CHIPS and Science Act is destined for Republican congressional districts."[11] So much for the caricature of Republicans as the party of fossil fuel addicts and climate skeptics. I do, however, have two major concerns related to the *execution* of the distributing manufacturing strategy in the US.

First, as I explained in Part II, "if you build it, they will come" doesn't work in manufacturing. It's not enough to build agile factories powered by clean energy in every region or even county that churn out innovative products. You also need to build a *market* that creates the *demand* to absorb the stuff you are producing locally. I would like to see more market-shaping schemes like the Hydrogen Demand Initiative (H2DI) emerge in all US regions. HD2I is a ground-breaking effort led by the Energy Futures Initiative Foundation in partnership with S&P Global, Intercontinental Exchange, Dentons, and the MIT Energy Initiative to develop demand-side hydrogen markets across the US. HD2I's goal is to mobilize private investments to de-risk and accelerate the deployment of clean hydrogen produced by the H2Hubs in various US regions.[12]

Second, we need to distribute clean manufacturing across the US with a social consciousness. All 3,143 counties can potentially benefit from PBIP programs. And yet, some counties *deserve* PBIP projects more than others because of their dire socioeconomic needs. Public and private investments that bolster industrial development across the US must be not only place-based but also *equity*-based. The trillion-dollar question is, "How can governments and companies *prioritize* their place-based industrial strategies?" Kailin Graham and Christopher Knittel, two MIT researchers, have an answer. Graham and Knittel have created a detailed "employment carbon footprints" map that identifies the US counties where jobs and local economies are most tied to fossil fuels and therefore will be the most affected by the transition to renewable energy (see Figure 12.1). In their study, Graham

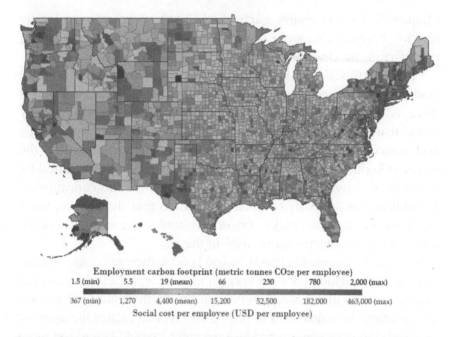

Figure 12.1 Overall employment carbon footprints (ECFs) in metric tonnes of carbon dioxide equivalent (CO$_2$e) per employee at the county level across the US.
Source: Graham and Knittel, 2024 / National Academy of Sciences.

and Knittel "demonstrate that efforts to target communities in the US Inflation Reduction Act leave a significant number of the most carbon-intensive regions of the country behind."[13] Their work offers policy-makers "much-needed data on employment vulnerability that can be used to target future just transition policy" and "makes the case for place-based policy approaches when considering how best to support communities through the energy transition."[14]

Triple Regeneration: Revitalizing the Soul of the Heartland

In a landmark study published in May 2019 by ReGenFriends, 8 out of 10 American consumers surveyed preferred engaging with "regenerative" businesses rather than "sustainable" ones. Nils-Michael Langenborg, cofounder of ReGenFriends, believes that US consumers are well ahead of US businesses who have still not grasped the enormous economic opportunities inherent in regeneration. Langenborg's favorite quote is that of Alexandre Ledru-Rollin, a French politician who coled the French Revolution of 1848: "I have to follow them, since I am their leader."

As an American, I am proud to note that progressive US companies like Danone North America, Interface, General Mills, and Patagonia are heeding US consumers' clarion call to regenerate people, communities, and the planet altogether. In doing so, these US firms are leapfrogging their European rivals who are still focused on becoming sustainable (by just recycling their waste and reducing emissions). In Part III, I showed how visionary US firms are practicing "triple regeneration" with a holistic approach to renew, restore, and grow people, places, and the planet simultaneously.

In addition to US businesses, forward-thinking think tanks and nonprofits are also spearheading bold initiatives to regenerate underserved communities across America by boosting local economies; enhancing the physical, mental, and financial health of people who live there; and enabling communities to harness the power of digital tools and transition to renewable energy.

Heartland Forward (HF) is a nonpartisan and nonprofit "think and do tank" based in Bentonville, Arkansas. HF works with states and local communities in America's heartland to improve their education and training, spur entrepreneurship and stimulate business creation, provide access to affordable health care, and boost the attractiveness and competitiveness of their region. For HF, America's heartland comprises 20 states in the Midwest, the East South Central, and the West South Central – making-up some of the largest cities and thriving rural communities across America.

Forty-two million Americans lack access to a reliable internet connection, curbing their ability to contribute to a digital economy. Studies show a strong link between high-speed internet availability and economic growth. According to a 2021 Deloitte study, if there had been even a 10% increase in broadband access across the US in 2014, the US would have created 875,000 additional jobs by 2019 and $186 billion more in economic output.[15]

To close the digital divide in the heartland, in 2021, HF launched the Connecting the Heartland initiative to expand high-speed internet across Arkansas, Illinois, Ohio, Tennessee, and Oklahoma. For instance, HF formed the Arkansas Connectivity Coalition with 15 local partners and state government leadership to expand digital equity and broadband workforce opportunities across the Natural State. In June 2023, Arkansas received $1 billion from the federal government for "transformational" internet improvements in the state.

In the US, 75% of all venture capital has gone to just three states, all on the coasts. Of $150 billion invested in capital funds, only 2% goes to women, and black founders receive just 1%. To spur inclusive entrepreneurship and stimulate business creation in the hinterland, HF is supporting the Builders + Backers Idea Accelerator.[16] This 90-day program offers a proven on-ramp to entrepreneurship, helping participants (which HF calls *builders*) put their business ideas into action and scale. Each participant is eligible for funding up to $5,000.

HF is keen to challenge and shift America's negative and condescending perception of its own heartland. In an optimistic report titled "The Emergence of the Global Heartland," HF researchers write:

> In the national media, the Heartland represented a region, as the *New York Times* described it, as "not far from forsaken," a depopulating place where the American dream has come and gone. Others have seen the region as an unreconstructed mecca for intolerance, one that had few immigrants and poor race relations and seems destined to suffer for it. As one professor at Vanderbilt suggested recently, the region was "dying from whiteness" and that its "politics of racial resentment is killing America's heartland." Perhaps it is time to change that narrative. Over the past decade, the Heartland's share of the foreign-born population has risen from 23.5% in 2010 to 31.1% in 2019. This shift can be seen in many Heartland communities, some such as Louisville, KY, Columbus, OH, and Nashville, TN, have seen their immigrant populations swell more than 40% from 2010 to 2019, often helping to reverse generations of demographic decline. They are now growing their foreign-born populations faster than such well-known historic immigrant hubs as New York, Los Angeles, San Francisco, Boston, and Philadelphia.[17]

As an immigrant myself, I spent 20 years in Boston, New York, and the Bay Area. I long believed the cosmopolitan coastal areas were the leading innovation hubs in the US. My perspective radically shifted when I read in *Financial Times* the 2023 ranking of the best US cities for international business.[18] Here is the list of top 10 best US cities for foreign multinationals to do business: Houston (TX), Pittsburgh (PA), Plano (TX), Irving (TX), Dallas (TX), Miami (FL), Austin (TX), Charlotte (NC), Greensboro (SC), and Seattle (WA). During the 20th century, Houston was known as the energy capital of the world. Now, Houston aspires to become the energy *transition* capital of the world by 2040.[19] Houston plans to lead this transition to green energy *frugally* by cleverly repurposing and reusing its existing assets and know-how honed for oil and gas. As the *Financial Times* notes, "Houston boasts unrivaled technical expertise in energy, including manufacturing, engineering, trading markets, and complex industrial project management. It also has a robust energy infrastructure and the nation's biggest port by tonnage." Houston's frugal pivoting from oil and gas to clean energy can yield huge dividends. McKinsey & Company estimates that Houston can "grow its share of energy transition capital from about 6% in 2020 to as much as 15% in 2040, reaching $250 billion annually."[20]

In December 2023, I interviewed Ross DeVol, CEO of Heartland Forward, for this book. I was living then in Lyon, France, and DeVol was based in Bentonville, Arkansas. Prior to joining HF, DeVol had served 20 years as chief research officer at Milken Institute, a think tank based in Los Angeles. DeVol and I traded jokes on how we both left big metros – Los Angeles in his case and New York and Paris for me – to come live in human-scale cities (Bentonville and Lyon) to prove to ourselves that we can keep driving our thought leadership without residing in a big US coastal city or a cosmopolitan European capital. For DeVol, America's heartland is now entering the golden age of innovation-fueled economic regeneration, as evidenced by a new HF report on America's evolving geography of innovation coauthored by Richard Florida, a leading urban studies theorist who coined the term *creative class*.[21]

As DeVol explained to me,

The heartland has a strong tradition at making things. It is capitalizing on its core industrial strength to build the next-gen tech innovation ecosystems centered on clean energy, advanced mobility, cutting-edge materials, robotics, and

advanced manufacturing – all of which involve making physical products. While Silicon Valley entrepreneurs create "ethe-
real innovations" that operate in the cloud (computing),
heartland innovators develop "grounded solutions" that
improve our material life here on Earth. Today, the levels of
venture capital investment flowing into Austin, Texas, and
Chicago are comparable to Silicon Valley's in 1995. Forty percent of America's leading-edge research universities are based
in the heartland. They will anchor the industry-transforming
innovation ecosystems of the 21st century.[22]

DeVol used Tulsa, Oklahoma to prove his point.

During the 1920s, Tulsa, Oklahoma, came to be known as the
oil capital of the world. A century later, it is emerging as America's
"most inclusive tech community." To avoid repeating the mistake of
Silicon Valley, which failed to actively promote diversity, Tulsa is
consciously building an innovation ecosystem that is deliberately
inclusive from the get-go. I call it a *natively diverse tech hub*.
Founded with support from the George Kaiser Family Foundation,
the Tulsa Innovation Labs (TIL) is leading a coalition of public, private, and nonprofit partners who leverage the city's existing assets
and strengths to create inclusive workforce and economic development projects in four emerging tech clusters: virtual health, energy
tech, advanced air mobility, and cyber. TIL calls them *Tulsa's
tech niche*.[23]

Enlightened entrepreneurs like Tyrance Billingsley II are using
the power of tech to regenerate the wounded soul of Tulsa. Billingsley is a descendant of the survivors of the 1921 Tulsa Race Massacre.
From May 31 to June 1, 1921, white supremacists burned and
destroyed businesses and residences in Tulsa's Greenwood District,
which was at that time one of the wealthiest black communities in
the US and known as *Black Wall Street*. In just two days, 35 square
blocks of the black neighborhood were burnt to ashes by the racist
assailants.[24] In 2021, the centennial of the 1921 Tulsa Race Massacre,
Billingsley founded Black Tech Street as an organization that aims to
revive the innovation spirit of Black Wall Street by regenerating it as
a tech-powered, wealth-creating movement led by black entrepreneurs. "We're working to rebirth Black Wall Street as a premier Black

innovation economy, but also catalyze this movement that sees Black people embrace tech as a mechanism to build wealth and impact the world," notes Billingsley, who has spoken before US congress on AI's transformative impact on the future of work.[25] According to "The Road to Zero Wealth" report, if current trends continue, the median African American household wealth will fall to $0 (yes, *zero* dollar!) by 2053.[26] America aims to become a "net-zero emissions" nation by 2050. But it can't afford to become a "net-zero wealth" nation for its minorities. We need more initiatives like Black Tech Street to empower black entrepreneurs to contribute to, and benefit from, the American tech dream.

Reimagine Appalachia (RA) is a diverse coalition of policy experts, community leaders, and labor organizations from West Virginia, Kentucky, Ohio, and Pennsylvania who have developed a blueprint for Appalachia's green transition. This blueprint notes, "Immense wealth (was) extracted from Appalachia over the past centuries. The Ohio River Valley of the Appalachian region has fueled the prosperity of other regions while we have suffered. Many of our communities rank in the bottom 10% nationally for their high unemployment and poverty rates and low incomes."[27] RA is keen to unleash and harness the Appalachian ingenuity to transform the region from an extractive economy to "a 21st century sustainable economy" that will generate local wealth, retrain fossil fuel workers for clean energy and green manufacturing jobs, and create inclusive economic opportunities for minorities for generations to come.

RA strives to attract public and private investments in several key initiatives that would support Appalachia's equitable transition. These sustainable, job-creating initiatives include restoring damaged lands and waters, modernizing the electric grid and decentralizing clean energy production, bolstering green manufacturing (like electric vehicle production and alternatives to single-use plastic), building a sustainable transportation system, restoring wetlands, promoting regenerative agriculture and ecotourism, and absorbing greenhouse gases with natural landscapes.

Amanda Woodrum, codirector of RA, explained to me how the Appalachian region can undertake its green transition *frugally* by repurposing Appalachia's existing infrastructure and skills. "We can turn our shuttered coal plants from liabilities into assets by repurposing them as eco-industrial parks where companies share energy, waste, and resources synergistically using circular economy processes. Fossil fuel workers in our region have foundational skills that can be leveraged to create a clean manufacturing hub. Our rich natural landscapes can absorb carbon via reforestation and wetland restoration while growing local farms and food networks. Our goal is to heal our land and our people, regenerate our economy, and create sustainable local wealth by creatively leveraging the natural, physical, human resources we already got."[28] Woodrum is right. A report by the Lawrence Berkeley National Laboratory explains how coal assets in Appalachia can be repurposed for a decarbonized digital economy by, for instance, using reclaimed mine lands for clean energy projects and hosting data centers that can be cooled with groundwater in mines and adjacent aquifers.[29]

■ ■ ■

In 2014, when he was vice president, President Joe Biden told an audience at Harvard Kennedy School: "The United States today faces threats that require attention. But we face no existential threat to our way of life or our security. Let me say it again: We face no existential threat – none – to our way of life or our ultimate security. You are twice as likely to be struck by lightning as you around to be affected by a terrorist event in the United States."[30] Ten years later, in 2024, Biden's optimistic outlook is proving to be wrong: the US is facing not one but *two* existential threats: exploding social inequalities and the climate crisis. Only a frugal economy can enable all 3,143 US counties across the US to overcome this dual challenge and secure their future.

For Americans who are used to "supersizing" everything, the term *frugal* is scary: it sounds like "downsizing" the American way of life (what the French call *déclassement*, the downgrading of one's social status). But as Chapter 11 and this chapter show, *frugal* doesn't mean *less*, but *better with less*. The visionary entrepreneurs, think tanks, academics, businesses, nonprofits, and government agencies who are building *frugal economies* across all 3,143 US counties are just striving to bring dignity and a decent quality of life to all

340 million people who call America home. And they do so by *valorizing* – creating value from – all available local resources, including human talent, so they don't go to waste. A frugal economy offers *all* US citizens an inclusive and sustainable pathway to realize the American dream.

Conclusion: The Rise of Frugal Natives

According to "Joyful Frugality," an insightful report published by Havas Red in May 2023, two-thirds of mainstream consumers worldwide believe they could be happy in a more frugal world. For them, frugality is aspirational. Only 13% of consumers view frugality negatively, as if it's similar to going back to the Middle Ages.[1] A frugal world is not defined by privation and sacrifice but rather by liberty and purpose. As the Havas report points out, "We want to live with less to have more: a more meaningful existence. More free time. More financial security and psychological freedom. More faith that our planet will survive."[2]

As I read this Havas report, I had a sense of déjà vu. In the 1970s and 1980s, I grew up in Pondicherry, a small town in South India where water was rationed (due to severe droughts) and electricity was intermittent (due to an unreliable grid). My family didn't own a car and my house was devoid of TV, fridge, and other electric appliances. I used my bike to get around in the town and we cooked at home using only the fresh ingredients available in the local market every day. For me, frugality was a way of life. There was nothing special about it. As a kid, I didn't complain about our frugal lifestyle. I didn't celebrate it either as a noble virtue.

Even today, as I turn 54, I still live frugally. I don't own a car or a home (and never will) and all my belongings fit in a single suitcase (which is practical to shift home every few years, as I am a nomad by nature). In 2023, my income was less than what I earned in 1999 when I started my career in the US (clearly, I failed to live up to the American dream!). I could certainly earn 10 times more but I choose not to. I prefer living *better* with *less*. I want to put every ounce of my vital energy to good use – like writing this soulful book, rather than chasing well-paid but senseless consulting and speaking gigs. (I recently declined the request from a big European bank to give a talk to the children of their wealthy private banking clients on the value of . . . frugality!) Today, my existence is frugal but fruitful.

I am not the only one sticking to a frugal lifestyle that is rich in meaning and modest in means. Since the Great Recession of 2008–2009, a growing number of millennials have willingly downsized their material existence so they can lead a simpler life. Their role models are Joshua Fields Millburn and Ryan Nicodemus, two Gen Yers who are the leading proponents of "minimalism": they advise their 20 million followers on social media how to live a meaningful life by owning less stuff.[3] Gen Z, which represents 25% of the world's population today and will account for 30% of workers in 2030, is way more frugal than previous generations. Worried about the deteriorating socioeconomic conditions and the worsening climate crisis, the values-driven and future-oriented Gen Zers save big time, spend mindfully, and vote with their wallet for brands that genuinely improve society and the planet.[4]

The Gen Zers are redefining the very notions of "American dream" and "middle class" and what constitutes a good life. As Adam Hardingham, the young CEO of digital marketing firm Rivmedia, points out, "To us, being middle class isn't just about material comforts like a nice house and cars. It's more about having stability, security, and freedom. Sure, a good salary is important, but we're also looking at the big picture, things like healthcare we can afford, education without the burden of debt, and a healthier planet."[5]

Just like the millennials, the Gen Zers are *digital natives*, a term coined by Marc Prensky to designate those born after 1980 and who grew up in an environment suffused with digital media and technology.[6] By contrast, Gen Xers like me and baby boomers are *digital immigrants* who were brought up in a pre-internet world dominated by print and television. In the same vein, I believe millennials and Gen Xers are *frugal natives*: they possess an innate social and ecological awareness that drives them to eschew selfish hyper-consumption and embrace a balanced, eco-friendly lifestyle that enables them to live better with less. Conversely, the Gen Xers and baby boomers are frugal immigrants: they need to first unlearn their profligate habits, which is akin to their mother tongue, and then learn to practice frugality, which is like a new foreign language they find complex and unappealing. This explains why when I mentioned the title of this book to CEOs, policymakers, and academics aged 45 or above, they all warned me, "Are you sure you want to use *frugal* in the title?

Because *frugal* has a negative connotation." On the contrary, when I interviewed the millennials who run most of the startups mentioned in this book, they all unanimously said, "I love your book title. *Frugal* is the new cool!"

The millennials and Gen Zers, as frugal natives, will be the main architects of the frugal economy that will gradually emerge over the next two decades. The millennials pioneered and shaped the consumer-to-consumer sharing economy in the 2010s (Airbnb was founded by three millennials). In coming years, as they assume leadership roles in big companies, millennials will engage their organizations actively in business-to-business sharing, hence replacing competition with cooperation as the new core corporate value. Millennials will also lead the next industrial revolution by scaling out manufacturing and building hyper-local value networks, which mirror the decentralized nature of the internet and social media, which millennials grew up with.

If Gen Yers erect the first and second pillars of the frugal economy, it is Gen Zers who will establish its third column: triple regeneration. Acutely and viscerally aware of the climate urgency, Gen Zers, soon to become the single largest group of consumers and employees, will heap pressure on businesses to go beyond sustainability and regenerate people, places, and the planet synergistically. According to surveys done by ReGenFriends in 2019 and in 2020, a vast majority of Gen Z consumers find the term *sustainable* too passive and want businesses to build a regenerative economy that heals, restores, and grows communities and natural ecosystems.[7] Brands that merely aim for *net-zero* emissions won't impress Gen Zers, who will vote with their wallet for *net-positive* brands that do greater good to society and nature. As conscious workers, Gen Zers will shun employers with a stand-alone corporate social responsibility department in favor of companies that use their core business model to revitalize ailing communities and restore dwindling biodiversity. Rather than militate for *degrowth* – a popular concept being thrown around to rein in the excesses of capitalism – the pragmatic Gen Zers will root for a holistic and balanced growth model that I described in Chapter 9 as *regenerative development*.

Michael Luchs, a professor at William & Mary, and David Glen Mick, a professor at the University of Virginia, are trailblazing practical research on *consumer wisdom*, which they define as "the pursuit

of well-being for oneself and for others through mindful management of consumption-related choices and behaviors."[8] For Luchs and
Mick, consumption is neither good nor bad in itself. It's just a tool
that can contribute – or not – to individual and collective well-being,
depending on the level of wisdom of the person – the consumer –
using that tool. Luchs and Mick, along with Kelly L. Haws, a researcher
at Vanderbilt University, have developed a self-assessment question-
naire based on six dimensions that measures your consumer wisdom, which are the key traits of a wise person who consumes in a
way that enhances their own well-being while contributing to the
greater good.[9] According to Luchs, "wise consumers successfully
consider a bigger picture focused on who they want to be and how
they want to live. [They] also recognize that their resources and priorities change over time. But a constant theme is making intentional
choices that promote their well-being rather than merely reacting to
marketplace signals."[10] Luchs believes that consumer wisdom will
form the cornerstone of next-generation marketing, which will be
centered on "creating real, human-centered value – and then com-
municating it."[11]

I believe millennials and Gen Yers are wise consumers who strive
to live better with less. I trust they will use their consumer wisdom
to cocreate a frugal economy that genuinely benefits people, society,
and the planet. May this book serve as their guide to building a better
world with less.

Navi Radjou

Madrid, Spain

April 2024

Notes

Introduction

1. Bartels, M. (2023, September 13). Humans have crossed 6 of 9 "planetary boundaries." *Scientific American.* https://www.scientificamerican.com/article/humans-have-crossed-6-of-9-planetary-boundaries

2. Rockström, J., Steffen, W., Noone, K., Persson, Å., et al. (2009). Planetary boundaries: Exploring the safe operating space for humanity. *Ecology and Society, 14*(2), 32. http://www.ecologyandsociety.org/vol14/iss2/art32

3. Richardson, J., Steffen, W., Lucht, W., Bendtsen, J., Cornell, S. E., et al. (2023). Earth beyond six of nine planetary boundaries. *Science Advances, 9*(37). https://www.science.org/doi/10.1126/sciadv.adh2458

4. Radjou, N. (2014, October). Creative problem-solving in the face of extreme limits [Video]. TED Conferences. https://www.ted.com/talks/navi_radjou_creative_problem_solving_in_the_face_of_extreme_limits

5. Radjou, N. (2017, March 21). The genius of frugal innovation. TED Ideas. https://ideas.ted.com/the-genius-of-frugal-innovation

6. Crilly, T. (2011, July 8). No limits for Usain. *Maths and Sport.* https://sport.maths.org/content/no-limits-usain

7. Wikipedia contributors. (2024, February 13). Seven virtues. *Wikipedia.* Retrieved February 20, 2024, from https://en.wikipedia.org/w/index.php?title=Seven_virtues&oldid=1206815537

8. Stockholm Resilience Centre. (n.d.). Planetary boundaries. https://www.stockholmresilience.org/research/planetary-boundaries.html

Chapter 1

1. The World Bank. (2023, March 27). Global economy's "speed limit" set to fall to three-decade low. https://www.worldbank

.org/en/news/press-release/2023/03/27/global-economy-s-speed-limit-set-to-fall-to-three-decade-low

2. Ibid.

3. Earth Overshoot Day. (2023). How the date of earth overshoot day 2023 was calculated. https://www.overshootday.org/2023-calculation

4. Gillespie, L. (2024, January 24). Bankrate's 2024 annual emergency savings report. https://www.bankrate.com/banking/savings/emergency-savings-report

5. Eurostat. (2023, June 14). People at risk of poverty or social exclusion in 2022. https://ec.europa.eu/eurostat/web/products-eurostat-news/w/DDN-20230614-1

6. Doris, A., & Kacperczyk, O. (2019, May 22). Why female entrepreneurs are missing out on funding. London Business School. https://www.london.edu/think/iie-why-female-entrepreneurs-are-missing-out-on-funding

7. Kunthara, S. (2021, July 16). Black women still receive just a tiny fraction of VC funding despite 5-year high. *Crunchbase News*. https://news.crunchbase.com/diversity/something-ventured-black-women-founders

8. Kounis, N., Burgering, C., & Renoult, S. (2023, February 27). SustainaWeekly—The decoupling of emissions and economic growth. ABN Amro. https://www.abnamro.com/research/en/our-research/sustainaweekly-the-decoupling-of-emissions-and-economic-growth

9. McAfee, A. (n.d.). *More from less*. Book summary. https://www.andrewmcafee.org/books/more-from-less

10. Sogeti. (2020, September 23). Navi Radjou @ What Matters Now TV—Conscious Society [Video]. https://www.youtube.com/watch?v=MPm0Abmx3As

11. Radjou, N. (2020, August 6). The rising frugal economy. *MIT Sloan Management Review*. https://sloanreview.mit.edu/article/the-rising-frugal-economy

12. Monbiot, G. (2021, October 30). Capitalism is killing the planet—It's time to stop buying into our own destruction. *The Guardian*. https://www.theguardian.com/environment/2021/oct/30/capitalism-is-killing-the-planet-its-time-to-stop-buying-into-our-own-destruction

13. Beck, R., & Seru, A. (2019, December 21). Short-term thinking is poisoning American business. *New York Times*. https://www.nytimes.com/2019/12/21/opinion/sunday/capitalism-sanders-warren.html

14. Eldridge, S. (n.d.). Negative externality. *Encyclopaedia Britannica*. https://www.britannica.com/topic/negative-externality

Chapter 2

1. PwC. (2014, August). The sharing economy: How will it disrupt your business? https://pwc.blogs.com/files/sharing-economy-final_0814.pdf

2. This chapter and the next two draw heavily on a report written by the author titled "The B2B Sharing Revolution" published by the French think tank Terra Nova in November 2021. The report's content is reused here with Terra Nova's permission.

3. Radjou, N. (2021, April 14). The sharing economy's next target: Business-to-business. *Fast Company*. https://www.fastcompany.com/90624859/the-sharing-economys-next-target-business-to-business

4. Flexe. (2021, October 22). Report: Flexe reduces operational costs, increases revenue. https://www.flexe.com/articles/report-flexe-reduces-operational-costs-increases-revenue

5. McConnell, E. (2024, January 20). Office space hits highest vacancy rate since 1979. Yahoo! Finance. https://fr.finance.yahoo.com/news/office-space-hits-highest-vacancy-182339589.html

6. Convoy. (2021, November 8). 35% of the time the truck next to you on the highway is empty—That's a really big deal for the environment. https://convoy.com/blog/empty-miles-versus-electric-vehicles

7. MIT. (n.d.). Why 95% of new products miss the mark (and how yours can avoid the same fate). https://professionalprograms.mit.edu/blog/design/why-95-of-new-products-miss-the-mark-and-how-yours-can-avoid-the-same-fate

8. Fallon-O'Leary, D. (2023, November 1). The state of the B2B sharing economy. https://www.business.com/articles/b2b-sharing-economy

9. Asonibarev, P. (n.d.). Hello tractor. MIT Solve. https://solve.mit .edu/challenges/circular-economy/solutions/9522

10. Our Projects. (n.d.). Digital Green. https://digitalgreentrust .org/our-projects/

11. Chen, Z. (2021). Sharing employee: B2B employment model in the era of Coronavirus disease 2019 and implication for human resource management. *Frontiers in Psychology, 12.* https://doi .org/10.3389/fpsyg.2021.714704

12. Lendel, I., Piazza, M., & Madeline, F. (2021, September). The effect of the COVID-19 pandemic on Ohio manufacturing. Cleveland State University, Levin College of Public Affairs and Education. https://engagedscholarship.csuohio.edu/cgi/viewcontent.cgi? article=2742&context=urban_facpub

13. Circular Economy Foundation. (2024). Circular economy strategies can cut global emissions by 39%. https://www.circle-economy.com/news/circular-economy-strategies-can-cut-global-emissions-by-39

14. Eurostat. (2023, August). Road freight transport by journey characteristics. https://ec.europa.eu/eurostat/statistics-explained/ index.php?title=Road_freight_transport_by_journey_characteristics

15. Convoy. (2019, October 10). Automated reloads are reducing empty miles carbon emissions by 45%. https://convoy.com/blog/ automated-reloads-reducing-empty-mile-carbon-emissions

16. BlaBlaCar. (2019, March 27). Carpooling saves more than 1.6 million tonnes of CO_2 a year, whilst doubling the number of people traveling. https://blog.blablacar.com/newsroom/news-list/zeroemptyseats

17. Dana Clare Redden, founder of Solar Stewards, email interview with the author, January 19, 2024.

Chapter 3

1. Friis Møller, H.-M., & Randers, L. (2022, August 17). Industrial symbiosis and the circular economy of water. IWA. https://iwa-network.org/industrial-symbiosis-and-the-circular-economy-of-water

2. Why industrial symbiosis makes sound business sense. (n.d.). *Chemical Industry Journal.* https://www.chemicalindustry

journal.co.uk/why-industrial-symbiosis-makes-sound-business-sense

3. SCALER Project. (2020, May). Quantified potential of industrial symbiosis in Europe. https://www.scalerproject.eu/wp-content/uploads/2020/06/D3.5_SCALER_Quantified-potential-of-industrial-symbiosis-in-Europe_v1.0.pdf

4. CBRE. (2021, June 22). CBRE forecasts 300m sq ft of additional European logistics space will be needed by 2025 to meet rising e-commerce demand. https://news.cbre.co.uk/cbre-forecasts-300m-sq-ft-of-additional-european-logistics-space-will-be-needed-by-2025-to-meet-rising-e-commerce-demand

5. Helmore, E. (2023, August 19). Fears grow for property sector as WeWork scrambles to stay afloat. *The Guardian*. https://www.theguardian.com/business/2023/aug/19/wework-busines-new-york-london-rental-market

6. Breteau, P. (2023, January 28). Who could live without a car? Five graphs breakdown French people's daily journeys. *Le Monde*. https://www.lemonde.fr/en/france/article/2023/01/28/who-could-do-without-a-car-five-graphs-to-analyze-french-people-s-daily-journeys_6013438_7.html

7. Cheater, A. (n.d.). Why having a green supply chain has become a necessity. Kinaxis Blog. https://www.kinaxis.com/en/blog/why-having-a-green-supply-chain-has-become-a-necessity

8. Presutti, C. (2024, February 16). Patients wait for life-saving medications. *Voice of America*. https://www.voanews.com/a/patients-wait-for-life-saving-medications-/7490139.html

9. United States Senate Committee on Homeland Security & Governmental Affairs. (2023, March). Short supply: The health and national security risks of drug shortages. https://www.hsdl.org/c/abstract/?docid=876660

10. AARP. (2023, August 10). New report: Top Medicare Part D drugs have more than tripled in price since entering market. https://press.aarp.org/2023-08-10-New-Report-Top-Medicare-Part-D-Drugs-Have-More-Than-Tripled-in-Price-Since-Entering-Market

11. Khandekar, A., & Satija, B. (2022, March 3). Civica aims to launch low-cost insulin in U.S. by 2024. *Reuters*. https://www.reuters.com/business/healthcare-pharmaceuticals/civica-aims-launch-low-cost-insulin-us-by-2024-2022-03-03

12. Dan Liljenquist, chairman of Civica's board of directors, interview with the author, February 14, 2020.

13. CEBA. (2023, November 22). CEBA comments to SBTI emphasize role of market certificates in grid decarbonization. https:// cebuyers.org/blog/ceba-comments-to-sbti-emphasize-role-of-market-certificates-in-grid-decarbonization

14. World Economic Forum. (2024, January 8). First Movers Coalition: Over 95 members send world's largest clean demand signal for emerging climate technologies. https://www.weforum .org/impact/first-movers-coalition-worlds-largest-clean-demand-signal-climate-technologies

15. ESG News. (2022, October 18). Walmart, Ørsted and Schneider Electric announce first cohort for renewable energy supply chain program. https://esgnews.com/walmart-orsted-and-schneider-electric-announce-first-cohort-for-renewable-energy-supply-chain-program

16. Eurofound. (2015, March 12). New forms of employment. https://www.eurofound.europa.eu/en/publications/2015/new-forms-employment

17. Keller, J. R., Kehoe, R. R., Bidwell, M., Collings, D., & Myer, A. (2021). In with the old? Examining when boomerang employees outperform new hires. *Academy of Management Journal, 64,* 1654–1684.

18. NAAME. (n.d.). Supporting businesses and people to maximise their shared potential. https://naame.co.uk/talent-sharing-platform

19. Wilthagen, T., & Tros, F. H. (2004). The concept of flexicurity: A new approach to regulating employment and labour markets. *Transfer, European Review of Labour and Research, 10*(2).

20. Christophe Rebours, founder and CEO of InProcess, interview with the author, March 14, 2014.

21. Atluri, V., Dietz, M., & Henke, N. (2017, July 12). Competing in a world of sectors without borders. *McKinsey Quarterly.* https://www .mckinsey.com/capabilities/quantumblack/our-insights/competing-in-a-world-of-sectors-without-borders

22. USPTO. (2019). Intellectual property and the US economy (3rd. ed.). https://www.uspto.gov/sites/default/files/documents/uspto-ip-us-economy-third-edition.pdf

23. Rivette, K. G., Nothhaft, H. R., & Kline, D. (2000). Discovering new value in intellectual property. *Harvard Business Review*. https://hbr.org/2000/01/discovering-new-value-in-intellectual-property

24. Business Wire. (2016, March 22). Levi Strauss & Co. open sources water innovation techniques to public. https://www.businesswire.com/news/home/20160322005444/en/Levi-Strauss-Co.-Open-Sources-Water-Innovation-Techniques-to-Public

25. Bhatti, Y., Prabhu, J., & Harris, M. (2020, June 23). Frugal innovation for today's and tomorrow's crises. *Stanford Social Innovation Review*. https://ssir.org/articles/entry/frugal_innovation_for_todays_and_tomorrows_crises

26. Kleiner, A. (2004, November 30). Recombinant Innovation. *strategy+business*. https://www.strategy-business.com/article/04404

27. Weitzman, M. L. (1998). Recombinant growth. *The Quarterly Journal of Economics, 113*, 331–360. https://doi.org/10.1162/003355398555595

28. Dutz, M. A. (2007). Unleashing India's innovation: Toward sustainable and inclusive growth. World Bank. http://hdl.handle.net/10986/6856

29. World Economic Forum. (2021, January 22). What is stakeholder capitalism? https://www.weforum.org/agenda/2021/01/klaus-schwab-on-what-is-stakeholder-capitalism-history-relevance

30. Tata Group. (2018). In loop with success. https://www.tata.com/newsroom/circular-economy-initiatives-tata-group-companies

Chapter 4

1. Shalal, A. (2023, March 27). World Bank warns of "lost decade" in global growth without bold policy shifts. *Reuters*. https://www.reuters.com/markets/world-bank-warns-lost-decade-global-growth-without-bold-policy-shifts-2023-03-27

2. Peter G. Peterson Foundation. (2023, July 27). Healthcare spending will be one-fifth of the economy within a decade. https://www.pgpf.org/blog/2023/07/healthcare-spending-will-be-one-fifth-of-the-economy-within-a-decade

3. Rakshit, S., McGough, M., & Amin, K. (2024, January 30). How does U.S. life expectancy compare to other countries? The Peterson-KFF Health System Tracker. https://www.healthsystemtracker.org/chart-collection/u-s-life-expectancy-compare-countries

4. The concept of value-based health care (VBHC) was introduced in 1966 by Avedis Donabedian, a physician and professor at the University of Michigan. It was later expounded by Michael Porter, a professor of management at Harvard Business School, in a book he coauthored with Elizabeth O. Teisberg, *Redefining Health Care: Creating Value-Based Competition on Results,* which was published by Harvard Business School Press in 2006.

5. European Commission, Directorate-General for Health and Food Safety. (2019). Defining value in "value-based healthcare"—Opinion by the Expert Panel on effective ways of investing in Health (EXPH). https://data.europa.eu/doi/10.2875/148325

6. Holder, J. (2023, March 13). Tracking coronavirus vaccinations around the world. *New York Times.* https://www.nytimes.com/interactive/2021/world/covid-vaccinations-tracker.html

7. The World Bank. (2022, June 30). Eastern and Southern Africa's COVID-19 vaccination journey. https://www.worldbank.org/en/news/immersive-story/2022/06/30/unlocking-supply-and-overcoming-hesitancy-eastern-and-southern-africa-s-covid-19-vaccination-journey

8. World Health Organization. (n.d.). The mRNA vaccine technology transfer hub. https://www.who.int/initiatives/the-mrna-vaccine-technology-transfer-hub

9. Hamzelou, J. (2023, January 5). What's next for mRNA vaccines. *MIT Technology Review.* https://www.technologyreview.com/2023/01/05/1066274/whats-next-mrna-vaccines

10. World Health Organization. (2023, April 20). mRNA Technology Transfer Programme moves to the next phase of its development. https://www.who.int/news/item/20-04-2023-mrna-technology-transfer-programme-moves-to-the-next-phase-of-its-development

11. Petro Terblanche, CEO of Afrigen Biologics, email interview with the author, January 16, 2024.

12. Business & Sustainable Development Commission. (2017). Better business, better world. https://unglobalcompact.org/library/5051

13. United Nations. (2023, September 19). Annual cost for reaching the SDGs? More than $5 trillion. https://news.un.org/en/story/2023/09/1140997

14. United Nations. (2023, July 5). Developing countries face $4 trillion investment gap in SDGs. https://news.un.org/en/story/2023/07/1138352

15. United Nations. (2023, February 17). Guterres calls for G20 to agree $500 billion annual stimulus for sustainable development. https://news.un.org/en/story/2023/02/1133637

16. The World Bank. (2024, January 9). Global economy set for weakest half-decade performance in 30 years. https://www.worldbank.org/en/news/press-release/2024/01/09/global-economic-prospects-january-2024-press-release

17. Oxfam International. (2024, January 15). Wealth of five richest men doubles since 2020 as five billion people made poorer in "decade of division," says Oxfam. https://www.oxfam.org/en/press-releases/wealth-five-richest-men-doubles-2020-five-billion-people-made-poorer-decade-division

18. The Fifth National Climate Assessment. (2023). https://nca2023.globalchange.gov

19. Yenet, A., Nibret, G., & Tegegne, B. A. (2023). Challenges to the availability and affordability of essential medicines in African countries: A scoping review. *ClinicoEconomics and Outcomes Research, 15*, 443–458.

20. Gotev, G. (2017, June 8). Soft drink cold chain delivers vaccines to Africa's most remote corners. EURACTIV. https://www.euractiv.com/section/health-consumers/news/soft-drink-cold-chain-delivers-vaccines-to-africas-most-remote-corners

21. The voice of truth. (n.d.). *The selected works of Mahatma Gandhi* (Vol. V). https://www.mkgandhi.org/voiceoftruth/cooperation.htm

22. Athena Aktipis, associate professor at Arizona State University, interview with the author, January 31, 2024.

Chapter 5

1. Stallard, M. (2023, April 3). How slavery made Manchester the world's first industrial city. *The Guardian*. https://www.theguardian .com/news/ng-interactive/2023/apr/03/cotton-capital-how-slavery-made-manchester-the-worlds-first-industrial-city

2. Wikipedia contributors. (2023, December 16). Cottonopolis. *Wikipedia*. Retrieved February 19, 2024, from https://en.wikipedia .org/w/index.php?title=Cottonopolis&oldid=1190267512

3. Murray's Mills. (n.d.). Our Manchester. https://manchesterhistory .net/manchester/tours/tour15/area15page30.html

4. Schofield, J. (2020, April 23). The story of Manchester architecture: Part two 1800–1850. *Confidentials: Manchester*. https://confidentials .com/manchester/the-story-of-manchester-architecture-part-two-1800-1850

5. Textiles Gallery. (n.d.). Science and Industry Museum in Manchester. https://www.scienceandindustrymuseum.org.uk/ whats-on/textiles-gallery

6. History. (2010, April 26). Automobile history. https://www .history.com/topics/inventions/automobiles

7. Sugrue, T. J. (n.d.). Motor City: The story of Detroit. The Gilder Lehrman Institute of American History. https://ap.gilderlehrman .org/history-by-era/politics-reform/essays/motor-city-story-detroit

8. Ford Model T-1911. (n.d.). The Heritage Society at Sam Houston Park. https://www.heritagesociety.org/ford-model-t

9. Hoekstra, K. (2022, April 25). Ford Model T: The invention of the world's first affordable car. *History Hit*. https://www.historyhit .com/ford-model-t-the-invention-of-the-worlds-first-affordable-car

10. Wikipedia contributors. (2023, September 23). Ford River Rouge complex. *Wikipedia*. Retrieved February 19, 2024, from https:// en.wikipedia.org/w/index.php?title=Ford_River_Rouge_ complex&oldid=1176657361

11. History & Timeline. (n.d.). The Henry Ford. https://www .thehenryford.org/visit/ford-rouge-factory-tour/history-and-timeline

12. Hongbin, C. (2021, January 21). Chinese manufacturing must grow in strength, not just size. *ThinkChina*. https://www.thinkchina .sg/chinese-manufacturing-must-grow-strength-not-just-size

13. Xinhua (2022, June 14). China accounts for 30 pct of global manufacturing output. https://english.news.cn/20220614/f75a6 59ffbd04651b95b4d154fd0e9e5/c.html

14. Made in China? (2015, March 12). *The Economist*. https://www .economist.com/leaders/2015/03/12/made-in-china

15. McGee, P. (2023, January 17). How Apple tied its fortunes to China. *Financial Times*. https://www.ft.com/content/d5a80891-b27d-4110-90c9-561b7836f11b

16. Shepard, W. (2016, July 14). A look inside Shenzhen's high-tech empire. *Forbes*. https://www.forbes.com/sites/wadeshepard/ 2016/07/14/a-look-inside-shenzhens-high-tech-empire

17. Liu, J. (2022, November 30). China's Zhengzhou, home to world's largest iPhone factory, ends Covid lockdown. Other cities do the same. CNN.com. https://edition.cnn.com/2022/11/30/tech/ china-apple-foxconn-zhengzhou-lifts-lockdown-hnk-intl/index .html

18. Kane, M. (2023, November 27). BYD rolled out its 6 millionth plug-in vehicle. InsideEVs. https://insideevs.com/news/698054/ byd-rolled-out-6-millionth-plugin-vehicle

19. He, L., & Isidore, C. (2024, January 2). China's BYD is selling more electric cars than Tesla. CNN.com. https://edition.cnn .com/2024/01/02/cars/china-byd-ev-sales-increase-tesla-intl-hnk/index.html

20. Sheffi, Y., & Rice, J. B. Jr. (2005, October 15). A supply chain view of the resilient enterprise. *MIT Sloan Management Review*. https://sloanreview.mit.edu/article/a-supply-chain-view-of-the-resilient-enterprise

21. Radjou, N. (2000, July). *Manufacturing deconstructed*. Forrester Research.

22. Radjou, N. (2002, March). *Adapting to supply network change*. Forrester Research.

23. US Senate Committee on Finance. (2019, August 7). Grassley urges HHS, FDA to implement unannounced inspections of foreign drug manufacturing facilities. https://www.finance.senate .gov/chairmans-news/grassley-urges-hhs-fda-to-implement-unannounced-inspections-of-foreign-drug-manufacturing-facilities

24. Braw, E. (2020, March 4). Blindsided on the supply side. *Foreign Policy*. https://foreignpolicy.com/2020/03/04/blindsided-on-the-supply-side

25. Orlik, T., Rush, J., Cousin, M., & Hong, J. (2020, March 6). Coronavirus could cost the global economy $2.7 trillion. Here is how. *Bloomberg*. https://www.bloomberg.com/graphics/2020-coronavirus-pandemic-global-economic-risk

26. Wikipedia contributors. (2024, February 7). Manufacturing. *Wikipedia*. Retrieved February 19, 2024, from https://en.wikipedia.org/w/index.php?title=Manufacturing&oldid=1204702651

27. Les Echos. (2020, November 18). Morbihan: les couturières de L'Usine invisible lancent leurs masques pour enfants. https://www.lesechos.fr/pme-regions/bretagne/morbihan-les-couturieres-de-lusine-invisible-lancent-leurs-masques-pour-enfants-1265962

28. Radjou, N. (2020, July 3). Frugal lessons from Indian makers who created 1 million face shields super fast. LinkedIn. https://www.linkedin.com/pulse/frugal-lessons-from-indian-makers-who-created-1-million-navi-radjou

29. Hanson, K. (n.d.). Repurposing in the Buckeye State. SME. https://www.sme.org/smemedia/humans-of-manufacturing/ohio-manufacturing-alliance-to-fight-covid-19

30. Greenhouse gas emissions from a typical passenger vehicle. (n.d.). United States Environmental Protection Agency. https://www.epa.gov/greenvehicles/greenhouse-gas-emissions-typical-passenger-vehicle

31. Frédéric Mourier, founder of Avatar Mobilité, interview with the author, July 12, 2022.

32. Murati, A. (2013, November 13). La voiture grande consommatrice de matières premières. *L'argus*. https://www.largus.fr/actualite-automobile/la-votiure-grande-consommatrice-de-matiasres-premiasres-3299370.html

33. Naughton, K. (2024, January 4). Why America's car buyers are rethinking EVs. *Bloomberg*. https://www.bloomberg.com/news/articles/2024-01-04/high-ev-prices-charging-worries-push-us-car-buyers-to-hybrids

34. Distributed energy generation market size, share global analysis report, 2023–2030. (n.d.). Facts & Factors Research. https://www.fnfresearch.com/distributed-energy-generation-market

35. Microgrids. (n.d.). Montgomery County. https://www.montgo merycountymd.gov/DGS-OES/MicroGrids.html

36. Enel. (2023, November 30). The new grids: Smart and open to all. https://www.enel.com/company/stories/articles/2023/11/modernizing-grids-increasing-prosumers

37. Decode39. (2023, November 23). How Italy's renewables leader is rethinking green grids design. https://decode39.com/8284/enel-green-grids-design

38. Pacific Northwest—Blue Lake Rancheria. (n.d.). Northern Arizona University. https://www7.nau.edu/itep/main/tcc/Tribes/pn_rancheria

39. Sherriff, L. (2023, December 4). Native Americans are building their own solar farms. BBC.com. https://www.bbc.com/future/article/20231204-native-americans-are-building-their-own-solar-farms

40. Eisenstein, P. A. (2022, December 20). Tesla to add $1B plant in Mexico. *The Detroit Bureau.* https://www.thedetroitbureau.com/2022/12/report-tesla-to-add-1b-plant-in-mexico

41. US: Future-proofing vertical farms' electricity access through microgrids. (2024, February 19). HortiDaily.com. https://www.hortidaily.com/article/9547675/us-future-proofing-vertical-farms-electricity-access-through-microgrids

42. Power Africa. (2018, November 26). Eaton microgrid solution saves 40% in energy costs. https://medium.com/power-africa/eaton-microgrid-solution-saves-40-in-energy-costs-ee8d32ae138c

43. CORDIS. Final report summary—F³ FACTORY (Flexible, Fast and Future Production Processes). https://cordis.europa.eu/project/id/228867/reporting

44. The results speak for themselves. (n.d.). Bright Machines. https://www.brightmachines.com

45. Selzler, M. L. (2020, September 11). Chisel away the superfluous. Medium.com. https://myrnalselzler.medium.com/chisel-away-the-superfluous-78b682a7b9f5

46. Friedland, E., & Healy, K. (2023, April 17). How sustainable is 3D printing? *Sustainable Plastics.* https://www.sustainableplastics.com/news/how-sustainable-3d-printing

47. Madeleine, P. (2023, January 12). What can we expect from the additive manufacturing market over the next 5 years? *3Dnatives.*

https://www.3dnatives.com/en/additive-manufacturing-market-next-5-years-120120234

48. Fast Radius, a SyBridge Brand. (2022, January 19). Fireside chat: The impact of microfactory production [Video]. https://www.youtube.com/watch?v=UrogsGhK6HE

49. Rajan, R. (2020, April 3). How to save global capitalism from itself. *Foreign Policy*. https://foreignpolicy.com/2020/04/03/save-global-capitalism-localism-deglobalization

Chapter 6

1. Circle Economy Foundation. (2023). The circularity gap report 2023. https://www.circularity-gap.world/2023

2. McGinty, D. G. (2021, February 23). 5 opportunities of a circular economy. World Resources Institute. https://www.wri.org/insights/5-opportunities-circular-economy

3. du Besse, A. (2019, May 22). The NYC curb-to-market challenge: An opportunity for a better circular economy. Impakter. https://impakter.com/the-nyc-curb-to-market-challenge-an-opportunity-for-a-better-circular-economy

4. Our story. (n.d.). Circular Economy Manufacturing. https://www.circulareconomymfg.com/about

5. Does a garment really travel around the world before it is bought? (n.d.). Decathlon. https://sustainability.decathlon.com/un-vetement-fait-il-vraiment-le-tour-du-monde-avant-detre-achete

6. Nadiv, R., Kanar, V., & Turkowski, M. (2023, June 29). If a circular economy is the goal, microfactories are the solution. World Economic Forum. https://www.weforum.org/agenda/2023/06/if-a-circular-economy-is-the-goal-microfactories-are-the-solution

7. Wright, D. (2023, June 7). Re-Fresh. Global's revolution: Transforming textile trash into eco-treasures. Startup to Follow. https://www.startuptofollow.com/article/re-fresh-global-s-revolution-transforming-textile-trash-into-eco-treasures

8. Wikipedia contributors. (2024, February 4). Bioeconomy. *Wikipedia*. Retrieved February 19, 2024, from https://en.wikipedia.org/w/index.php?title=Bioeconomy&oldid=1203297405

9. European bioeconomy robust as bio-based industry turnover jumps to 780 billion EUR. (2021, October 5). *Bioplastics Magazine*.

https://www.bioplasticsmagazine.com/en/news/meldungen/20211005-European-bioeconomy-robust-as-bio-based-industry-turnover-jumps-to-780-billion-EUR.php

10. Cumbers, J. (2022, September 12). White House unveils strategy to grow trillion dollar U.S. bioeconomy. *Forbes.* https://www.forbes.com/sites/johncumbers/2022/09/12/white-house-inks-strategy-to-grow-trillion-dollar-us-bioeconomy

11. China maps out measures to develop $3.28t bioeconomy by 2025. (2022, May 10). *Global Times.* https://www.globaltimes.cn/page/202205/1265272.shtml

12. World Business Council for Sustainable Development. (2020, November 23). The circular bioeconomy: A business opportunity contributing to a sustainable world. https://www.wbcsd.org/Archive/Factor-10/Resources/The-circular-bioeconomy-A-business-opportunity-contributing-to-a-sustainable-world

13. For this case study, the author interviewed Caroline Pétigny, CSR and communication director at AFYREN, March 28, 2023.

14. Africa is bringing vaccine manufacturing home. (2022, February 9). *Nature.* https://www.nature.com/articles/d41586-022-00335-9

15. BioNTech achieves milestone at mRNA-based vaccine manufacturing site in Rwanda. (2023, December 18). BioNTech. https://investors.biontech.de/news-releases/news-release-details/biontech-achieves-milestone-mrna-based-vaccine-manufacturing-0

16. BioNTech mRNA vaccine manufacturing facility, Rwanda. (2023, February 15). Pharmaceutical Technology. https://www.pharmaceutical-technology.com/projects/biontech-mrna-facility-rwanda

17. EduardH. (2023, November 16). Innovations in decentralized manufacturing of advanced therapies. Supply Chain Management Blogs by SAP. https://community.sap.com/t5/supply-chain-management-blogs-by-sap/innovations-in-decentralized-manufacturing-of-advanced-therapies/ba-p/13580192

18. RNA technology to support decentralization and production autonomy. (n.d.). Univercells. https://www.univercells.com/what-we-do/casestudy/RNA-technology-to-support-decentralization-and-production-autonomy

19. What is carbon capture and storage and how does it work? (n.d.). Global CCS Institute. https://www.globalccsinstitute.com/resources/ccs-101-the-basics

20. Wikipedia contributors. (2024, January 6). Carbon capture and utilization. *Wikipedia*. Retrieved February 19, 2024, from https://en.wikipedia.org/w/index.php?title=Carbon_capture_and_utilization&oldid=1193865838

21. Carbon removal. (n.d.). World Resources Institute. https://www.wri.org/initiatives/carbon-removal

22. What is carbon removal? (n.d.). American University. https://www.american.edu/sis/centers/carbon-removal/what-it-is.cfm

23. Lebling, K., Leslie-Bole, H., Byrum, Z., & Bridgwater, L. (2022, May 2). 6 things to know about direct air capture. World Resources Institute. https://www.wri.org/insights/direct-air-capture-resource-considerations-and-costs-carbon-removal

24. Dickie, G. (2023, January 19). Global carbon dioxide removal totals 2 billion tonnes per year - report. *Reuters*. https://www.reuters.com/business/environment/global-carbon-dioxide-removal-totals-2-billion-tonnes-per-year-report-2023-01-19

25. Lindsey, R. (2024, April 9). Climate change: Atmospheric carbon dioxide. Climate.gov. https://www.climate.gov/news-features/understanding-climate/climate-change-atmospheric-carbon-dioxide

26. The State of Carbon Dioxide Removal report is available at https://www.stateofcdr.org

27. Tutton, M. (2023, June 23). Concrete is a huge source of carbon emissions. These researchers are working to make it greener. CNN. https://www.cnn.com/2023/06/16/world/concrete-carbon-emissions-researchers-working-to-make-it-greener-climate-scn-spc/index.html

28. Heirloom. (2023, February 3). CO_2 removed from the atmosphere by Direct Air Capture is permanently stored in concrete for the first time. https://www.heirloomcarbon.com/news/co2-removed-from-the-atmosphere-by-direct-air-capture-is-permanently-stored-in-concrete-for-the-first-time

29. Clancy, H. (2020, October 28). Carbontech is getting ready for its market moment. GreenBiz. https://www.greenbiz.com/article/carbontech-getting-ready-its-market-moment

Chapter 7

1. Radjou, N., & Prabhu, J. (2015). *Frugal innovation*. Profile Books.
2. McKinsey & Company. (2021, November 12). The value of getting personalization right—or wrong—is multiplying. https://www .mckinsey.com/capabilities/growth-marketing-and-sales/our-insights/the-value-of-getting-personalization-right-or-wrong-is-multiplying
3. WARC. (2021, October 6). Lack of emotional connection costs brands. https://www.warc.com/content/feed/lack-of-emotional-connection-costs-brands/3738
4. Bain & Company. (2023, November 13). Consumers say their environmental concerns are increasing due to extreme weather; study shows they're willing to change behavior, pay 12% more for sustainable products. Press release. https://www.prnewswire.com/news-releases/consumers-say-their-environmental-concerns-are-increasing-due-to-extreme-weather-study-shows-theyre-willing-to-change-behavior-pay-12-more-for-sustainable-products-30198 5233.html
5. Koop, A. (2023, July 19). Does "made in America" still matter to consumers? *Visual Capitalist*. https://www.visualcapitalist.com/made-in-america-vs-made-in-china
6. America is ready for reshoring. Are you? (2022). 2022 Reshoring Index. Kearney research report. https://www.kearney.com/service/operations-performance/us-reshoring-index
7. McLaughlin, E., & Peterson, D. M. (2023, November 02). A reshoring renaissance is underway. *MIT Sloan Management Review*. https://sloanreview.mit.edu/article/a-reshoring-renaissance-is-underway
8. Reshoring Initiative 1H 2023 Report. (2023). Geopolitical risk and industrial policy drive reshoring and FDI announcements. https://reshorenow.org/content/pdf/1H2023_RI_Report.pdf
9. Makena, K. (2022, August 9). Biden signs $280 billion CHIPS and Science Act. *The Verge*. https://www.theverge.com/2022/8/9/232981 47/biden-chips-act-semiconductors-subsidies-ohio-arizona-plant-china
10. Martin, E. (2023, September 11). The many challenges facing France's reindustrialization. *Geopolitical Intelligence Services*. https://www.gisreportsonline.com/r/france-reindustrialization

11. Deutsch, J. (2023, July 25). EU enacts €43 billion Chips Act in bid to boost production. *Bloomberg.* https://www.bloomberg.com/news/articles/2023-07-25/eu-enacts-43-billion-chips-act-in-bid-to-boost-production

12. Porter, M. (1985). *Competitive advantage: Creating and sustaining superior performance.* Free Press.

13. American Compass. (2024, January 11). The American rejection of globalization. https://americancompass.org/the-american-rejection-of-globalization

14. Halassi, S., Semeijn, J., & and Kiratli, N. (2019). From consumer to prosumer: A supply chain revolution in 3D printing. *International Journal of Physical Distribution & Logistics Management, 49*(2), 200–216. https://doi.org/10.1108/IJPDLM-03-2018-0139

15. Fisher, L. M. (2006, November 30). Alvin Toffler: The thought leader interview. *strategy+business.* https://www.strategy-business.com/article/06408

16. Radjou, N., Prabhu, J., & Ahuja, S. (2012). *Jugaad innovation.* Jossey-Bass.

17. Anderson, C. (2012). *Makers: The new industrial revolution.* Crown Business.

18. Winn, Z. (2023, June 5). How MIT's fab labs scaled around the world. *MIT News.* https://news.mit.edu/2023/how-mits-fab-labs-scaled-around-world-0605

19. Radjou & Prabhu, *Frugal innovation.*

20. Young, J. (2022, June 30). What is Blue Ocean? Definition in markets and characteristics. *Investopedia.* https://www.investopedia.com/terms/b/blue_ocean.asp

21. What are scope 3 emissions and why do they matter? The Carbon Trust. https://www.carbontrust.com/our-work-and-impact/guides-reports-and-tools/what-are-scope-3-emissions-and-why-do-they-matter

22. Cox, E., & Herman, C. (n.d.). Tackling the scope 3 challenge. PwC. https://www.pwc.com/gx/en/issues/climate/scope-three-challenge.html

23. Rajan, Q. (2022, August 25). What are scope 1, 2, and 3 emissions. https://www.esganalytics.io/insights/what-are-scope-1-2-and-3-carbon-emissions

24. Rosenbaum, E. (2021, August 18). Climate experts are worried about the toughest carbon emissions for companies to capture. CNBC. https://www.cnbc.com/2021/08/18/apple-amazon-exxon-and-the-toughest-carbon-emissions-to-capture.html

25. Science Based Targets. (2024, March 7). Business ambition for 1.5°C campaign—Final report. https://sciencebasedtargets.org/resources/files/SBTi-Business-Ambition-final-report.pdf

26. Loh, I. (2022, October 14). Why companies struggle with scope 3 measurement. Unravel Carbon. https://www.unravelcarbon.com/blog/companies-struggle-scope-3-measurement

27. Deloitte. (2024, March 6). Executive summary of the SEC's landmark climate disclosure rule. https://dart.deloitte.com/USDART/home/publications/deloitte/heads-up/2024/sec-climate-disclosure-requirements-ghg-emissions-executive-summary

28. Blatter, J. (n.d.). Glocalization. Britannica Money. https://www.britannica.com/money/glocalization

29. Lawrence Livermore National Laboratory. (2023, December 11). New analysis outlines national opportunities to remove CO_2 at the gigaton scale. https://www.llnl.gov/article/50686/new-analysis-outlines-national-opportunities-remove-carbon-dioxide-gigaton-scale

30. The Roads to Removal website (https://roads2removal.org) offers interactive maps that highlight the opportunities for CO_2 removal in all 3,143 counties across the US.

31. Oak Ridge National Laboratory. (2023, December 11). New report outlines opportunities to remove CO_2 at the gigaton scale. https://www.ornl.gov/news/new-report-outlines-opportunities-remove-co2-gigaton-scale

32. Rawlings, I. (2022, October 10). The first vertical hydroponic greenhouse in North America. *Mountain Living*. https://www.mountainliving.com/the-first-vertical-hydroponic-greenhouse-in-north-america

33. Farm-to-fork in 24 hours. Visit Jackson Hole. https://visitjacksonhole.com/farm-to-fork-in-24-hours

34. Chesbrough, H. (2003). *Open innovation: The new imperative for creating and profiting from technology*. Harvard Business Press.

35. Radjou, N. (2004, June 17). *Innovation networks*. Forrester Research.

36. Wikipedia contributors. (2023, August 2). Living lab. *Wikipedia*. Retrieved February 20, 2024, from https://en.wikipedia.org/w/index.php?title=Living_lab&oldid=1168427807

37. Act4gaz. (2022, March 4). Living labs: une démarche d'innovation ancrée dans les territoires. GRDF. https://act4gaz.grdf.fr/living-labs-une-demarche-dinnovation-ancree-dans-les-territoires

38. Messad, P. (2022, December 8). GRDF chief: France is on track to exceed its biomethane goals. *Euractiv*. https://www.euractiv.com/section/energy/interview/grdf-chief-france-is-on-track-to-exceed-its-biomethane-goals

39. Biomethane: The future of natural gas. (n.d.). GRDF. https://www.grdf.fr/english/biomethane-main-projects

40. McLaughlin, E., & Peterson, D. M. (2023, November 2). A reshoring renaissance is underway. *MIT Sloan Management Review*. https://sloanreview.mit.edu/article/a-reshoring-renaissance-is-underway

41. Huriez, T., Boël, E., Prat, A., & Bouillon, J.-M. (2024). *La permaindustrie*. Eyrolles.

42. Kevin O'Marah, cofounder of Zero100, interview with the author, December 11, 2023.

43. Chabanel, B., Florentin, A., Laville, E., & Richard, A. (2023). *L'entreprise hyper-locale - Réinventer les modèles économiques à partir des territoires*. Pearson France.

44. Library of Congress Blogs. (2019, January 25). BFU: Inspired by Ben Franklin. https://blogs.loc.gov/inside_adams/2019/01/bfu-inspired-by-ben-franklin

45. Benjamin Franklin's inventions. (n.d.). The Franklin Institute. https://fi.edu/en/science-and-education/benjamin-franklin/inventions

Chapter 8

1. Ellen MacArthur Foundation. (2013). Towards the circular economy: Opportunities for the consumer goods sector (Vol. 2). https://www.ellenmacarthurfoundation.org/towards-the-circular-economy-vol-2-opportunities-for-the-consumer-goods

2. Ibid.

3. Waste-free world. (n.d.). Unilever. https://www.unilever.com/planet-and-society/waste-free-world/strategy-and-goals

4. Questions and answers: End-of-life vehicles. (n.d.). European Commission. https://ec.europa.eu/commission/presscorner/detail/en/qanda_23_3820

5. Murati, A. (2013, November 13). La voiture grande consommatrice de matières premières. *L'argus*. https://www.largus.fr/actualite-automobile/la-votiure-grande-consommatrice-de-matiasres-premiasres-3299370.html

6. End-of-life vehicles regulation. (n.d.). European Commission. https://environment.ec.europa.eu/topics/waste-and-recycling/end-life-vehicles/end-life-vehicles-regulation_en

7. Jaguar Land Rover upcycles aluminum to cut carbon emissions by a quarter. (n.d.). Jaguar Land Rover. https://media.jaguarlandrover.com/news/2020/08/jaguar-land-rover-upcycles-aluminium-cut-carbon-emissions-quarter

8. Momentum in our operations and supply chain. (n.d.). Levi Strauss & Co. https://www.levistrauss.com/sustainability-report/climate

9. The AIA 2030 Commitment. (n.d.). The American Institute of Architects. https://www.aia.org/design-excellence/climate-action/zero-carbon/2030-commitment

10. Copernicus. (2023, September 5). Summer 2023: The hottest on record. https://climate.copernicus.eu/summer-2023-hottest-record

11. Harvey, F. (2023, May 17). World likely to breach 1.5C climate threshold by 2027, scientists warn. *The Guardian*. https://www.theguardian.com/environment/2023/may/17/global-heating-climate-crisis-record-temperatures-wmo-research

12. How the Earth overshoot day 2023 was calculated. (n.d.). Earth Overshoot Day. https://www.overshootday.org/2023-calculation

13. How many Earths? How many countries? (n.d.). Earth Overshoot Day. https://overshoot.footprintnetwork.org/how-many-earths-or-countries-do-we-need

14. Jaynes, C. H. (2023, March 22). Global freshwater demand will exceed supply 40% by 2030, experts warn. World Economic Forum. https://www.weforum.org/agenda/2023/03/global-freshwater-demand-will-exceed-supply-40-by-2030-experts-warn

15. McKinsey & Company. (2023, November 7). Striking the balance: Catalyzing a sustainable land-use transition. https://www.mckinsey.com/industries/agriculture/our-insights/striking-the-balance-catalyzing-a-sustainable-land-use-transition

16. Guynup, S. (2023, June 5). Global study of 71,000 animal species finds 48% are declining. Mongabay. https://news.mongabay.com/2023/06/global-study-of-71000-animal-species-finds-48-are-declining

17. UNEP. (2021, October 5). Rising sea surface temperatures driving the loss of 14 percent of corals since 2009. https://www.unep.org/news-and-stories/press-release/rising-sea-surface-temperatures-driving-loss-14-percent-corals-2009

18. World Economic Forum. (2023, September 20). 5 ways we can promote nature-positive cities: These mayors around the world are calling for action. https://www.weforum.org/agenda/2023/09/beyond-net-zero-the-rise-of-nature-positive-cities

19. World Economic Forum. (2021, June 23). What is "nature positive" and why is it the key to our future? https://www.weforum.org/agenda/2021/06/what-is-nature-positive-and-why-is-it-the-key-to-our-future

20. CBS News. (2023, November 29). U.S. life expectancy rose in 2022 by more than a year, but remains below pre-pandemic levels. https://www.cbsnews.com/news/us-life-expectancy-up-2022

21. Ibid.

22. Kekatos, M. (2023, November 29). Number of suicides in the US in 2022 reaches record level: CDC. https://abcnews.go.com/Health/number-suicides-us-2022-reaches-record-level-cdc/story?id=105204012

23. France 24. (2023, December 22). Fighting poverty in Europe: Meet the people who are making a difference. https://www.france24.com/en/tv-shows/talking-europe/20231222-fighting-poverty-in-europe-meet-the-people-who-are-making-a-difference

24. Oxfam International. (2023, January 16). Richest 1% bag nearly twice as much wealth as the rest of the world put together over the past two years. https://www.oxfam.org/en/press-releases/richest-1-bag-nearly-twice-much-wealth-rest-world-put-together-over-past-two-years

25. Financial Health Network. (2023, September 13). Financial Health Pulse 2023: Share of financially vulnerable Americans grows to 17% of population, climbing to pre-pandemic levels.

https://finhealthnetwork.org/financial-health-pulse-2023-share-of-financially-vulnerable-americans-grows-to-pre-pandemic-levels

26. Langenborg, N.-M. (2020, March 8). 8 of 10 customers want regenerative. Can a billion people be wrong? LinkedIn. https://www.linkedin.com/pulse/8-10-customers-want-regenerative-can-billion-people-langenborg-gmba

27. Nils-Michael Langenborg, co-founder of ReGenFriends, interview with the author, March 26, 2020.

28. Simard, S. (2016, June). How trees talk to each other. TED Talk. https://www.ted.com/talks/suzanne_simard_how_trees_talk_to_each_other

29. Grant, A. (2013, April). In the company of givers and takers. *Harvard Business Review*. https://hbr.org/2013/04/in-the-company-of-givers-and-takers

30. Polman, P., & Winston, A. (2021, September–October). The net positive manifesto. *Harvard Business Review*. https://hbr.org/2021/09/the-net-positive-manifesto

31. Ibid.

32. Thomson, E. A. (2021, March 29). Accounting for firms' positive impacts on the environment. *MIT News*. https://news.mit.edu/2021/handprints-accounting-firms-positive-impacts-environment-0329

33. Danone North-America regenerative agriculture program. (n.d.). Danone corporate. https://regenerative-agriculture.danone.com/projects/danone-north-america-regenerative-agriculture-program

34. Natura Campus Blog. (n.d.). Amazon tree which was cut down to make brooms, survives, turning into a moisturizer. http://www.naturacampus.com.br/cs/naturacampus/post/2017-05/amazon-tree-which-was-cut-down-?lang=en_US

35. Radjou, N. (2020, October 24). Beyond sustainability: The regenerative business. *Forbes*. https://www.forbes.com/sites/naviradjou/2020/10/24/beyond-sustainability-the-regenerative-business

36. Baumeister, D., & Miller, N. (2023). Can the built environment function like nature? *Field Actions Science Reports, 25*, 36–41. https://journals.openedition.org/factsreports/7186

37. Biomimicry 3.8 - Interface. A design revolution is here. https://biomimicry.net/project-positive

38. Monty Hamilton, founder and CEO of Sparq, interview with the author, August 5, 2020.

39. Sanford, C. (2020, March 11). The regenerative life: A non-heroic approach to change. Porchlight. https://www.porchlightbooks .com/blog/changethis/2020/the-regenerative-life-a-non-heroic-approach-to-change

40. Critical help for Carol Sanford. (n.d.). GoFundMe. https://www .gofundme.com/f/critical-help-for-carol-sanford

41. 8 principles of a regenerative economy. (n.d.). Capital Institute. https://capitalinstitute.org/8-principles-regenerative-economy

42. Institute for New Economic Thinking. (2022, January 27). Regenerative economics: A necessary paradigm shift for a world in crisis. https://www.ineteconomics.org/perspectives/podcasts/ regenerative-economics-a-necessary-paradigm-shift-for-a-world-in-crisis

43. Wahl, D. C. (2017, March 15). Sustainability is not enough: We need regenerative cultures. *Medium*. https://designforsustain ability.medium.com/sustainability-is-not-enough-we-need-regenerative-cultures-4abb3c78e68b

44. Wahl, D. C. (2021, July 10). Sensitivity to scale, uniqueness of place and local culture. *Medium*. https://designforsustainability .medium.com/sensitivity-to-scale-uniqueness-of-place-and-local-culture-82e184678c9c

45. Présences. (2023, June 1). Isabelle Delannoy: l'économie régénérative, une autre vision pour l'avenir. https://www .presences-grenoble.fr/actualites-economie-verte-smart-city-grenoble/isabelle-delannoy-l-economie-regenerative-une-autre

46. Ibid.

47. Piersma, B. (2021, November 30). Book review: *Green Swans: The Coming Boom in Regenerative Capitalism*. University of Groningen. https://www.rug.nl/rudolf-agricola-school/community/blog/ book-review-green-swans-the-coming-boom-in-regenerative-capitalism

48. To learn about Project Regeneration initiated by Paul Hawken, visit https://regeneration.org

49. Radjou, N. (2018, June 20). Before we reinvent the economy, we must reinvent ourselves. Fast Company. https://www

.fastcompany.com/40587024/before-we-reinvent-the-economy-we-must-reinvent-ourselves

50. Ibid.
51. Régénération. (n.d.). *Larousse.* https://www.larousse.fr/dictionnaires/francais/régénération
52. Mason, C., & Dunnill, P. (2008). A brief definition of regenerative medicine. *Regen Med, 3*, 1–5.
53. Friar, G. (2019, June 17). The science of self-repair: Regeneration research at Whitehead Institute. Whitehead Institute. https://wi.mit.edu/news/science-self-repair-regeneration-research-whitehead-institute
54. Ibid.

Chapter 9

1. CERN Document Server. (2004, July 5). Lord Shiva statue unveiled. https://cds.cern.ch/record/745737?ln=en
2. Wikipedia contributors. (2023, December 18). Tandava. *Wikipedia.* Retrieved February 27, 2024, from https://en.wikipedia.org/w/index.php?title=Tandava&oldid=1190463056
3. Frawley, D. (2017, June 13). The primacy of Shakti. Vedanet. https://www.vedanet.com/the-primacy-of-shakti
4. Quote from *Cosmos* by Carl Sagan. (n.d.). Goodreads. https://www.goodreads.com/quotes/601581-the-hindu-religion-is-the-only-one-of-the-world-s
5. Fritjof Capra. (2004, June 20). Shiva's cosmic dance at CERN. https://www.fritjofcapra.net/shivas-cosmic-dance-at-cern
6. Spanda—The Supreme Divine Resonance. (n.d.). Tantramag. https://tantramag.com/philosophy/kashmir-shaivism/spanda-the-supreme-divine-resonance
7. Guite, M. (2017, January 26). The beatitudes: A little lifting of the veil. https://malcolmguite.wordpress.com/tag/the-sermon-on-the-mount
8. Lea, R. (2023, August 21). Are we really made of "star stuff" and what does that even mean? Space.com. https://www.space.com/we-are-made-of-star-stuff-meaning-truth
9. Jean-François Caron, former mayor of Loos-en-Gohelle (2001–2023), interview with the author, November 3, 2022.

10. Damien. (2022, June 25). A Loos-en-Gohelle, la transition comme seul avenir possible. Tikographie. https://www.tikographie.fr/2022/06/25/a-loos-en-gohelle-la-transition-comme-seul-avenir-possible

11. Nord-Pas de Calais Mining Basin. (n.d.). UNESCO World Heritage Centre. https://whc.unesco.org/en/list/1360

12. Horizons Publics. (2022, August 29). Jean-François Caron: La transition n'est pas une affaire technologique, c'est d'abord un changement de regard. https://www.horizonspublics.fr/environnement/jean-francois-caron-la-transition-nest-pas-une-affaire-technologique-cest-dabord-un

13. Perdrigeat, J. (2021). Décréter l'implication des citoyens ne suffit pas, il faut pouvoir l'organiser. *Cahiers de l'action, 57,* 61–67. https://doi.org/10.3917/cact.057.0061

14. Banque des Territoires. (2019, November 14). Loos-en-Gohelle amplifie les initiatives citoyennes grâce au fifty-fifty. https://www.banquedesterritoires.fr/loos-en-gohelle-amplifie-les-initiatives-citoyennes-grace-au-fifty-fifty

15. Sen's Capability Approach (n.d.). *Internet Encyclopedia of Philosophy.* https://iep.utm.edu/sen-cap

16. Les démonstrateurs nationaux de la conduite du changement: des villes en transition dans les Hauts-de-France. (n.d.). ADEME. https://librairie.ademe.fr/developpement-durable/4955-les-demonstrateurs-nationaux-de-la-conduite-du-changement-des-villes-en-transition-dans-les-hauts-de-france.html

17. Tourisme en Transition. (2021, March 15). Jean-François Caron, maire de Loos-en-Gohelle, témoigne de la transition de sa commune. https://tourisme-en-transition.fr/jean-francois-caron-maire-de-loos-en-gohelle-temoigne-de-la-transition-de-sa-commune

18. Radjou, N., Prabhu, J., & Ahuja, S. (2023). *L'innovation jugaad—Edition augmentée.* Diateino.

19. Claquin, A. (2023, June 21). Jean-François Caron: "Pour changer le monde, passons par le local!." *La Croix.* https://www.la-croix.com/Debats/Jean-Francois-Caron-changer-monde-passons-local-2023-06-21-1201272449

20. To learn about *La Fabrique des Transitions,* visit its website https://fabriquedestransitions.net.

21. Kate, M. (2023, November 9). Three big reasons Americans haven't rapidly adopted EVs. *BBC*. https://www.bbc.com/worklife/article/20231108-three-big-reasons-americans-havent-rapidly-adopted-evs

22. Cheminade, P. (2024, February 21). Trois ans après, le label du Bâtiment frugal bordelais est toujours en chantier. *La Tribune*. https://objectifaquitaine.latribune.fr/business/immobilier/2024-02-21/trois-ans-apres-le-label-du-batiment-frugal-bordelais-est-toujours-en-chantier-990527.html

Chapter 10

1. Ayurveda: Does it really work? (n.d.). WebMD. https://www.webmd.com/balance/ayurvedic-treatments

2. Ayurveda. (n.d.).John Hopkins Medicine. https://www.hopkinsmedicine.org/health/wellness-and-prevention/ayurveda

3. I explain the impact of Ayurveda on my life in my TEDx Talk "My Inner Journey to Freedom." https://www.ted.com/talks/navi_radjou_my_inner_journey_to_freedom

4. Take the quiz offered by the Chopra Center to determine your own doshas: https://webapp.chopra.com/en/public-dosha-quiz

5. Varsakiya, J., Kathad, D., & Shingadiya, R. (2018). Rasayana-rejuvenation: Unique therapy of Ayurveda for long living. *World Journal of Pharmaceutical Research, 492*. https://wjpr.net/abstract_file/10372

6. Rea, S. (2020, January 29). Cultivating Ojas with Ayurveda. Banyan Botanicals blog. https://www.banyanbotanicals.com/info/blog-the-banyan-insight/details/cultivating-juiciness-with-ayurveda

7. What is Ayurveda? (n.d.). Kerala Ayurveda. https://www.keralaayurveda.us/courses/about/what-is-ayurveda

8. Wikipedia contributors. (2023, November 8). *Collapse: How societies choose to fail or succeed. Wikipedia*. Retrieved February 28, 2024, from https://en.wikipedia.org/w/index.php?title=Collapse:_How_Societies_Choose_to_Fail_or_Succeed&oldid=1184191945

9. Han, B.-C. (2021, April 12). The tiredness virus. *The Nation*. https://www.thenation.com/article/society/pandemic-burnout-society

10. Bunting, M. (2011, November 10). Small is beautiful—An economic idea that has sadly been forgotten. *The Guardian*. https://www.theguardian.com/commentisfree/2011/nov/10/small-is-beautiful-economic-idea

11. A–Z of indigenous terms. (n.d.). Deakin University. https://www.deakin.edu.au/students/student-life-and-services/indigenous-students/glossary-of-indigenous-terms/az-list-of-terms

12. About Regenerative Songlines Australia. (n.d.). https://www.regenerative-songlines.net.au/about

13. Ibid.

14. What is bioregionalism? (n.d.). State University of New York College of Environmental Science and Forestry. https://www.esf.edu/cbbrs/about.php

15. Thackara, J. (2019). Bioregioning: Pathways to urban-rural reconnection. *She Ji: The Journal of Design, Economics, and Innovation, 5*(1), 15–28. https://doi.org/10.1016/j.sheji.2019.01.002

16. What is bioregioning? (n.d.). Bioregioning Tayside. https://bioregioningtayside.scot/about

17. Cooper, C., & Hubbard, E. (2022, March 29). Growing bioregioning through community science. ArcGIS StoryMaps. https://storymaps.arcgis.com/stories/19a53ccdaff341c7a0dd7651564184e6

18. Hendrickson, C., Muro, M., & Galston, W. A. (2018, November). Countering the geography of discontent: Strategies for left-behind places. *Brookings Report*. https://www.brookings.edu/articles/countering-the-geography-of-discontent-strategies-for-left-behind-places

19. Ibid.

20. Iammarino, S., Rodríguez-Pose, A., & Storper, M. (2019). Regional inequality in Europe: Evidence, theory and policy implications. *Journal of Economic Geography, 19*(2), 273–298. http://eprints.lse.ac.uk/87491

21. Rodríguez-Pose, A., Storper, M., & Iammarino, S. (2018, July 13). Regional inequality in Europe: Evidence, theory and policy implications. VoxEU CEPR. https://cepr.org/voxeu/columns/regional-inequality-europe-evidence-theory-and-policy-implications

22. Ratnatunga, M., & Feldman, M. (2023, November 9). Place-based economic development: A guide for implementation. Heartland Forward. https://heartlandforward.org/case-study/place-based-economic-development-a-guide-for-implementation

23. Dweck, C. (2016, January 13). What having a "growth mindset" actually means. *Harvard Business Review*. https://hbr.org/2016/01/what-having-a-growth-mindset-actually-means

24. Place-based policies for the future. (n.d.). OECD. https://www.oecd.org/regional/place-based-policies-for-the-future.htm

25. Ibid.

26. Carnegie Council for Ethics in International Affairs. (2013, October 30). Mass flourishing: How grassroots innovation created jobs, challenge, and change. https://www.carnegiecouncil.org/media/series/39/20131028-mass-flourishing-how-grassroots-innovation-created-jobs-challenge-and-change

27. Miller, K. (2020, December 8). The triple bottom line: What it is & why it is important. Harvard Business School Online's Business Insights blog. https://online.hbs.edu/blog/post/what-is-the-triple-bottom-line

28. Mortari, L. (2022). *The philosophy of care*. Springer Nature.

29. Wikipedia contributors. (2024, February 27). Triskelion. *Wikipedia*. Retrieved February 28, 2024, from https://en.wikipedia.org/w/index.php?title=Triskelion&oldid=1210597649

30. Moniz-Barreto, P., & Maestroni, M. (2024). *Régénération!* Les Ouvreurs de Monde.

31. Elgin, D. (2018, April 30). Humanity's most urgent challenge. *DailyGood*. https://www.dailygood.org/story/1978/humanity-s-most-urgent-challenge-duane-elgin

32. Meiji Yasuda. (n.d.). Management message. https://www.meijiyasuda.co.jp/english/about-us/management_message.html

33. Ibid.

34. Ibid.

35. A new approach for the life-insurance industry. (n.d.). *Nature*. https://www.nature.com/articles/d42473-022-00221-y

36. Japan's average life expectancy is 84 years and it may be linked to their food habits. *News18*. https://www.news18.com/news/

buzz/japans-average-life-expectancy-is-84-years-and-it-may-be-linked-to-their-food-habits-report-3298271.html

37. Yasuda, Management message.

38. Sheetz, M. (2017, August 24). Technology killing off corporate America: Average life span of companies under 20 years. CNBC. https://www.cnbc.com/2017/08/24/technology-killing-off-corporations-average-lifespan-of-company-under-20-years.html

39. Daepp, M., Hamilton, M., West, G., & Bettencourt, L. (2015). The mortality of companies. *Journal of the Royal Society, Interface, 12.* https://doi.org/10.1098/rsif.2015.0120

40. This case study on Eileen Fisher is adapted from an article originally published by the author in the Fall 2021 issue of *Rotman Management Magazine.*

41. Paradis, T. (2023, December 15). Why designer Eileen Fisher set an unachievable sustainability goal. *Business Insider.* https://www.businessinsider.com/eileen-fisher-goal-become-fully-sustainable-brand-2023-11

42. Zahniser, E. (2023, October 10). Sustainable fashion GOAT: Eileen Fisher. Fabrics store blog. https://blog.fabrics-store.com/2023/10/10/sustainable-fashion-goat-eileen-fisher

43. Draznin, H. (2020, January 6). Eileen Fisher built a fashion empire. Her employees now own nearly half of it. CNN Business. https://edition.cnn.com/2020/01/06/success/eileen-fisher-profit-sharing-fashion-boss-files/index.html

44. Yotka, S. (2020, April 22). The biggest thing we can do is reduce—Eileen Fisher shares a vision for a sustainable future. *Vogue.* https://www.vogue.com/article/eileen-fisher-amy-hall-sustainabiity-horizon-2030

45. Altitude Sports. (2022, April 14). Patagonia wants you to know how your clothes are made. https://www.altitude-sports.com/a/blog/patagonias-buy-less

46. Horner, I. (2019, March 6). Conscious consumerism: Fast fashion fuelling fashion failure? Greenpop. https://greenpop.org/conscious-consumerism-fast-fashion-fuelling-fashion-failure

47. Segran, E. (2023, September 7). Eileen Fisher's new CEO wants you to buy fewer clothes. Fast Company. https://www.fastcompany.com/90948608/eileen-fishers-new-ceo-wants-you-to-buy-fewer-clothes

48. Satran, R. (2023, April 8). Eileen Fisher is back. Her fans are younger than ever. *The Wall Street Journal*. https://www.wsj.com/articles/eileen-fisher-young-fans-gen-z-minimal-style-922f34a

Chapter 11

1. How many Earths? How many countries? (n.d.). Earth Overshoot Day. https://overshoot.footprintnetwork.org/how-many-earths-or-countries-do-we-need

2. U.S. Environmental Footprint Factsheet. (n.d.). University of Michigan Center for Sustainable Systems. https://css.umich.edu/publications/factsheets/sustainability-indicators/us-environmental-footprint-factsheet

3. Perry, M. J. (2016, June 05). New US homes today are 1,000 square feet larger than in 1973 and living space per person has nearly doubled. American Enterprise Institute. https://www.aei.org/carpe-diem/new-us-homes-today-are-1000-square-feet-larger-than-in-1973-and-living-space-per-person-has-nearly-doubled

4. Venditti, B. (2023, January 27). Visualizing U.S. consumption of fuel and materials per capita. *Visual Capitalist*. https://www.visualcapitalist.com/visualizing-u-s-consumption-of-fuel-and-materials-per-capita

5. National overview: Facts and figures on materials, wastes and recycling. (n.d.). EPA. https://www.epa.gov/facts-and-figures-about-materials-waste-and-recycling/national-overview-facts-and-figures-materials

6. Rauturier, S. (2024, February 2). Everything you need to know about waste in the fashion industry. Good on you. https://goodonyou.eco/waste-luxury-fashion

7. Hausfather, Z., & Friedlingstein, P. (2023, December 5). Analysis: Growth of Chinese fossil CO_2 emissions drives new global record in 2023. https://www.carbonbrief.org/analysis-growth-of-chinese-fossil-co2-emissions-drives-new-global-record-in-2023

8. Scott, M. (2023, August 30). Does it matter how much the United States reduces its carbon dioxide emissions if China doesn't do the same? Climate.gov. https://www.climate.gov/news-features/climate-qa/does-it-matter-how-much-united-states-reduces-its-carbon-dioxide-emissions

9. Ibid.

10. Adcox, G., & Fraser, C. (2024, February 27). Public perceptions of carbon dioxide removal in Wyoming, Texas, Louisiana, and Colorado. National Wildlife Federation. https://www.nwf.org/en/Educational-Resources/Reports/2024/Public-Perceptions-of-Carbon-Dioxide-Removal-in-WY-TX-LA-CO

11. Frugal. *Merriam-Webster.* https://www.merriam-webster.com/dictionary/frugal

12. Holman, H. R. (2020). The relation of the chronic disease epidemic to the health care crisis. *ACR Open Rheumatology, 2*(3), 167–173. https://doi.org/10.1002/acr2.11114

13. Witters, D. (2023, May 17). US depression rates reach new highs. Gallup. https://news.gallup.com/poll/505745/depression-rates-reach-new-highs.aspx

14. Health and economic costs of chronic diseases. (n.d.). CDC. https://www.cdc.gov/chronicdisease/about/costs/index.htm

15. Brenan, M. (2023, January 17). Record high in U.S. put off medical care due to cost in 2022. Gallup. https://news.gallup.com/poll/468053/record-high-put-off-medical-care-due-cost-2022.aspx

16. Hardy, A. (2024, January 12). Health insurance and medical costs are set to surge again in 2024. *Money.* https://money.com/health-insurance-premiums-increase-2024

17. 2022–2031 National health expenditure projections. (n.d.). CMS. https://www.cms.gov/newsroom/press-releases/cms-office-actuary-releases-2022-2031-national-health-expenditure-projections

18. Berwick, D. M., & Hackbarth, A. D. (2012). Eliminating waste in US health care. *JAMA, 307*(14), 1513–1516. https://doi.org/10.1001/jama.2012.362

19. Perry, S. (2017, September 12). U.S. physicians say up to 30 percent of medical services are unnecessary. *MinnPost.* https://www.minnpost.com/second-opinion/2017/09/us-physicians-say-30-percent-medical-services-are-unnecessary

20. Shrank, W. H., Rogstad, T. L., & Parekh, N. (2019). Waste in the US health care system: Estimated costs and potential for savings. *JAMA, 322*(15), 1501–1509. https://doi.org/10.1001/jama.2019.13978

21. The Center for Health Care Transformation and Innovation (CHTI) at Penn Medicine. (n.d.). https://chti.upenn.edu/about

22. Roy Rosin, chief innovation officer at Penn Medicine, interview with the author, February 19, 2020.

23. Radjou, N. (2020, December 20). Penn Medicine pioneers frugal healthcare. https://www.linkedin.com/pulse/penn-medicine-pioneers-frugal-healthcare-navi-radjou

24. Miller, J. (2022, November 1). No place like home. *Penn Medicine News.* https://www.pennmedicine.org/news/publications-and-special-projects/penn-medicine-magazine/fall-winter-2022/no-place-like-home

25. Comprehensive support for individuals struggling with opioid use disorder. (n.d.). Penn Medicine. https://chti.upenn.edu/core

26. Our program. (n.d.). Grameen America. https://www.grameenamerica.org/program

27. Kobara, J. E. (2015, February 3). Macro impact coming from microloans in LA. *HuffPost.* https://www.huffpost.com/entry/macro-impact-coming-from-microloans-in-la_b_6263972

28. Bellucci, A., Borisov, A., & Zazzaro, A. (2010). Do male and female loan officers differ in small business lending? A review of the literature. MoFiR, *Working Paper 47.*

29. Our impact. (n.d.). Grameen America. https://www.grameenamerica.org/impact

30. Leveraging social capital to expand women's financial opportunities. (n.d.). Grameen America.

31. What is psychological capital? (n.d.). MindTools. https://www.mindtools.com/aocqqad/what-is-psychological-capital

32. Leveraging social capital to expand women's financial opportunities.

33. Schaberg, K., Holman, D., Becerra, M.V.Q., & Hendra, R. (2022). Pathways to financial resilience. MDRC. https://www.mdrc.org/work/publications/pathways-financial-resilience

34. Muckerheide, M. (2023, October 26). The finance gap for women entrepreneurs is $1.7 trillion. Here's how to close it. World Economic Forum. https://www.weforum.org/agenda/2023/10/women-entrepreneurs-finance-banking

Chapter 12

1. The total economic impact of Flexe logistics programs. (n.d.). Flexe. https://www.flexe.com/whitepaper/tei-of-flexe-logistics-programs

2. PR Newswire. (2022, August 18). Governors Stitt, Hutchinson partner to create super region for advanced mobility in the heartland. https://www.prnewswire.com/news-releases/governors-stitt-hutchinson-partner-to-create-super-region-for-advanced-mobility-in-the-heartland-301608582.html

3. Shideler, D., & DeVol, R. (2023, May 11). Regional collaboration drives economic development: Tulsa and Northwest Arkansas' FLAME proposal. *Heartland Forward Report.* https://heartlandforward.org/case-study/regional-collaboration

4. About NSF Engines. (n.d.). NSF. https://new.nsf.gov/funding/initiatives/regional-innovation-engines/about-nsf-engines

5. NSF, EDA announce official coordination on regional innovation programs.(n.d.).NSF.https://new.nsf.gov/news/nsf-eda-announce-official-coordination-regional

6. Muro, M., Maxim, R., Parilla, J., & Briggs, X. S. (2022, December 15). Breaking down an $80 billion surge in place-based industrial policy. *The Brookings Institution Report.* https://www.brookings.edu/articles/breaking-down-an-80-billion-surge-in-place-based-industrial-policy

7. Ibid.

8. Tomlinson, V. (2021, March 17). Arrival announces new microfactory producing electric delivery vans in Charlotte. Arrival. https://arrival.com/news/Arrival-Announces-New-Microfactory-Producing-Electric-Delivery-Vans-in-Charlotte

9. Regional clean hydrogen hubs. (n.d.). Department of Energy. https://www.energy.gov/oced/regional-clean-hydrogen-hubs-0

10. Biden-Harris administration announces $7 billion for America's first clean hydrogen hubs, driving clean manufacturing and delivering new economic opportunities nationwide. (n.d.). Department of Energy. https://www.energy.gov/articles/biden-harris-administration-announces-7-billion-americas-first-clean-hydrogen-hubs-driving

11. Chu, A., Roeder, O., & McCormick, M. (2023, August 13). Republican districts dominate US clean technology investment boom. *Financial Times.* https://www.ft.com/content/06fcd3dd-9c39-48d3-bb08-6d75d34b5ed1

12. Dentons collaborates with premier energy innovators to form hydrogen demand initiative. (n.d.). Dentons. https://www.dentons .com/en/about-dentons/news-events-and-awards/news/2024/ january/dentons-collaborates-with-premier-energy-innovators

13. Graham, K., & Knittel, C. R. (2024). Assessing the distribution of employment vulnerability to the energy transition using employment carbon footprints. *Proceedings of the National Academy of Sciences of the United States of America, 121*(7), e2314773121. https://doi.org/10.1073/pnas.2314773121

14. Ibid.

15. Cooper, A. (2023, July 27). Real life-changer. *Arkansas Democrat Gazette.* https://www.arkansasonline.com/news/2023/jul/27/ real-life-changer

16. The idea accelerator—The new on-ramp to entrepreneurship. (n.d.). Builders & Backers. https://www.buildersandbackers .com/building/about-idea-accelerator

17. Kotkin, J., Schill, M., Del Rio, K. L., Cox, W., Kurimska, A., & Del Rio, C. L. (2021, May 26). The emergence of the global heartland. *Heartland Forward Report.* https://heartlandforward.org/case-study/the-emergence-of-the-global-heartland

18. Chu, A., & Hawkins, O. (n.d.). Houston overtakes Miami as best place for foreign businesses in annual FT-Nikkei ranking. *Financial Times.* https://ig.ft.com/us-cities-index

19. McKinsey & Company. (2022, October 14). The energy transition capital of the world: Houston's opportunity to win by catalyzing capital formation. https://www.mckinsey.com/capabilities/ sustainability/our-insights/the-energy-transition-capital-of-the-world-houstons-opportunity-to-win-by-catalyzing-capital-formation

20. McCormick, M. (2023, November 7). Houston takes top spot in FT-Nikkei rankings by moving beyond oil. *Financial Times.* https:// www.ft.com/content/8854bb17-938d-4dd5-88a8-c1605a4c5bce

21. Florida, R., & King, K. (2023, November 28). America's evolving geography of innovation: How the heartland region

can lead the way of industry transforming technology. *Heartland Forward Report.* https://heartlandforward.org/case-study/americas-evolving-geography-of-innovation-how-the-heartland-region-can-lead-the-way-on-industry-transforming-technology

22. Ross DeVol, president and CEO of Heartland Forward, interview with the author, December 13, 2023.

23. Tulsa has the ingredients to be the next tech hub. (n.d.). TIL. https://www.tulsainnovationlabs.com/about

24. Wikipedia contributors. (2024, March 4). Tulsa race massacre. *Wikipedia.* Retrieved March 4, 2024, from https://en.wikipedia.org/w/index.php?title=Tulsa_race_massacre&oldid=1211723915

25. Blake, A. (2024, February 7). Tulsa man uses technology to rebuild Black Wall Street. *2 News Oklahoma.* https://www.kjrh.com/news/local-news/tulsa-man-uses-technology-to-rebuild-black-wall-street

26. Prosperity Now. (2017, September). The road to zero wealth—How the racial wealth divide is hollowing out America's middle class. https://prosperitynow.org/resources/road-zero-wealth

27. Reimagine Appalachia. (n.d.). A new deal that works for us. https://reimagineappalachia.org/wp-content/uploads/2020/09/ReImagineAppalachia_Blueprint_092020.pdf

28. Amanda Woodrum, co-director of Reimagine Appalachia, interview with the author, February 12, 2024.

29. Sartor, D., Shen, B., & Shehabi, A. (2023, November). Repurposing coal assets for a decarbonized digital economy. *Lawrence Berkeley National Laboratory Report.* https://eta.lbl.gov/publications/repurposing-coal-assets-decarbonized

30. The White House. (2014, October 3). Remarks by the vice president at the John F. Kennedy forum. https://obamawhitehouse.archives.gov/the-press-office/2014/10/03/remarks-vice-president-john-f-kennedy-forum

Conclusion

1. 4 key findings from the "joyful frugality" prosumer report. (n.d.). Havas Red. https://havasred.com/4-key-findings-from-joyful-frugality-prosumer-report

2. Havas Red. (2023). Joyful frugality. *Prosumer Report.* Havas Red.

3. About the minimalists. (n.d.). https://www.theminimalists.com/about

4. To understand Generation Z today is to glimpse a radically different future. (2024, January 15). Telefónica. https://www.telefonica.com/en/communication-room/blog/to-understand-generation-z-today-is-to-glimpse-radically-different-future

5. Blake, S. (2023, December 25). Gen Z doesn't agree $74K is middle class. *Newsweek.* https://www.newsweek.com/gen-z-middle-class-salary-difference-money-views-1854720

6. Wikipedia contributors. (2024, February 12). Digital native. Wikipedia. Retrieved March 15, 2024, from https://en.wikipedia.org/w/index.php?title=Digital_native&oldid=1206581397

7. Langenborg, N.-M. (2020, March 8). 8 of 10 customers want regenerative. Can a billion people be wrong ? LinkedIn. https://www.linkedin.com/pulse/8-10-customers-want-regenerative-can-billion-people-langenborg-gmba

8. Luchs, M. G., & Mick, D. G. (2018). Consumer wisdom: A theoretical framework of five integrated facets. *Journal of Consumer Psychology, 28,* 365–392. https://doi.org/10.1002/jcpy.1037

9. You can measure your own consumer wisdom using the self-assessment tool developed by Michael Luchs, David Glen Mick, and Kelly L. Haws. (2021). https://wmsas.qualtrics.com/jfe/form/SV_81VsSPLyEl1NKL4

10. Karwath, R. (2018, November 12). Wise consumers show the way to better living, professor finds. Raymond A. Mason School of Business at William & Mary. https://mason.wm.edu/news/2018/wise-consumers-show-the-way-to-better-living-professor-finds.php

11. Ibid.

Acknowledgments

My sincere gratitude goes to Stuart Crainer and Des Dearlove, cofounders of Thinkers50, who motivated me to write this book. Stuart and Des were aware that, since 2016, I was working on a book on how to reinvent our society to make it humane, fair, and ecologically sound. I wanted to integrate Western science and philosophy and Eastern spiritual traditions to create an original framework that describes the operating model of an enlightened society.

Being a procrastinator par excellence, or rather an obsessive perfectionist, I spent four years researching and developing this book, but struggled to get it out. Stuart and Des kept nudging me to publish this book at some point. But I felt a strong resistance in me.

Then COVID-19 happened. I was living in New York in 2020. I was aghast to see the "richest economy," that is, America, unable to rapidly produce and deliver life-saving masks and respirators. I understood that the US was a giant economy with feet of clay. I realized that when it comes to the economy, *size does not matter*. What matters is not how giant your economy is, but how well you wield it to create a deep impact in your society.

In 2021, Thinkers50 ranked me as one of the top 50 management thinkers in the world. Stuart and Des congratulated me and with a gentle smile told me, "Navi, you really need to write THAT book." That's when it hit me. "That" book in question was not the book that I *wanted* to write on how to build a better *society*. What mattered was not what *I wanted* to write, but what the world urgently *needed* me to write. On hearing Stuart and Des, I felt a calling: I *had* to write a book on how to build a better *economy*!

In high-school and in college, I studied, excelled at, and loved economics. I had a humanistic view of economics and believed in its salutary power to elevate everyone, especially the underprivileged. But since I immigrated to the US in 1999, I gradually became disillusioned with economics and its capacity to heal and uplift all citizens. I saw how America was enslaved to "dismal economics" that put profit above people and the planet. Worse, as COVID-19 blatantly revealed, the "big" US economy lacked the agility to respond to societal needs rapidly and effectively.

I felt compelled to write a book that provocatively associates *frugal* with *economy*. *Frugal economy* sounds like an oxymoron for profligate Americans, although Ben Franklin, one of our founding fathers, extolled the virtue of frugality. A frugal economy is exactly what the US, as well as declining European nations, desperately need right now to tackle the dual challenges that threaten the Western world: exploding social inequalities and the climate crisis. I want to sincerely thank Stuart and Des for urging me to write a book on "noble economics," hence restoring my own faith in the field of economics.

I also want to thank Jeanenne Ray at Wiley who commissioned this book and agreed to edit and publish it swiftly on an accelerated schedule. I am indebted to Sunnye Collins who, as developmental editor, "read my mind" and offered me valuable suggestions to improve the style and content of this book. I am grateful to Susan Geraghty for her careful copyediting and Rene Caroline for the meticulous typesetting. Thank you, Michelle Hacker, Casper Barbour, and Gabriela Mancuso, for addressing all my questions regarding permissions and coordinating efficiently this book project so I could meet the tight deadline without compromising quality.

About the Author

Navi Radjou is a French-American innovation and leadership scholar who has advised businesses and governments worldwide over the past 30 years.

He has served as a Fellow at the University of Cambridge's Judge Business School (UK) and as a vice president at Forrester Research, a technology research and consulting firm based in Cambridge, Massachusetts.

Since 2021, Navi has been ranked by Thinkers50 as one of the 50 most influential management thinkers in the world.

In 2013, Navi won the prestigious Thinkers50 Innovation Award, given to a management thinker who is redefining the way we think about and practice innovation.

He spoke at TED Global 2014 on frugal innovation (over 2 million views).

Navi is coauthor of *Frugal Innovation*, published by The Economist, as well as the global bestseller *Jugaad Innovation* and *From Smart to Wise*, both published by Jossey-Bass, an imprint of Wiley.

He is a much-sought-after keynote speaker and widely quoted in the international media.

Born and raised in Pondicherry, India, he holds dual French-American nationality. He studied at Ecole Centrale Paris and Yale School of Management. He is a life-long student of Yoga, Ayurveda, and Vipassana (mindfulness) meditation. He lives in Madrid, Spain.

Index

50-50 program, 134, 136

A

Adaptive supply networks, need, 65–69
Additive manufacturing, 77
Ad hoc (tactical) employee sharing, 40
Advanced B2B sharing, 39
AfricVac 2121 vaccine, usage, 54
AFYREN, 82–83
  biorefinery, 82f
  Mitr Phol partnership, 83
Afyren, upcycling example, 33
Agile processes, HYLOVAN usage, 106f
Agility
  gaining, 75–76
  increase, 19
Airbnb, 17, 189
Aktipis, Athena, 58
Aliveness, 151–152
  economy, goal, 152
  maximization, 124
  triple regeneration, impact, 150
Amazon, natural/cultural biodiversity regeneration (Natura), 121
American dream, Gen Zer redefinition, 188
American Rescue Plan Act (ARP), 175
Americans, mental health (deterioration), 165
Anderson, Chris, 98

Appalachia
  coal assets, repurposing (Lawrence Berkeley National Laboratory explanation), 184
  infrastructure/skills, repurposing, 183–184
Arias, Elizabeth, 117
Artificial intelligence (AI), usage, 17
Atlassian (software company), 41
Automotive sector, material usage (percentage), 114
Awareness, expansion, 131–133
Ayurveda (medicine system), 141, 148

B

Bartering, 36
BarterPay, transactions, 36
Basic B2B sharing, 39
Battery electric vehicles (BEVs), 65
Bergson, Henri, 1
Biden, Joe, 184
Billingsley II, Tyrance, 182–183
Bilum, upcycling example, 32
Biodiversity, reduction, 116
Bioeconomy, impact, 81–83
Biomimicry, 126
BioNTainer, flexible product manufacture, 84
BioNTech, vaccine production, 84
Bioregionalism (philosophy), 146
Bioregional Learning Centre, 146
Bioregional regeneration, 145
BioWin (health cluster), 85

233